Women

and

Health

Series

Raymond G. DeVries

Making Midwives Legal

Childbirth, Medicine, and the Law

Second Edition

Ohio State University Press
Columbus

Library of Congress Cataloging-in-Publication Data

DeVries, Raymond G.
  Making midwives legal : childbirth, medicine, and the law /
Raymond G. DeVries.
        p.   cm. — (Women and health)
  Originally published: Regulating birth. 1985. With new pref.
and epilogue.
  Includes bibliographical references and index.
  ISBN 0-8142-0703-0 (paper : alk. paper)
  1. Midwives—Legal status, laws, etc.—United States.
  2. Midwives—United States.   3. Obstetrics—United States.
  I. DeVries, Raymond G.   Regulating birth.   II. Title.   III. Series.
  IV. Series: Women & health (Columbus, Ohio)
  KF2915.M5D48   1996
  344.73'0415—dc20
  [347.304415]   96-6312
                                                            CIP

Type set in ITC Garamond Book by G&S Typesetters, Inc., Austin,
Texas.

The paper used in this publication meets the minimum requirements of American National Standard for Information Sciences—
Permanence of Paper for Printed Library Materials. ANSI Z39.48-
1992.

9 8 7 6 5 4 3 2 1

To C. A.

Contents

Series Editors' Preface

We are pleased to add *Making Midwives Legal: Childbirth, Medicine, and the Law* to our Women and Health Series. When Raymond DeVries's book (then entitled *Regulating Birth: Midwives, Medicine, and the Law*, Temple UP, 1985) first appeared a decade ago, it provided a way to help readers understand the debates erupting over the legal regulation of midwives. The issues raised by the book continue to be relevant both to scholars and to the general public. As the close of the twentieth century brings new concerns about the financing and regulation of health care, and as decisions about birth are increasingly negotiated not only between women and health care workers but between managed care companies and state legislatures, the place of midwives in the health care system continues to draw our attention.

DeVries's analysis highlights the dilemma of traditional midwifery in the United States in the late twentieth century. It documents the seemingly intractable contradiction that has troubled and continues to trouble this profession—namely, that in seeking to promote and strengthen legalized midwifery, proponents often create regulatory boundaries that stem its spread. Consequently, the regulations governing midwifery restrict some women's access to their preferred health care practitioner, while at the same time offering hope for a more humane health care system.

Making Midwives Legal thus remains a significant and relevant sociological work; in addition, it has become an important historical work. In this edition Raymond DeVries gives us a new preface and epilogue. Together they update the book and provide some timely comparisons between the situations in the United States and in other nations. Students, scholars, practitioners, and general readers will find much to reflect upon as they consider the practice and regulation of midwifery in contemporary America.

Preface

Doe maar gewoon, dat is gek genoeg
(Just act normally, that is crazy enough)
—Dutch proverb

This research began nearly twenty years ago, in the mid-1970s, a time when many of us were full of the hope that we could change the way Americans viewed and experienced birth. We were a motley crew—feminists, members of the religious right, "back-to-the-earth" types, pro-family crusaders, peace activists, and libertarians—truly strange bedfellows. Collectively, we were referred to as "the alternative birth movement," giving us a home among the many movements that populated the American social landscape in the sixties and seventies. The better-known movements of that era—the civil rights movement, the women's liberation movement, the antiwar movement—were, in fact, our inspiration. Compared with the task of overturning centuries-old discriminatory laws or taking on the military-industrial complex, our mission seemed easy. We were confident we could "de-medicalize" pregnancy and childbirth, making a place for birth at home and for midwife-assisted birth. The need for change seemed so obvious, so rational, who could resist? One need not have been a commune-dwelling hippie to see that the American way of birth made no sense: it was costly, inefficient, and subjected women to needless, often painful, medical interventions.

Our strategy for the childbirth revolution was twofold. On the local level, we pressured hospitals to revise their policies, making room for more natural, less technological birth practices. (Down with routine shaving, mandatory IVs, electronic fetal monitoring, routine episiotomies, drugs to speed—or slow—labor, separation of mothers and babies, infant formula! Up with alternative birthing rooms, fathers and siblings at birth, "bonding," breast-feeding!) On the state level, we organized and lobbied for the rewriting of medical practice acts in order to create an independent profession of midwifery. (Bring back the midwives!)

We were working against the grain, and we knew it. In American society it was decidedly abnormal to define birth as a normal, healthy process. The American view of birth was shaped by an obstetric science convinced that birth is fraught with risk; according to obstetricians, birth can be seen as "normal" only in retrospect, after technology has guided a woman around the dangers of deformed fetuses, prolonged labor, decelerating heart tones, excessive bleeding, difficult presentations, torn perinea, retained placentas, and the like.

What seemed so obvious to us, alas, seemed exotic and dangerous to nearly everyone else, including, unfortunately, the vast majority of childbearing women. We expected opposition from physicians and hospitals, but we were not prepared for either the resistance or the apathy we found among the very women we wished to help. As the decade wore on, our campaign to re-form American birth practices found few successes. We saw only cosmetic changes in hospital policies. And in spite of our grassroots organizing, we saw our innovative proposals for the licensing of midwives fail again and again. We began to see that the alternative birth movement was hopelessly overmatched. Given the economic, political, and cultural power of the medical profession, there was little we could do to establish a "new" profession of midwifery or a "new" view of birth.

The failure of the alternative birth movement fell hardest on midwives. It was their hope to establish themselves as independent professionals, emulating the model of midwifery care found in some European nations. Instead, they were forced either to become a part of the world of obstetrics or to be content with a peripheral role, living in the shadow of questionable legitimacy. Nurse-midwives chose the former strategy, working under the supervision of physicians. This decision gave them a legitimate place in American medicine, but it led to accusations of selling out and co-optation. "Lay" midwives did not sell out. They refused formal education based in obstetric science and avoided entanglement in medical hierarchies. They retained their purity but were dismissed as countercultural throwbacks in a world moving away from the libertarian excesses of the sixties toward the staid conformism of the Reagan-Bush eighties. Midwifery, with its promise of a more natural view of birth, seemed destined to remain nothing more than an anomaly in America.

By the mid-1980s the alternative birth movement was largely dissipated, content with the relatively small victories of birthing rooms, freestanding birth centers, rooming-in, and staff midwives. American obstetrics had made some minor concessions, but it remained firmly in control of the birth experience.

In the second half of the 1980s, new hope for changing the American approach to birth arose from an unexpected quarter. Physician control of American medicine was challenged not by the alternative birth movement (or any other consumer movement) but by private enterprise. The *business* of medicine was gaining control over the *practice* of medicine. More and more medical decisions were being made not by M.D.s but by M.B.A.s. We sociologists began to analyze the "coming of the corporation" and the "proletarianization of the medical profession." We wondered aloud if physicians, working as salaried employees of health care corporations, could retain control of their turf.

The transfer of control over medical decision-making from physicians to administrators was a promising development for America's midwives and childbearing women. Independent midwifery offered cost-conscious health care managers an alternative to high-tech, high-cost obstetrics: an alternative as safe (or safer) than obstetric care,[1] with the extra benefit of high levels of client satisfaction. Watching from the sidelines, the remnants of the alternative birth movement were convinced that the clinically irrational resistance of physicians to midwives (i.e., an opposition to midwives stemming not from questions of safety but from fear of competition) could not survive the cool rationality of business managers. It was only a matter of time before obstetricians would be hoisted on their own petard of excessive, costly intervention.

In 1996, ten years into the managed care revolution, physicians continue to lose control to administrators. The medical citadel is crumbling, and yet, almost inexplicably, childbirth remains in the hands of obstetricians. American obstetrics survived the alternative childbirth movement and managed care essentially unchanged: today, more than 20 percent of all births in the United States are accomplished surgically; in spite of research suggesting negative effects, epidural anesthesia is increasingly popular and is used routinely by healthy women, a trend that has led to a new specialty in "obstetric anesthesiology"; electronic fetal monitoring remains the norm. Midwives have found a niche working in inner cities and in rural locations—medically underserved areas—but they attend less than 5 percent of the nation's births. The view of birth represented by midwifery remains marginal.

The staying power of the status quo in American obstetrics is best illustrated by the plight of a group of midwives in New York City. In that city's public hospitals, nurse-midwives provide a majority of the care for birthing women. Not surprisingly, midwives were brought into the system (in the late 1970s) because they were less expensive than physicians. An early assessment of their work showed them to be providing high quality care. The perinatal mortality rates for the midwifery service were lower than the average in New York City and in the nation, in spite of the fact that their clients had little or no prenatal care and inadequate nutrition (Haire, 1981). We proponents of alternative birth saw their success as further proof of the wisdom of changing our system of childbirth. If nothing else, here was compelling evidence for administrators seeking cost-efficient care.

This evidence notwithstanding, in 1995, a team of investigative reporters for the *New York Times*, looking to explain poor perinatal outcomes in New York City, turned their gaze to that which seemed out of place in American medicine: midwives. In a three-part exposé, the authors maligned midwives and the insufficient use of obstetric technology as the culprits for poor obstetric results. When the maternity care system is not functioning well, it is not the system that is to blame, rather it is the insufficient application of the system. Too many perinatal deaths? The solution must be more technology, more intervention. Following this logic, the authors faulted the midwives for their low rate of Caesarean sections, 12.9 percent, and asked why it was not closer to the city average of 23.1 percent.

In a letter of response to the exposé, an epidemiologist offers another way to think about the problem: "Among other causes for [the high number of perinatal] deaths, you blame insufficient use of birth technologies such as electronic fetal monitoring and Caesarean section, and midwives who do not function properly. These are . . . complaints of American obstetricians who wish to divert blame from themselves. . . . Underlying New York's maternity care crisis is an *unfounded faith in birth technology*. In your . . . article is the statement that 'a fetal monitor malfunctioned, making it impossible to determine the baby's condition.' Before there was a monitor there was a stethoscope. The monitor should only complement the stethoscope" (Wagner, 1995, emphasis added; see also Marsico, 1995). Using evidence from European countries—where both Caesarean section and perinatal mortality rates are low—the letter writer characterizes the problems in New York City as the result of an overdependence on technology rather than of too little use of that technology. He argues that the proper use of technology requires the careful separation of healthy and high-risk mothers, reserving technological solutions for difficult cases. In New York City, misplaced faith in technology results in too little care in the selection of cases (if all births are high risk it makes no sense to separate them) and the improper use of obstetrical support (private patients get more attention from specialists than do public patients).

This story demonstrates that increased use of midwives and a shift to home birth will require more than a simple policy decision from an M.B.A. What is needed is a new way of thinking about birth. Our American conception of birth is deeply rooted in our culture. We might be willing to move birth from the delivery room to an LDR (one room that combines labor, delivery, and recovery) and to shorten the hospital stay after birth, but it is more difficult to re-envision birth as normal, to jettison the medical interpretation of this critical life event. In retrospect, it is clear that the kind of change we were seeking two decades ago was at least as radical as the changes demanded by the civil rights and antiwar movements. We were asking for a new view of our bodies, of our relation to technology, of our sense of "home," of gender, of family. We were asking not just for social change but for cultural change.

The role played by culture in shaping the care given at birth was not as apparent to me when I wrote the first edition of this book in 1984. Since then, I spent a year researching maternity care in the Netherlands. The Dutch have a sophisticated and modern medical system, in which, interestingly, midwives and home births remain an important part of perinatal care. In 1992, midwives attended 45.8 percent of the births in the Netherlands, and 31.5 percent of all births occurred at home (Centraal Bureau voor de Statistiek, CBS, 1992). This is contrary to the logic of professions (those with more power—physicians—will move to control the turf of those with less power—midwives) and to the logic of technology (the technological imperative: if the technology exists, it will be used). According to the conventional wisdom of medical sociology, the advance of medical systems and the development of medical specialties lead, inevitably, to the hospitalization of birth. But this has not happened in the Netherlands. Why?

The most common explanation of this phenomenon focuses on the structure of Dutch medical care: historians and sociologists point to early legislation that favored midwives, to an insurance system that gives midwives an advantage over their competitors, and to a well-developed program of postpartum care in the home (Hingstman, 1994). These (and other) factors have played a part in the current system, but still we are left asking, "Why did this structure emerge in the Netherlands and not elsewhere?" To answer that question we must look beyond structure to the unique culture of the Netherlands.

A complete analysis of the role of culture in generating and sustaining Dutch maternity care is the subject of a longer study. But a few examples can help illustrate the way culture shapes health care. Taken alone, none of the cultural features listed below—ideas about home, gender, and solidarity—can account for maternity care in the Netherlands; but taken together they create a context that allowed the current system to develop and persist.

The Dutch system of birth is nurtured by a view of home and family different from that found in the United States. As van Daalen points out, the family "nuclearized" earlier in the Netherlands than elsewhere, making birth a private event, not suitable for the public setting of clinic or hospital (van Daalen, 1988; 1993). The Dutch idea of the *gezin* (or nuclear family)[2] coincided with, and overlapped, Dutch notions of domesticity and home. In his analysis of our modern conception of "home," Rybczynski (1986) concludes that the idea of home as a place of comfort and refuge for the nuclear family was created by the Dutch. Schama (1988) confirms this analysis, noting that in the seventeenth and eighteenth centuries the Dutch were renowned for their domesticity. Homes were small, tidy, and the center of family life—a perfect setting for birth.

Not surprisingly, Dutch beliefs about home and family are tied to prevailing views of gender. The position of women in the Netherlands is somewhat paradoxical: women are regarded as strong and independent and yet remain tethered to the family. Trying to explain this paradox, historians have turned to the peculiar economy of the Netherlands. Dutch ideas about the family grew up in an economy centered on trading, fishing, and farming, each of which demanded strong roles for women in the context of family. Consequently, the idea that home is the appropriate place for women survived longer in the Netherlands than elsewhere. Dutch women differ from their European sisters in the persistence of high fertility rates and the relative slowness with which they entered the paid workforce.[3] The domestic sphere, including childbirth, belongs to women. Except in unusual circumstances, birth should be kept in this sphere.

In comparison with the United States, Dutch culture places far greater emphasis on solidarity. Long-running battles against nature, in the form of rising waters, and against a series of foreign occupiers required the Dutch to develop systems of cooperation. By way of contrast, we Americans, with our endless frontier, learned to cherish rugged individualism. The Dutch emphasis on solidarity is the foundation for cooperation between midwives and physicians and for an approach to health care where resources are managed cooperatively, for the good of all citizens. A maternity care system that reserves a place for home birth is not the ideal of all mothers in the Netherlands, some of whom are convinced that it is better (safer, cleaner) to give birth in the hospital; but it is tolerated because it is in the interest of the population at large.

Independent midwifery and home birth were able to survive in the Netherlands because the cultural soil there could sustain them. The cultural soil in the United States is not nearly as hospitable, and it is no small task to rework it.

The first edition of this book, *Regulating Birth*, was published in 1985. My analysis gave me little cause for optimism, but I stubbornly clung to my belief that careful study of earlier efforts to improve the position of midwives—looking at what worked and what did not work—would provide the information needed for the creation of an independent and successful profession of midwifery in the United States. It was my naive hope that by 1996 *Regulating Birth* would be nothing more than a curiosity: evidence that there was once a time when midwife-attended birth was the exception, when even healthy women in labor were "managed" with continuous electronic fetal monitoring and anesthesia, when those choosing to have their babies at home were accused of child abuse. Sadly, my book remains relevant. Sociological lessons learned in the seventies and eighties continue to be useful to childbirth reformers of the nineties who are looking for a better way of birth.

Although the alternative birth movement and managed care have had little success in altering American obstetrics, all hope is not lost. Elsewhere in the world, midwifery is being (re)established as the best approach to birth. Most notable are changes taking place in Canada and the United Kingdom. In 1993 the British government released its report, *Changing Childbirth*, which recommended that the National Health Service move to a model of maternity care where midwives serve as "lead professionals" (Department of Health, U.K.). The province of Ontario recently introduced a model of midwifery care based on that found in the Netherlands, using Dutch midwives as consultants to set up education programs and practice guidelines. These programs, in other English-speaking countries, will doubtless generate new data (in English-language journals) showing the benefits of midwife care. As evidence of the efficacy of midwifery mounts and as costs increasingly impinge on interventionist obstetrics, perhaps even in American culture birth will regain its status as a normal and healthy life event. It is in the interest of continuing the struggle against a system of maternity care that is costly, inefficient, painful, and dangerous that this book is being republished.

A few notes on this second edition. First, a comment on the use of this book. My study of midwives is nothing more or less than a work of sociology in the tradition of C. W. Mills. I point to connections between biography and history, demonstrating that "private troubles" are, in fact, "public issues." The problems faced by one woman whose birth seems unnecessarily difficult are not hers alone. Her difficulty is part and parcel of a medical system and a culture that together define appropriate and inappropriate birth. In its original edition, this book found an audience among medical sociologists and those working in health policy and public health. It is my hope that the appearance of this work in a paperback version will allow the audience to expand: to midwives, to consumers, to students in other fields. Students of medicine, nursing, women's studies, and the sociology of occupations, the sociology of organizations, and the sociology of law all have something to learn from the midwife's campaign for legitimacy. This book will also be useful to historians of women, health care, and nursing who wish to understand the complicated struggles of women and midwives to regain control of birth in the latter decades of the twentieth century.

Second, a word about words. When I was writing the first edition of the book, midwives who were not "certified nurse-midwives" proudly called themselves "lay midwives." The term was seen as an act of resistance against the overly technical and cold approach of medical "professionals." Not long after the book was published, however, many lay midwives decided that the term *lay* created an image of incompetence. Within a few years the term *lay* was abandoned, replaced by a collection of new names: practical midwife, empirical midwife, traditional midwife, community midwife, direct-entry midwife, or sometimes, simply, midwife. For reasons related to the needs of the (re)production of the text, the term *lay midwife* remains in this edition. My apologies to those who find it offensive.

Finally, a few acknowledgments are in order. This second edition would not have been possible without the persistent efforts of Karen Reeds, editor at Rutgers University Press. Her belief in the value of this work led her to push until it found the light of publication. Support for the new research reported in this edition came from the Fogarty Center of the National Institutes of Health (Grant number F06-TW01954), NIVEL (Netherlands Institute for Health Care Research), and from a collection of faculty development grants from St. Olaf College. As with the first edition (and with all academic work), I was cajoled, nurtured, humored, and otherwise supported by a collection of family and friends. Noteworthy in this effort were Sjoerd Kooiker, Annemiek Cuppen, Rebeca Barroso, Dana Quealy, my friends on the ASPO/Lamaze board of directors (who are keeping up the fight for more humane and safer birth), Steve Polansky, Alvin Handelman, and Jesse, Rocky, Anna, and Charlotte.

Acknowledgments

Spanning almost seven years, this study is intertwined with a part of my life that included the births of my three children, at least four different jobs, and four different residences. In the course of this nomadic, eventful existence I have accumulated several personal and intellectual debts. My greatest debt is to the subjects of the study—the midwives, parents, physicians, legislators, lobbyists, and employees in various state departments of health and state medical societies—who were willing to have a nosey sociologist poke around in their affairs. In most research of this type, certain subjects become more than subjects. The friendships I developed with Jan McNabb, Patricia Ternahan, and Anita Pandolphe Ruchman helped to enrich both this study and my life.

My friends in the academic world also contributed to this effort. Those familiar with the work of Ed Lemert and Julius Roth will see their ghosts wandering these pages. When I was a graduate student, Lemert and Roth infected me with the "dis-ease" of sociology, an incurable ailment that causes discomfort by forcing its victims to question everything they had previously taken for granted. The disease is contracted by watching others work and seeing the freshness in their views of the world. These men have a way of offering new insights into some of our oldest institutions: law and medicine. My study benefits from these insights. In addition, Lyn Lofland, Gary Hamilton, George Annas, Allan Solares, and Robert Clark provided editorial advice, suggestions, and moral support. Sheryl Ruzek has followed my study from its earliest phases. Given her knowledge of the literature in women's health I could have found no better editor for this book. Her investment in this work is responsible for much of what is good here. Additional editorial assistance offered by Janet Francendese, Jennifer French, Dorothy Wertz, and Irv Zola made this a more readable, logical work.

The making of a book requires all sorts of mundane assistance provided by the unsung heroes in the production of knowledge. In my case these heroes include Betty Fleming, Jackie Meers, Wava Fleming, and Mary Lee Burdette.

Having money makes the research process much easier. The major support for this work was a grant from the Law and Social Sciences program of the National Science Foundation (#SES-8107980). Some of the data used here are from a study of alternative birth centers funded by a grant from the National Health Care Management Center at the University of Pennsylvania. A Regents Fellowship from the University of California and a Faculty Grant from the Westmont College Alumni Association were also instrumental in the preparation of the manuscript. Important, informal support was given by Delbert and Maybelle Jones who met many essential family needs (like groceries) during the course of this study. Henry and Jeanette DeVries offered unfailing support in prayer.

These acknowledgments would not be written—nor would I be a sane person—if not for the deep support given by Charlotte DeVries. This truly was a joint effort. The fact that I am listed as sole author is the result of the arrogance of academic custom. The technical assistance, editorial comments, emotional support, and nurturing she offered form the true substructure of research. All else is superstructure. Finally, thanks to Anna, Rocky, and Jesse, who constantly remind me where reality is when I start to float away.

For His glory.

Raymond G. DeVries

Introduction

For the last decade American midwives have struggled to reclaim a place in birth, to recapture the heritage of woman "with woman" during childbearing. But the heritage they seek can not be resurrected in the same form as it was interred earlier in this century. As midwifery regains popularity it may become more common to find women with women in the birthing process, but it is no longer possible for midwives and their clients to be truly alone in the lying-in chamber. In the modern world medicine and law are constant—perhaps unwelcome—companions at birth. Advances in medical science change the practices of all but the most isolated of midwives and laws in most states limit the clientele and technology available to these practitioners. The midwife's "bag" now contains the instruments of modern medicine and her vocation is now defined by statute. The worlds of medicine and law were of little concern to turn-of-the-century midwives; today's midwives can not practice without attending to these worlds.

What does it mean to attend to the worlds of medicine and law? Surely it implies being informed of the laws which regulate midwifery and having knowledge of medical developments relevant to birth. But that is not enough. Today's practicing midwife—as well as consumers of maternity care and the advocates and detractors of midwifery—must have a sociological understanding of the way law and medicine interact with and affect her profession. The future of midwifery, the very nature of the profession, is shaped by these worlds. And in turn, medicine and law are influenced by midwifery and the changes in society responsible for its renewed popularity.

In the following pages, I explore the laws which regulate midwives, considering how such laws came to be and the way these laws affect midwifery. My interest in, and concern for, midwifery grew out of a personal investigation of maternity care. When my wife and I learned that we were expecting our first child we explored various alternatives for birthing. Northern California offered us a number of options. The choices ranged from a home birth (with or without the assistance of a birth attendant of some sort) to the more conventional hospital birth (incorporating everything from "natural childbirth" to Caesarean section).

The exploration of available options began to arouse my sociological curiosity, and the decision to engage a certified nurse-midwife marked the beginning of my professional research. I had assumed midwifery to be an anachronistic profession, and was anxious to explore both its history and its recent resurgence. My early work involved a comparison of the medically educated, certified nurse-midwife and the self-taught lay midwife (DeVries, 1982). From there I branched into a study of institutional innovation in the treatment of birth (DeVries, 1979a; 1979b; 1980; 1984) and an investigation of birth as an example of "existence transition" (DeVries, 1981). As is evident, I was quickly drawn into aspects of the subject only vaguely connected with my role as expectant father. Although my personal experience offered useful data, I was also forced to get into the field to gather comparative and background information.

Our second and third children were born during the course of the research. By the time of the second pregnancy we were convinced that the best attendant at this birth would be a lay midwife. Our second child was born in California and our third in Massachusetts. Both were attended by lay midwives. Comparison of my children's births—one attended by a certified nurse-midwife, the other two by lay midwives—has provided my wife and me with new insights into American medicine.

My fascination with law and its relationship to society naturally drew my attention to the interaction between law and midwifery. Preliminary study of the laws that govern midwives revealed great diversity in state regulations. This diversity—although disconcerting to midwives and their supporters—offered an ideal research setting in which to compare the origin and impact of different regulatory measures. After review of the laws in several states I decided that Arizona, Texas, and California provided an ideal comparison because of their varied regulations—ranging from licensure in Arizona, through loose control in Texas, to outright prohibition in California.

The variety of regulation in these three states allowed me to set up a loose, quasi-experimental research design (see Cook and Campbell, 1979). I wanted to gather information both on the creation of laws that regulate midwifery and on the effect of such laws on the way midwives practice. The first objective led me to explore how the need for advice from "medical authorities" on the part of legal institutions influenced the nature of midwife regulations. The second led me to the field itself; I was looking for variations in the quality and style of care, the cost of midwifery services, the availability and accessibility of midwives, and the willingness of established medical professions to work with lay midwives. In devising my quasi-experimental design, California—because of its lack of formal regulation—became the control, with Texas and Arizona representing degrees of regulation.

My exploration of midwife regulation began with a close look at the current laws in the three states. I was concerned with what the laws allow, what they prohibit, and the relationship between the statutes and the reality of day-to-day practice. Other topics included the degree to which the law is an example of "friendly" or "hostile" licensing (that is, do lay midwives govern themselves or are they placed under the control of medical or nursing boards?), the origin of the law, and the justifications used to gain its passage. I also examined past and current legislation to determine how changes in the bill accommodated the demands of various interest groups. Specific data that provided insight into all these matters included: 1) descriptive statistics on the number of births and the practitioner in attendance; 2) information relevant to midwife licensure drawn from the media, newsletters of various organizations, medical journals, and state archives; and 3) interviews with legislators, lobbyists from medical professional groups, and representatives from midwife and consumer groups.

Information about the effect of licensure came from detailed interviews and observation. I conducted interviews with midwives, their clients, and medical professionals who work with midwives. My earlier historical study of midwife regulation (DeVries, 1982) indicated that licensure significantly affected both styles of practice and the kind of client who would employ a midwife. With this in mind, my observations and interviews were structured to collect information on: 1) the routines and practices of the lay midwife (What are the limitations set up by the law? Do midwives adhere to them? Does licensure expand or restrict the midwife's prerogatives and behavior with regard to medical procedure? Is interaction with physicians facilitated or hindered by licensing law? Will physicians continue to work with unlicensed midwives once a licensing law is passed?); 2) the nature and attitude of the lay midwife (Does licensure alter the kind of individual drawn to the occupation? Does the medical training necessitated by licensure change the lay midwife's attitude toward the efficacy of medicine?); and 3) the nature and motivations of the clientele who seek the services of the lay midwife (What are their motivations? Does the nature of the clientele change when the practice is given state sanction? If so, does this change the nature of the practice of lay midwifery?). I also observed midwives on their daily rounds—which included watching their interactions with clients, other midwives, and physicians—in order to check and clarify data supplied in interviews.

My research began with an obvious handicap: I was a male investigating a female-dominated occupation. Not only are most midwives women, but *all* their clients are women. Feminist sensitivities, in which the intentions of all males are suspect, compounded the difficulties. Interestingly, I faced greatest opposition from several women in the academic world who thought it inappropriate for a male to study what they perceived as a uniquely female issue.

As expected, the problem of gender limited my access on certain occasions. For instance, I delayed my arrival at a midwife educational workshop because part of the workshop included instruction on the insertion of catheters and the midwives were going to practice on each other. I am not the first researcher to face this problem. In his report of a meeting of Mississippi midwives in 1948, Ferguson (1950: 93) reports that the male physician accompanying him grew nervous when it appeared the midwives were about to demonstrate how to give an enema. In an informative article on this problem, Daniels (1967) discusses the difficulties she encountered as a female civilian researching the military. She suggests that while being a "low caste stranger" is hardly ideal for a researcher, it does provide some unique opportunities and insights. In my own case, for example, I discovered that midwives often went out of their way to explain matters they thought would be unclear to a male. Some midwives were also anxious to include me in their activities as their "token male"; an offer of apprenticeship I received was an example of this. The midwives felt it would be nice to have an apprentice who could relate to fathers.

When I sought financial support for this research I immediately confronted problems with the university's human subjects committee (more formally referred to as the Institutional Review Board or IRB). Research involving human subjects in almost any capacity — even as the subjects of interviews or observations — must gain the approval of the local IRB. The IRB was hesitant to approve my research plan because I was gathering information on an illegal activity (midwifery in California), information that potentially could be used to indict and convict some of the subjects of my study. I finally won aproval by convincing the IRB that my results would not be published until well after the statute of limitations for the offenses I observed had run out. The delay, however, damaged my chances of acquiring funding by forcing me to submit grant proposals "pending IRB approval."

The problem of "sentimentality" in social research is another difficulty I faced. Becker (1964: 4) uses the term "sentimentality" to refer to "a disposition on the part of the researcher to leave certain variables in a problem unexamined." He defines "conventional sentimentality" as that which takes for granted the dominant assumptions of a society, and "unconventional sentimentality" as that which leaves unchallenged assumptions of society's marginal groups. It is the task of the researcher to take a neutral, disinterested position on the phenomena under study, but as we well know, this task is difficult, if not impossible, to achieve completely.

All field researchers experience a tension between the "research self" and the "social self." The *researcher* sets out to gather interesting, high-quality data, but soon the *person* grows involved in an array of relationships with his subjects that range from close and affectionate to openly hostile. Of course, a good researcher knows how to blend the research and social selves in order to maximize both the quality of the study and the quality of his life, but even the most facile of investigators is constantly forced to balance personal and professional interests in the field. A bittersweet reality of qualitative research is that the subjects of investigation often become friends. The friendships are rewarding, but the researcher is afraid of "going native" and suffers the guilt of using information given on the basis of friendship. As Davis (1961) points out, the subjects the researcher feels closest to are usually the subjects that are most thoroughly used (that is, exploited).

I established some rewarding friendships with the midwives who were my subjects. As a result, it is likely that I exhibit a trace of "unconventional sentimentality" which leaves unquestioned parts in favor of the midwives' point of view. But let me suggest that if I lean toward unconventional sentimentality it only serves to counteract the conventional sympathies toward medicine that pervade our society.

The issue of sentimentality raises some interesting problems. To what extent, for example, does sentiment govern the recommendations of researchers? When pressed for specific policy recommendations, do analysts base their advice on how it will affect their subjects (that is, their new friends) or is such advice grounded solely on the outcomes of their scientific study? In many studies the research evidence supports policy changes beneficial to the subjects in question, but this is not always the case.

My own research offers an example where the policy suggested by the data differed from what many of the subjects perceived as their own best interests. As my research progressed, the conclusions I was drawing were not always welcome news among my midwife friends. Most of these friends did not question the essential validity of my findings—that licensure would alter, and perhaps destroy, the uniqueness of lay midwifery—but nevertheless disagreed with the full implications of my work. They agreed that licensure was potentially dangerous, but felt certain the bills they supported would prove less destructive.

Most of my midwife friends were unwilling to accept the implications of my evidence—that is, that lay midwifery should remain unlicensed, hence illegal. To accept that notion would require them to live under the continued threat of prosecution, even persecution. Several midwives in California had in fact run afoul of the law around the time of my research. The case that most frightened my friends was that of Rosalie Tarpening, a midwife who came to the attention of the authorities when she attended a birth where the infant died. Her arrest and subsequent jailing offered stark evidence of the danger of remaining unlicensed. Although convinced of the truth of my findings, this incident and similar cases made it difficult to ask my friends to live by this truth.

The dilemma came to a head when I was asked by a group of California midwives to help devise a strategy to gain passage of a licensing bill in that state. How could I, a supporter of midwifery, contribute to a campaign I was convinced would spell doom for that profession? On the other hand, how could I refuse to contribute to a cause that, if successful, would make the lives of my friends more tolerable? In this case, I let my heart rule my head and threw myself into working for the passage of the licensing bill. I planned, lobbied, marched, phoned, and did all those things associated with mobilizing a constituency behind legislation. I must admit that I took my researcher's notebook with me wherever I went, but I genuinely worked for passage of this bill.

The failure of the bill in its three versions left me with mixed feelings. All the people I worked with were disappointed, and I understood their frustration. On the other hand, I felt that the defeat, which allowed midwifery to continue in its unique but threatened status, was a paradoxical victory for the profession. It is the nature of this paradox, the true dilemma of licensure, that I explore in this book.

In the following chapters I examine several aspects of the relationship between midwives, medicine, and the law. I begin in Chapter 1 by exploring some common sense, but inaccurate, views of medical licensure. In that chapter I discuss the implications of licensure for the provision of health care. Specific consideration of midwifery begins in Chapter 2, where I lay the foundation for analysis of modern laws governing midwifery by reviewing the history of midwife regulation. There have been several excellent histories of midwifery in recent years (for example, Litoff, 1978; Donnison, 1977) but none have focused exclusively on regulation. In Chapter 3 I look at successful and unsuccessful attempts to get midwife licensing laws passed by legislatures in Arizona, Texas, and California. My focus lies on the social setting and the key players in the creation and evolution of these laws. Chapter 4 considers the impact of the various regulatory schemes on the practice of midwives. Here I examine the direct and indirect changes initiated by law.

Chapter 5 explores the ways regulatory law influences the social and legal nature of disciplinary actions. In the conclusion, Chapter 6, I comment on the relationship of law and medicine and outline some of the consequences of alternative policies for regulation.

Regulating Birth

Chapter 1

Midwifery, Medicine, and the Law

In the sixteenth century science gradually started to displace traditional views and practices of childbirth. As science shed more light on the birth process and as technology allowed increasing intervention in birth, midwifery became a more regulated and less popular occupation. Physicians developed and controlled new technologies for monitoring and intervening in birth, and with the use of law to define medical practice, technical control became legal control. These legal and medical developments forever altered the relationship between physicians and midwives and changed the practical nature of their respective professions.

In this chapter I discuss how medical licensure—as an example of the interaction of medicine and law—has affected the claim of physicians for exclusive privileges with regard to technology and techniques. I focus on the role of medical licensing in protecting public as well as professional interests and critically review prevailing views of licensure.

Common Sense and Medical Licensure

In our society, common sense is a prized possession. It speaks of a person's practical knowledge, the ability to quickly comprehend a situation and take appropriate action. But there is also a dark side to

common sense. The utility of common sense is derived from simpli-
fication, and common sense understandings of the world do not often square with reality because they take so much for granted. In
the area of medical licensure there are at least *two* common sense
views of reality—"public" common sense and "sociological" common sense—each with an element of truth, but neither telling the
whole story.[1]

"Public" common sense tells us that the licensing of medical personnel guarantees the quality of health care and thereby protects
the citizenry. In her discussion of this view, Hodgson (1977:
664–74) points out that the state attempts to protect the health of
its citizens by licensing orthodox practitioners and prohibiting unorthodox practice. Such a procedure is seen as having several positive functions: 1) it prevents the delay of effective treatment; 2) it
protects a gullible public from fraud; 3) it standardizes treatment
according to objective criteria; and 4) it avoids undue economic
costs to the patient and society. Most informed observers concur
on the desirability of these goals, and some admit that to a certain
extent licensure accomplishes them. However, others note that
closer inspection of licensing laws in operation belies common
sense. These more cynical observers claim that licensure is unable
to fully obtain its objectives, and point out the costs imposed by using licensure to achieve these ends. Much of this critique is based
on an alternative variety of common sense developed by sociol-
gists.

The first two objectives of licensure—preventing the delay of
effective treatment and protecting the gullible—seem easy to
prove, but only at first glance. The treatment of cancer provides a
case in point. What separates "effective" from "fraudulent" treatment? Surgery, radiation, and chemotherapy are the conventional
treatments of cancer, but in certain cases they appear no more effective than the unorthodox metabolic therapy (see Hodgson,
1977: 666). More relevant for our discussion, we find similar difficulties when considering the appropriate location for giving birth,

with debates being waged over the relative safety of the conventional hospital birth as opposed to the unconventional home birth (see Yankauer, 1983; Adamson and Gare, 1980; McQuarrie, 1980; Annas, 1978).

The goals of licensure, however praiseworthy, also tend to inhibit innovation. The standardizing of treatment is particularly culpable in this regard because it establishes a "standard of care" which defines the boundaries of acceptable medical practice. Practitioners who step over boundaries are liable to legal prosecution and social ostracism. This discourages experimentation with new techniques or with new categories of health personnel. Medical history is literally full of examples in which orthodox practitioners ostracize the discoverers of significant medical facts and theories. Included in this category are the discoverers of the circulation of blood, the germ theory of disease, smallpox vaccine, penicillin, the use of Vitamin C for the prevention of scurvy, and the use of Vitamin B for the prevention of pellegra (Hodgson, 1977: 668). Friedman (1962: 157) observes:

> There are many different routes of knowledge and learning and the effect of restricting the practice of what is called medicine and confining it as we tend to do to a particular group, who in the main have to conform to the prevailing orthodoxy, is certain to reduce the amount of experimentation that goes on and hence reduce the rate of growth of knowledge in the area.

Other individuals have noted that medical licensure restricts the innovative use of medical and paramedical personnel. Shyrock (1967) notes the claim of medical educators that conservative policies of medical examining boards hamper innovations in the training of health-care providers. In one of the most thorough studies on this topic yet conducted, Forgotson and Cook (1967: 750) conclude "that present legal regulation of health manpower restricts optimal allocation of tasks among members of the medical manpower matrix and operates as a barrier to experiments to train and utilize new categories of health professionals." McKinley (1973: 80) concludes that licensure laws play an important part in allowing professional groups "to question the propriety of and impede any social change initiated by [any outside] source."

The fourth policy goal of licensure—the avoidance of undue economic costs—also has unintended, negative consequences. While it ostensibly prevents unnecessary expense associated with ineffective treatments, licensure creates a professional monopoly which is capable of artificially inflating prices. Also, the emphasis on "effective treatment" works to suppress innovations which are potentially less costly than orthodox practice. As Hodgson (1977: 674) notes:

> Innovative alternatives to orthodox treatment represent potential contributions toward improving the public health. The converse of the proposition that some of yesterday's quackery is today's science is that some of today's orthodox practices will be tomorrow's barbarisms. Because risks to the patient's health are involved in the orthodox as well as the unorthodox, and because orthodox therapy can itself prove costly, government prohibition of medical alternatives may represent an additional cost in the form of potential benefits foregone or actual harm inflicted.

Another element in the public common-sense view of licensure is the belief that licensing is the most effective way of ensuring the discipline of errant practitioners. In theory, the licensing board—composed of experts drawn from the profession—is the only body capable of recognizing and correcting improper practice; moreover, the board is assumed to be eager to maintain an acceptable professional image. But, again, reality belies common sense. The most widely cited study of medical licensure and discipline (Derbyshire, 1969) found only 938 actions taken by licensing boards against physicians in the United States in the five year period between 1963 and 1967, although approximately 300,000 physicians were practicing at that time (National Center for Health Statistics, 1979).

These data indicate that "disciplinary action by medical boards is almost insignificant in terms of the universe of practicing physicians" (DHEW, 1971: 33). Another survey of medical discipline estimates that 1 to 3 percent of the physician population merit disciplinary action "within the legal concept of the problem" and that this percentage would increase dramatically "if one includes those who are delinquent within the broader field of ethical consideration" (McCleery et al., 1971: 69–70). Derbyshire (1969: 89) speculates that the "proportion of unscrupulous, unethical, delinquent, and incompetent physicians" is somewhere between 2 and 10 percent. If these estimates are accurate it is safe to conclude that licensing boards are not effective disciplinary mechanisms.

Implicit in the criticism of public common sense on licensure is another common sense understanding of the phenomenon which I label "sociological" common sense.

Modern social scientists, critical of earlier investigations that accepted the public common sense conclusion that licensing boards were necessary for improved health care (for example, see Sigerist, 1935), have called attention to a basic dilemma in licensure. These sociologists have noted that licensing laws, while attempting to guarantee quality and protect public health, have given professionals and their associations a restrictive monopoly over practice. Historical evidence of this dilemma is found in Carlson's (1970) observation that licensing laws have evolved in a monopolistic direction, moving from permissive laws—which merely prevent the use of a given title by the unlicensed—to mandatory laws—which made it a criminal offense for the unlicensed to take any action specifically reserved for licensed professionals.

Sociological common sense tells us that licensure laws do not exist solely for the protection of the public. Instead, and perhaps more importantly, they exist for protection of the profession. Within the last two decades social scientists have identified the accommodative relationship between the professional associations of medicine and the regulatory boards which govern them (for example, Carlson, 1970; *Iowa Law Review*, 1972). In a study of professional associations and the legal regulation of practice, Akers (1968: 480) comments on the "close interrelationship between the association and public regulatory agency. . . . It appears that their activities, personnel, facilities and even finances overlap to such an extent that it is not entirely correct to say that the association 'influences' the board's administration of public policy. . . . The cooperation between the two sometimes reaches the point of near identity."[2]

The sociological debunking of medical licensure has wide appeal, finding supporters among the very conservative and the very liberal, both in government and in the academy. For instance, comments from conservative economist Milton Friedman (1962: 58) sound much like Ivan Illich's (1976) radical indictment of modern medicine as a contributor to illness:

> I am myself persuaded that licensure has reduced both the quantity and quality of medical practice; that it has reduced the opportunities available to people who would like to be physicians, forcing them to pursue occupations they regard as less attractive; that it has forced the public to pay more for less satisfactory medical service, and that it has retarded technological development both in medicine itself and in the organization of medical practice. I conclude that licensure should be eliminated as a requirement for the practice of medicine.

Government acceptance of sociological common sense in these matters is found in a 1971 Department of Health, Education and Welfare report on the licensing of health personnel. After reviewing the many problems associated with licensure the report recommends a "two year moratorium on the enactment of legislation that would establish new categories of health personnel with statutorily-defined scopes of functions" (DHEW, 1971: 73–74). It concludes that licensing should not be extended to new types of health practitioners because it does not serve the public interest.

These two common-sense views of medical licensure have varied appeal to different categories of medical practitioners. Physicians—the chief beneficiaries of licensure according to sociological common sense—stress the validity of public common sense and are apt to write off its sociological counterpart as the exaggerated imaginings of social scientists. Consequently, the majority of physicians and their associations support the existing methods of licensure. Midwives, as well as other practitioners who travel under the label of "paraprofessional," often accept some combination of public and sociological common sense. They perceive licensure as necessary to assure the competence of individual practitioners, but also feel it grants too much authority to physicians. They believe that separate licensing laws establishing independent licensing boards could both erode the over-extended authority of physicians and establish credibility for their own professions. In this way they accept the sociological idea that licensure will grant special privileges to the occupation, but also embrace the public common-sense belief that paraprofessional licensure—unlike other forms of medical licensure—will serve the public interest.

Beyond Common Sense: An Interactive View of Medical Licensure

Both the public and sociological views of common sense are inadequate. The public view overemphasizes the extent to which licensure protects the public while it overlooks the role of licensure in protecting professional interests. In the sociological view, the emphases are reversed. Moreover, both views fail to account for how law and medicine interact—that is, how law affects (and in turn is affected by) medical practice.

Most analyses of the medicine-law interaction are written by physicians, ethicists, philosophers, or lawyers concerned with ethical dilemmas such as the right to die, informed consent, genetic engineering, or medical care for incompetent persons. Social scientists have thoroughly analyzed medical and legal institutions, but rarely have they explored the way these institutions interact.[3] Some scholars interested in the sociology of occupations have compared the medical and legal professions (see Heinz and Laumann, 1982: 333–42; Rueschemeyer, 1964), but very few studies have perceived the law-medicine relation as interactive.

This blind spot in research reflects sociologists' difficulty in deciding whether law shapes society or society shapes law. Works such as Sumner's (1960 [1906]) analysis of folkways, Ehrlich's (1936) treatise on the "inner order of associations," Hall's (1952) classic study of theft, law, and society, Schwartz and Miller's (1964) analysis of legal evolution and societal complexity, Chambliss' (1964) study of laws of vagrancy, and Massell's (1968) examination of imposed legal change in traditional society provide evidence that law depends on other social institutions. On the other hand, some social scientists and jurists view the law as an effective agent of change and have advocated the use of law for social engineering (see Ward, 1906; Pound, 1923: 141–65). This view of law can also be verified by empirical research. Studies of the impact of law on interracial relationships in the American South (see Woodward, 1966; Knoll, 1967; Hyman and Sheatsley, 1964), certain investigations of deterrence (see Gibbs, 1967; Tittle, 1969; Campbell and Ross, 1968), and research on the effects of legislation (Colombotos, 1969) indicate that law can indeed function as an instrument of social change.

Given this evidence it is reasonable to conclude, along with Akers and Hawkins (1975: 41), that law "is *interdependent* with other systems in society. Law is both shaped by and has an independent impact on society; it grows out of and is consistent with extant normative structures and can also influence them to change in one direction or another." In the case of medical licensure this implies that while medicine shapes the laws that govern it, those laws have an independent impact on medicine. Recognition of the interdependence of law and medicine places them in a larger social and cultural context and acknowledges that both institutions are shaped by that context.

Legal Controls on Medical Practice and Parental Authority

Kantorowicz (1958) has observed that areas ruled by the law must be "justiciable"—that is, the arrangements of nonlegal institutions must be understood in legal terms in order for laws to regulate them. Unfortunately, technological developments in modern society have outstripped the ability of legal institutions to comprehend them. Many nonlegal institutions, including medicine, have developed highly specialized bodies of knowledge that prevent penetration by legal institutions without some technical guidance. As a result, those who create and administer the law must consult "experts." Chemists and toxicologists give advice on laws governing the disposal of toxic substances, automobile engineers affect decisions concerning the inclusion of safety devices in passenger cars, and the counsel of medical experts helps determine the outcome of legal decisions related to health care. (This latter category is of particular import for midwifery, where obstetricians and other physicians have enormous *de facto* power over legislation and adjudication concerning midwives.) By default, these experts gain considerable control over their own field, a situation which raises the potential for conflict of interest; it makes legal decisions dependent on information and opinion which legal officials cannot evaluate independently. This "legal dependency," which is unique to modern society, influences both legal and technical institutions (see Stone, 1980: 161–63).

In medicine, legal dependency helps sustain a cultural authority which upsets more traditional patterns of authority. It is reasonable to assume that legal officials who make medical decisions let themselves be influenced by culturally dominant medical views. In America, as in other modern societies, allopathy has been accepted as the orthodox mode of medical treatment.[4] The elevation of allopathy—reflecting a basic trust in the progress of science and the benefits of technology—is the result of political and economic competition among various styles of medicine that occurred earlier in this century (see Starr, 1982: 30–144; Brown, 1979). Consequently, legal decisions in the legislatures and courts exhibit a bias toward allopathic practice.

The cultural dominance of allopathy has replaced more traditional forms of authority. For example, in recent years the courts have repeatedly denied parental authority to withhold "orthodox" treatments for illness or disease suffered by their offspring. In perhaps the most well-publicized case of this type, a Massachusetts court ordered the parents of Chad Green, a young leukemia victim, to stop unorthodox metabolic therapy and replace it with the more orthodox chemotherapy (393 N.E. 2d 836 1979; see also Horwitz, 1979). Law has also been invoked to prevent parents from substituting prayer and other religious rituals for orthodox medical treatment of sick children (Ostling, 1984). In these cases scientific, allopathic medicine is used as a basis to challenge traditional parental authority and to replace it with a more rationalized notion of parent-child relationships which recognizes separate rights of the child.

This challenge to parents' authority extends to the choice of how their children will be born. In a decision related to the practice of lay midwifery, the California Supreme Court stated (18 Cal. 3d 479 1976 at 638):

In recent years the constitutional right to privacy derived from the First, Fourth, Fifth, Ninth and Fourteenth Amendments has been substantially expanded to protect certain personal choices pertaining to childbearing, marriage, procreation and abortion. However, the right to privacy has never been interpreted so broadly as to protect a woman's choice of the manner and circumstances in which her baby is born.

The court then cites an interest in the rights of the unborn as articulated in *Roe v. Wade* as a valid reason to require all birth attendants to be licensed. At the end of her study of case law relevant to childbirth, Katz (1980) concludes that parents can be held liable for injury to their child resulting from a home birth. She states that in cases where the infant is seriously injured because of complications which could have been predicted and perhaps avoided in a hospital setting, the parents could be charged with

> child abuse, and if the infant dies, maybe for manslaughter, depending on the actual cause of death and its reasonable predictability. This potential liability is an attempt by the law to discourage people from having unassisted home births, and to encourage them to obtain an appropriate attendant for any homebirth, while seeking hospital care when reasonably necessary to protect the health and safety of the infant.[5]

In these and similar cases, court limits on once unquestioned parental authority is justified by citing the benefits of scientific medicine.

Thus technology allows medicine to use the power of law to shape social relationships. As Cottrell noted more than four decades ago, technology carries with it the potential for "monopolizability" by the occupational group controlling that technology (Cottrell, 1940: 36–38). He was speaking largely in terms of a technical monopoly (where only certain people had the skill to use the technology) but in the case of medicine this extends to a cultural monopoly in which only one style of medicine is felt to be appropriate. In this way cultural monopoly exists in happy interaction with legal monopoly. Each enhances and amplifies the other.

Rise of Medical Paraprofessions
Medicine uses technology to influence law, but it doesn't follow that medicine dominates law. Technology, after all, is a part of the larger context that influences both medical and legal institutions,

and the effect of technology on medicine is not always predictable. For instance, accompanying the growth of technological medicine are a variety of consumer movements that have forced professionals to reassess and "humanize" their treatments (see DeVries, 1984). The growth of medical technology also results in a new array of medical occupations. Much to the chagrin of many physicians, these medical technicians are clamoring for autonomy, seeking to claim jurisdiction over tasks that were once the private possession of medical doctors.

Law itself is an important part of the social context that shapes medicine. The legal environment shapes the actions of the medical community in at least two ways. First, it acts to constrain behavior directly. If one group seeks to dominate medical care, for instance, it must do so in terms of the legal system. The desire to dominate is subject to the wiles of the legislative arena and the technicalities of legal procedure. Admittedly, better organized professional groups have an advantage here, but their wishes are altered by, and structured in, a legal environment. Direct constraint is also visible in challenges to medical domination. For instance, the current concern with the rights of patients and legal limits on the proliferation of medical technology are evidence of the law's resistance to conventional medical authority. Second, and perhaps more important, the law indirectly constrains medical behavior by redefining relationships, altering attitudes, and initiating social change. Colombotos (1969) shows how law changed the attitudes and behavior of physicians in relation to Medicare. Similarly, Stone (1980) documents how the political and legal traditions of America and West Germany have affected medicine in those countries.

The licensing of midwives and other paraprofessionals offers perhaps the clearest view of the impact of law on medicine. It is no accident that sociological common sense, with its inflated view of the ability of medicine to control law, emerged from the study of physicians (see Shyrock, 1967; Freidson, 1970a; 1970b; Berlant, 1975; Larson, 1977). In contrast to these studies of physicians, sociological explorations of medical paraprofessions show law to be an important element in the shaping of those occupations (see Larkin, 1978; 1981; 1983; White, 1979). In his investigation of the licensure of radiographers in England, Larkin (1978: 852) concludes:

The medical division of labor is usually given its shape, formally speaking, in those controversies which centre on licensing arrangements. . . . The exercise of dominance implies also a careful deskilling of other health occupations insofar as their need for medical legitimacy will lead them to acquiesce in a re-definition of their role.

Of course there is the temptation to conclude that the laws which shape these paraprofessions are themselves shaped by medical orthodoxy—in the guise of physician organizations. To an extent this is true. Larkin (1983: 18) makes this point when he notes that licensing "[completes] a stage in the evolution of medical dominance." However, the newly created patterns of care also alter medicine. Sensitivity to the dynamic relationship between law and medicine derived from the study of midwifery and other medical paraprofessions makes one skeptical about sociological common sense.

Common Sense Disconfirmed:
The Licensing of Midwives

Laws that govern the practice of midwifery were first established during the European Middle Ages. With the development of new techniques and instruments for assisting birth, medical men created regulations to insure that midwives were competent in the new "science" of birth. Later, midwives themselves endorsed legislation as a way to protect and promote their profession.

Bringing midwifery into the twentieth century involved more

than updating the contents of the midwife's bag. The intrusion of law has proved equally important. In a society that defines and regulates medicine by law, midwives can achieve legitimate status only by accepting a place within medical statutes. In some instances this means seeking licensing legislation; in others it means attempting to prove that existing statutes do not prohibit midwifery. In either situation, laws necessarily alter midwives' established relationships with doctors, clients, and other midwives.

The current statutes in some states clearly specify that the practice of midwifery—including prenatal care, assistance at birth, and postpartum care—is forbidden to all but licensed physicians and their designated assistants. In other states no clear definition of midwifery exists, and because the provision of assistance at birth is not defined as the practice of medicine, midwives have what some have called "legality by default." Somewhere between these extremes lies the more common regulatory strategy of licensure that grants midwives the privilege to practice but prohibits their access to certain clientele, technology, and techniques.

Midwifery is considered one of a blossoming number of medical paraprofessions which includes physical therapists, nurse-practitioners, physician assistants, and other occupations sometimes referred to as "physician extenders." But midwifery is unique in at least two important ways: it has had a history independent of the medical profession; and its existence is characterized by the presence of more than one type of midwife. Other paramedical occupations arose to assist conventional medicine. These include nurses, physicians' assistants, respiratory therapists, occupational therapists, and other practitioners whose occupations were created with the intent of assisting or relieving the physician from some tedious task. Although midwives are now seen as adjuncts to physicians, historically midwifery was an autonomous profession. As will be evident in the following chapter, it is difficult to read the chronicle of midwifery's move from autonomy to domination by the medical profession without noticing the interaction of law and medicine.

Unlike other paraprofessions, the occupation of midwifery includes more than one category. While other paramedical occupations have singular and uniform descriptions of their practitioners, midwifery in the United States includes both certified nurse-midwives and lay or empirical midwives. A nurse-midwife is a Registered Nurse (R.N.) who has completed an additional course of training in obstetrics lasting between one and two years (see ACNM, n.d.). In 1984 there were an estimated 3,000 nurse-midwives in the United States who could legally practice in 51 of the 53 states and jurisdictions. In that year 28 schools offered training in nurse-midwifery and together they graduated about 250 students per year (ACNM, 1984). Lay midwives, on the other hand, have a more practical orientation toward birth and are often regarded as not being "true" medical practitioners. While a few schools do exist for lay midwives (see Baldwin, 1979b), their training is less formal and usually consists of some combination of apprenticeship and self-education. Because lay midwives often practice without a license—even in locations where licenses are issued—it is difficult to arrive at an accurate estimate of their numbers. The National Center for Health Statistics (1979: 164) reports that 2,534 lay midwives were practicing as of July 1975, but fails to take account of many midwives practicing without licenses. For instance, the California Department of Consumer Affairs (DCA) estimated that somewhere between 300 and 400 lay midwives were active in the state during 1977, although California does not license or register these practitioners. Literature from the alternative birth movement indicates that lay midwives are also active in several other states where, due to the lack of legal recognition, the National Center for Health Statistics claims no lay midwives exist (see Sallomi et al., 1981).

The regulations which control midwifery reflect the differences between the two categories of midwives. Thanks to the efforts of their professional association, the American College of Nurse-Midwives (ACNM), licensing laws for certified nurse-midwives are fairly uniform across states. On the other hand, lay midwives, with no effective national organization, are regulated by a unique set of statutes in each state. In fact the legal status of lay midwifery varies radically from state to state. According to one recent report, there were only five states in which lay midwifery is clearly legal. Nine states clearly prohibit lay midwives from practicing and the rest have a variety of ambiguous laws (see Sallomi et al., 1981).[6]

The existence of more than one type of midwife and the variation in laws which regulate their practices provide an ideal setting for a comparative study of the influence of medicine on law and the direct and indirect ways law shapes medicine. In fact, the comparison of various strategies for regulating midwives forms the major portion of this study. Arizona, Texas, and California were selected for this comparison for two reasons. First, as indicated above, these states represented the range of approaches for licensing lay midwives: California prohibited lay midwives from practicing; Texas allowed midwives to practice with the simple requirement that they register at the county courthouse; and Arizona had a licensing program which included mandatory education and certification exams. Second, at the time of the study all three were considering changes in their regulation of midwives, a fact which made the legislative strategies of several groups particularly visible.

Modern midwife regulations have much in common with their historic counterparts. The next chapter provides the groundwork for the comparison and analysis of contemporary regulations by examining early licensing laws and identifying the common themes in those laws. A major thesis that emerges from review of midwife regulations, both old and new, is that the dynamic relationship of law and midwifery holds serious consequences for the midwife's profession as well as for the provision of health care to women and their infants. For women in the upper and middle classes, these dynamics determine options available for childbirth. For women with limited incomes, the midwifery-law relationship can altogether eliminate choice. In fact, some minority groups resist licensure in the belief that the legitimation of midwifery would cut off poor women's access to physicians and force them to accept "second class care" at the hands of midwives.

Chapter 2

The Emergence of
Midwifery Regulation

The art of midwifery is undergoing a revival in the United States. At an earlier point in history, midwives were considered the only appropriate assistants for childbirth, which was "woman's business." The very thought of allowing a male physician into the lying-in chamber was appalling to the modest sensibilities of most women and their husbands. However, modesty and tradition eventually gave way to medical science, and by the middle of this century the overwhelming majority of births were attended in hospitals by male physicians. Midwifery was regarded as little more than the medically ignorant traditions carried on by a handful of midwives who served isolated pockets of our population—those who were cut off from the benefits of modern medicine by their remote geographic location, their immersion in cultures that had never abandoned the traditional approach to birth, or lack of resources. But in recent years this view has changed. At present, midwifery is emerging from the mists of folkore and disrepute into a modern and acceptable approach to childbirth. Somewhat ironically, midwife care, a form of health care with a centuries-long tradition, is now being offered as a nontraditional, an alternative approach to childbirth for all classes of women, not only the poor, the uneducated, or the immigrant.

Midwives and Other Birth Attendants[1]

Although the midwife currently plays an insignificant role in the United States, she was and still is the primary attendant in the majority of the world's births.[2] In her report, "Maternity Care in the World," Bayes (1968) estimates that two-thirds of all babies are born with the sole assistance of nonmedical personnel, many of whom are the cultural counterparts of the midwife. A number of Western European nations employ trained midwives to attend the majority of uncomplicated births (Josiah Macy, Jr. Foundation, 1968: 105–46). Sousa (1976: 117) estimates that midwives of one type or another are responsible for managing 80 percent of all human births.

Throughout her history in the Western world, the midwife has existed in a somewhat anomalous position. Although she has always been a desired companion to women in labor, she has at various times been accused of everything from ignorance to being in league with the devil. In parts of medieval Europe her social status was lower than that of the executioner, and in these same areas the son of a midwife faced exclusion from trade guilds because of his mother's profession (Forbes, 1966: 113). In later centuries she became the target of ambitious male practitioners who were armed with a variety of implements to assist and "ease" the process of childbirth.

References to midwives as a distinct occupational group extend at least as far back as the Jewish captivity in Egypt. The character of midwifery at that time is revealed by an account of the refusal of a group of midwives to obey an order by the Pharaoh to kill all male children born to the Hebrews. When the Pharaoh demanded an explanation for this disobedience, a spokeswoman for the group replied, "The Hebrew women are not as the Egyptian women; for they are lively and are delivered ere the midwives come in unto them" (Exodus 1:19). The Pharoah's acceptance of this rather lame excuse is enlightening, for as Samuel Gregory noted in 1848, "Even this tyrant dared not invade their sacred office to make special inquisition" (Gregory, 1974 [1848]: 7). Commenting on this episode, Litoff (1978: 3) makes a similar observation: "This passage indicated that the presence of a midwife was considered sufficient when an attendant at birth was necessary and that parturition was believed to be such a normal process that many births went unattended." The responsibility for the control and management of birth was beyond even kingly jurisdiction, belonging solely to the mother and her attendant.

The Western midwife's position began to erode in the sixteenth century with the advent of male forays into midwifery and the appearance of regulatory measures. The church was the primary agent of midwife regulation in medieval Europe. On the Continent this ecclesiastical licensure gave way to municipal systems of registration as early as 1452 (Donnison, 1977: 5), but in England church regulation persisted until the eighteenth century, when its power diminished, leaving midwifery essentially unregulated until early in the twentieth century. These first efforts to regulate midwifery were more concerned with its social and religious aspects than with the mastery of any specified body of knowledge; regulation consisted of little more than formal licensing itself and the "supression" of those who practiced without the proper certification.[3] The church's major interest was the prevention of witchcraft. Because midwives used herbs, potions, and spells to assist in delivery, they were often confused with, or assumed to be, witches. While the accusations of witchcraft were seldom well-founded, the consequences could be severe. Forbes (1966: 127) documents several cases and concludes: "It is difficult, even impossible to separate actual from imagined offenses but there can be no doubt of the utter vindictiveness toward any midwife who was suspect" (see also Oakley, 1976: 23–30).[4]

During the sixteenth and seventeenth centuries the midwife's control over birth began to be undermined by male intrusions in the lying-in chambers. At this point in history, male involvement in birth was largely reactive. Typically, barber-surgeons—who by virtue of guild membership had exclusive rights to the wielding of surgical instruments—were called to assist in the most complicated cases. These ministrations were often disastrous for the mother and child as well as for the reputation of the male attendant. This gradual encroachment by doctors and other males into a previously all-female domain met resistance, but technology favored the emerging masculine claim to the role of birth attendant. The invention of the forceps, with their promise of shortened labors and their monopoly by men, is generally acknowledged as the crucial factor in the male's rise to dominance in this field. Rousch (1979: 34) characterizes the forceps as "the fatal blow to the female midwives." Litoff (1978: 7) regards the development of the forceps as "the single most important event" in the displacement of midwives. Donnison (1977: 21–22), while she is careful to enumerate other factors that contributed to the decline of female midwifery, contends that "the introduction of the midwifery forceps . . . precipitated . . . rapid acceleration in . . . an existing trend." It is difficult to understand why midwives did not adopt the use of forceps in their practice. Wertz and Wertz (1977: 39) suggest:

> Legal restrictions stemming from the power of surgeon's guilds may have prevented it, and the simple force of custom, which associated men with instrumental interference, may have limited women's use of forceps. Men may have also refused to sell forceps to women, or women may have found that using early versions required a degree of physical strength they did not have.

It is also likely that female midwives were hesitant to identify themselves with techniques and intruments characteristic of male midwifery. Elizabeth Nihell, a famous eighteenth century English midwife, offered the following evaluation of William Smellie, one of the "fathers of modern obstetrics":

[He has] the delicate fist of a great horse god-mother of a he mid-wife. . . . His disciples [are] made out of broken barbers, tailors, or even pork butchers, for I knew myself one of this last trade, who after passing half his life in stuffing sausages, is turned an intrepid physician and man-midwife. See the whole pack open in full cry: to arms! to arms! is the word; and what are those arms by which they maintain themselves, *but those instruments, those weapons of death*! Would not one imagine that the art of midwifery was an art militare? (quoted in Aveling, 1977a [1872]: 122–23, emphasis added).

Except for her relative freedom from regulation, the situation of the midwife in America was similar to her counterpart in Europe. For instance, like their sisters in Europe, midwives in Colonial America were often suspected of practicing witchcraft. Anne Hutchinson, one of the more famous early American midwives, was accused of witchcraft and banished by the General Court of Massachusetts after assisting in the delivery of an anencephalic child (a child born without the frontal lobes of the brain—essentially brainless and headless).

The American midwife continued to play an important role at birth until the early twentieth century. At that point the medical profession turned its attention to her activities and found them lacking. The result was a "flood of articles and addresses on 'the midwife problem in ____'" which in turn spawned a rash of legislation restricting and regulating midwifery (see Kobrin, 1966). The effect of the medical establishment's attacks was dramatic. For example, the number of midwives practicing in New York City dropped from 1,700 in 1919 to 170 in 1939, and finally to just 2 in 1957 (Kobrin, 1966; Speert, 1968).

Professional rivalry was clearly a motive in the negative evaluation of midwives by medical professionals. Indeed, as Devitt (1979a: 366) points out, the choice of titles for the many critical articles published earlier in this century were variations of "the Midwife Problem" rather than the "Infant and Maternal Mortality Problem," thus reflecting the desire of physicians for the "expansion of [their] profession and the elimination of midwifery" (see also Devitt, 1979b; 1979c). Ostensibly, American physicians rejected the European idea of upgrading midwifery through education because it promulgated a "double standard of obstetrics," but actually they were concerned about the loss of income and access to cases used for teaching (Kobrin: 1966: 358). Consider this comment made by two American physicians regarding the passage of the 1902 midwifery licensing law in England:

> The Midwife Bill . . . has given England a fairly well-trained cleanly midwife, in place of the dirty midwife and the careless practitioner, but it has not instituted a new system, and in the light of modern medicine, it is of questionable advantage to the community, for it provides a double system in obstetrics, the midwife but scantily trained, depending upon the physician who is not certain to respond to her call. *Some 30,000 women have taken enough practice away from physicians to obtain a livelihood. Unquestionably the field of physicians has been invaded* and the community is the loser (Emmons and Huntington, 1911: 260, emphasis added).

As recently as 1968 a doctor reported to a conference on midwifery: "Let us be above board about it. We have a financial interest in delivering babies. If you don't include us in deliveries, we have no choice but to be obstructive to whatever thing you start" (Johnson, 1968: 95).

Two types of evidence confirm that the flurry of concern over midwives early in this century was more a consequence of physicians' fear of competition than a desire to protect the health of women and children. Devitt (1979c) has collected statistics on rates of maternal and infant mortality from several cities and states indicating that during the period from 1910 to the 1930s midwives performed as well as, or better than, physicians. For example, data from Newark, New Jersey, for the years 1915 and 1916 show that physician-attended births had strikingly higher rates of neonatal mortality (death under 30 days of age) and infant mortality (death within the first year of life) than births attended by midwives (De-vitt, 1979c: 171). Data from other locales are more equivocal, but in no case are midwives shown to be the direct cause of poor outcomes at birth. It is likely that the high mortality rates that prompted concern were due to the incompetence of general practitioners who had no training and little experience in birth (Yankauer, 1983). Writing about "Immigration and the Midwife Problem," Ira Wile (1912) noted that foreign-trained midwives working in the United States were better trained, offered better service, and charged less than the typical physician.

A second kind of evidence that sheds light on the opponents of midwifery is the continued presence of midwives among poor and minority populations and those in remote locations. Despite the poor health of these people, physicians regarded them as undesirable clientele and left their care to midwives. Although physicians generally opposed midwife training programs, they supported such programs for midwives who worked in the urban ghettoes and among the rural Southern poor (see Ferguson, 1950; Mongeau et al., 1961; Campbell, 1946). If the primary concern of physicians was the health of women and their babies, they would have pressed their services into these areas first and allowed midwives to practice among healthier populations. Holmes (n.d.) interviewed some "granny midwives" still working in isolated areas of the South and documented the important contributions they make to the community, not only in the area of health care, but in the preservation of tradition and in the provision of a sense of autonomy of poor blacks.

Despite all its setbacks, midwifery is currently making a comeback. The certified nurse-midwife is slowly gaining medical recognition and acceptance, and the lay midwife—who is often beyond legal or medical control—is gaining in popular appeal. The status of the American midwife is somewhat confounded by the fact that each state and jurisdiction establishes its own regulations. This creates the wide range of controls alluded to earlier, sometimes prohibiting all midwives, sometimes allowing only certified nurse-midwifery, and sometimes allowing the ambiguous "legality by default" (Forman, 1973; see also Forman and Cooper, 1976; HOME, 1976b; Rooks *et al.*, 1978; National Center for Health Statistics, 1979; Sallomi *et al.*, 1981; Cohn *et al.*, 1984).

Midwifery in the contemporary world exists in two basic forms: traditional practices continue in less industrialized countries, and in more advanced Western nations midwives have been gradually absorbed by the medical profession. Even in the Netherlands, a country often cited as an example of the feasibility of midwife-attended home birth (because its low infant and maternal mortality rates exist in conjunction with a large proportion of such births), midwives have recently experienced a significant decline in autonomy because of the decrease in the number of home births. The independent practices of Dutch midwives are disappearing as physicians in that country encourage more women to have their babies in the hospital (Laurillard-Lampe, 1981; van Arkel *et al.*, 1980).

Technology continues to play an important part in the midwife's loss of independence. Her noninterventionist stance—the belief that birth should progress naturally without artificial assistance—has suffered at the hands of medicine's new devices, from the invention of the forceps to the development of the fetal heart monitor. Necessary accommodations of midwifery to the advances of obstetric science have undermined opposition to organized medicine, bringing midwives under the supervision and control of the medical profession. However, the lay midwives who have emerged in America and elsewhere (for instance, Canada; see Thomas, 1979) are an important exception to this trend. They favor home birth and have serious reservations about the efficacy of technological intervention in the birth process. These lay practitioners perpetuate a significant bifurcation within the occupation. When pressed on the issue, it is not unusual for a member of one group to question whether the other group qualifies for the label of "midwives." For both groups, however, the regulation of midwifery has significantly influenced styles of practice. The following section looks more closely at the regulatory process, its effects on the role and status of the midwife, and the manner in which midwifery is regarded by the courts.

Midwife Licensure:
Recognition or Restriction?

In his analysis of laws licensing occupations during the period 1890–1910, Friedman (1965: 494–97) draws a distinction between "friendly" and "hostile" licensure. In the former, the licensing process is controlled by individuals drawn from the occupation being regulated; in hostile licensure, an occupation group is placed under outside control. Friedman offers the licensing of dentists in the state of Wisconsin as an example of friendly licensing; in that instance the authority was granted to a "state board of dental examiners" consisting of "five practicing dentists, at least three of whom shall be members of the Wisconsin state dental society." Hostile licensure is exemplified in the regulations placed on peddlers in the same state; "transient merchants" had to pay fifty dollars for a state license and were also responsible for local fees that could be as high as fifty dollars a day. These exorbitant fees were prompted by the complaints of local merchants who disliked the competition from migratory peddlers. The history of midwife licensure provides another example of hostile licensing. As Friedman (1965: 516) recognized, the weakness of midwifery as an occupation derives from vesting licensing in medical or nursing boards rather than in a board of midwife examiners.

There has been little focus on the effect of hostile licensing laws, either on the regulated occupation or on society at large. As noted above, most studies pertaining to medical licensure deal with physicians. It is exclusive emphasis on friendly licensure that leads to the conclusion that licensing always benefits an occupation.

Many historians of midwifery regard legal recognition as necessary for the survival of the occupation, and they also believe it will improve the quality of care. In her analysis of the British Midwives Act of 1902, Donnison (1977: 174–75) acknowledges that, thanks to its various restrictive clauses, the act, "which was to lay the basis for the present law relating to midwives, was like no other registration Act, before or since, and was to put the midwives in a uniquely disadvantaged position among the professions." However, she still concludes that without the act the midwife

> would most probably have vanished from the scene within the next fifty years, squeezed out by her medical competitors. Midwifery would then have become the sole prerogative of what is still . . . a predominantly male profession. Women would have suffered a double loss—the disappearance of a traditional female occupation, and the denial of female attendance in childbirth. Finally, from the standpoint of society in general, a medical monopoly of midwifery would have had important implications for the cost of obstetric care.[5]

Ann Oakley (1976: 51), another scholar with an interest in the history of midwifery, concurs: "The passing of the 1902 Midwives' Act in Britain ensured a future for female midwifery."

Subscribing to similar reasoning—reasoning steeped in common-sense understandings of licensure—lay midwives who are currently practicing have welcomed recent attempts to license their occupation, regarding such legislation as a means of improving quality and insuring their professional future. When one looks at the history and effects of midwife legislation in most Western nations, however, their optimism seems unfounded. The future secured by licensure may not be welcomed by those who struggle to secure it. To demonstrate the relationship between midwifery and the law, we shall look at the historical development of midwife licensing laws, with special attention to the factors behind the creation of the law, the sanctions available for enforcement, and the influence of the law on the occupation.

Although limited data make definitive statements difficult, it appears that early, church-sponsored systems of midwife registration had little impact on the occupation. The creation of an ecclesiastical licensing system reflected the church's desire to prevent midwives from coercing fees, giving abortifacients, practicing magic, or concealing information about birth events or parentages from civil or religious authorities. Further, the church was interested in insuring a proper baptism for infants who died in childbirth. The following excerpt from a midwife license issued by the bishop of London in 1588 illustrates the concerns of the church (Hitchcock, 1967: 75–76):

> FIRST that ye shalbe dilligente faithfull and redye to helpe everye woman travelinge of Childe as well the poore as the ritche and that in tyme of necessitie you shall not forsake and leave the poore woman and goe to the ritche. ITEM you shall neyther cause nor suffer anye woman to name or put other father to the Childe but onlye him that is the verye father indede thereof. ITEM you shall not suffer anye woman to . . . clayme anye other womans childe for her owne. ITEM ye shall not suffer any childe to be murdered maymed or otherwise hurte. . . . ITEM that ye shall not in anye wise use or exercise anye manner witchcraft charme Sorcerye invocations or other prayers then may seeme withe godes Lawes and the Queenes. ITEM ye shall not give anye Counsaile or minister anye herbe medcyne pocon or anye other thinge to anye woman beinge withe childe wherby she sholde destroye or caste out that she goethe withall before her tyme. ITEM ye shall not enforce anye woman by

paynes or by other ungodlye wayes or means to give you more for your paynes and labor in bringinge her abed then they wolde otherwise doe. . . . ITEM if anye childe be ded borne ye your selfe shall see yt buryed in suche secrett place as neyther hogge dogg nor anye other beste maye come to yt. . . . ITEM ye shall use your selfe in honeste behaviore unto other women beinge lawfully admitted to the room and office of a midwife in all thinges accordinglye. ITEM that ye shall trulye pute to my selfe or my deputye all suche women as ye shall knowe from tyme to occupie and exercise the rome of a midwife within the foresaid dioces and Jury of London without my licens and admission.

Receipt of an ecclesiastical license was not based on a demonstration of competency or dependent upon the completion of an educational program; it relied solely upon a woman's ability to prove her good character and willingness to take an oath of office (see Donnison, 1977: 6–7; Forbes, 1966: 143–49). The sanctions available to the church, which included the prohibition from practice, excommunication, and forced penance, were unevenly applied and largely ineffectual. In spite of the requirement that licensed midwives must report all women practicing without a license, several sources indicate that many midwives remained both unlicensed and unpunished (Hitchcock, 1967; Petrelli, 1971; Roberts, 1962; Donnison, 1977: 7, 22). There was at least one widely employed way of circumventing the law: "Since possession of a license was not required for practice as a 'deputy' to a licensed midwife, women might continue in this capacity for many years without enquiry into their mode of life" (Donnison, 1977: 7). In sum, possession of a church license did little to distinguish a licensed from an unlicensed midwife. Because the latter were still available and because prospective clients saw no advantage in retaining a licensed midwife, traditional modes of practice remained largely unchanged.[6]

Although the first known government-sponsored law regulating midwives was adopted in 1452, municipal regulation of midwives did not begin in earnest until the 1500s. Government sponsored regulation was the result of a different set of motivations and had more important consequences for the occupation. The laws sponsored by secular authorities grew from a concern for public health coupled with the new and "scientific" view of childbirth that was emerging in the sixteenth century. France's newly created hospital schools provided surgeons and midwives with the opportunity to observe many births and encouraged a rational approach to labor and parturition. The new science of midwifery seemed an improvement over the practices of the traditional midwife, which were regarded as potentially dangerous and governed by ancient superstition (see Wertz and Wertz, 1977: 31–33). For example, among the many books on childbirth published in the sixteenth and seventeenth centuries was that of Gervais de la Rousche (1567), entitled *The most important and sovereign science of the art and natural activity of the infant. In opposition to the most accursed and wicked incompetence of women who call themselves midwives or stepmothers, who by their ignorance are responsible for the deaths of many women and infants.* Faith in the scientific approach to birth gradually expanded, and municipal officials interested in the health of their population began to feel it necessary to require competence on the part of midwives. To accomplish this, earlier licensing procedures were revived and made more rigorous by the addition of a formal examination (given by either a physician or an experienced midwife) and/or the requirement of some form of education. An ordinance issued in the French municipality of Lille in 1568 is typical (cited in Petrelli, 1971: 282, emphasis added):

It came to our notice that several persons were daily assuming the cure of some difficult cases and practicing surgery and assisting in childbirth without having demonstrated their competence; from which follow deplorable accidents to the disadvantage of families and the loss of His Majesty's subjects. For this reason, we forbid very emphatically all persons . . . henceforth to assist in childbirth without previously having been presented to the authorities and without having been examined *by the experts*, who for this purpose will be delegated and commissioned by us, and without record of their approval and admission for the practice of midwifery.

Unlike ecclesiastical licensing, municipal regulation worked to limit the scope of the midwife's practice. Because these regulations recognized a body of knowledge related to birth that had been developed by physicians ("the experts" mentioned in the Lille ordinance), the midwife was placed in a subordinate position. In most instances she was required to send for the assistance of a doctor or surgeon in difficult births, and in certain locales she was prohibited from using hooks or other sharp instruments. Like earlier church-sponsored laws, many of these municipal licensing laws required the certified midwife to inform the authorities of any woman practicing midwifery without a license (Donnison, 1977; Petrelli, 1971). These various penalities associated with the violation of these laws included fines, prohibition from practice, imprisonment, and in certain cases, death. But as with earlier regulatory schemes, enforcement was difficult. Undoubtedly, municipal licensing laws reduced the number of uncertified midwives, but the gradual acceptance of the scientific approach to childbirth was far more important. The spreading public belief in the benefits of the new obstetric art suppressed the traditional midwife more effectively than the strongest legal penalties.[7]

With the rise of nation states in Europe, municipal systems of midwife regulation gradually gave way to state-sponsored licensing laws. Although the relative autonomy granted to midwives varied by country, the creation of state regulations in Europe established the midwife as a legitimate and permanent part of childbirth care, albeit in a subordinate role. In England and America, where there were only scattered instances of municipal regulation, the issue of state-mandated licensing did not arise until the turn of this century, and it often became the subject of bitter debate (see Donnison, 1977: 116–202; Litoff, 1978: 48–134; Kobrin, 1966). The desire of some doctors to use regulatory measures to subordinate and eventually eliminate midwifery provoked strong enmity in opponents in the controversy.

In England, proposals for the secular regulation of midwives had been made intermittently since 1616 (see Aveling, 1977a [1872]), but it was nearly three hundred years before a state-sponsored system of midwife licensing was enacted. The proposals for midwife registration made over that three-hundred-year span reflected the concerns of other European countries for improving competency and reducing maternal and infant death. In justifying one of his several regulatory schemes, Peter Chamberlen (1647, quoted in Donnison, 1977: 15) noted that the current licensing system required the testimony of "two or three Gossips . . . But of Instruction or Order amongst the Midwives, not one word." Another proponent of midwifery licensure, J. H. Aveling, observed that the history of this issue in England was marked by "a conviction often reiterated, and now and again vehemently urged—namely, *that it is necessary to give instruction to midwives, and a guarantee of their skill to the public*" (Aveling, 1977a [1872]: 14, emphasis in original).

A lack of consensus on the desirability of midwife registration among English doctors, midwives, and the public prevented the first serious proposal for midwife licensing (introduced in 1890) from becoming law. Modified versions of the bill introduced over the next twelve years met a similar fate. Many doctors opposed midwife registration bills on the grounds that midwifery would die a natural death if left alone. When it became evident that some form of midwife licensing law would eventually be enacted, these same doctors began to favor registration; but they sought to insure tight medical control over midwives. There was some opposition to registration among the midwives. The Manchester Midwives' Society, a group of sixty certified midwives from Manchester and surrounding areas, strongly objected to registration under medical control, seeing it as a "sacrifice" of the occupation (Donnison, 1977: 151). On the other hand, the London-based Midwives' Institute, which had a larger constituency and more political influence than the Manchester group, took the position that the "need for regulation in the interests of poor mothers was so great that, provided certain clauses safeguarding midwives' rights were retained, any Bill was better than nothing" (Donnison, 1977: 153). The wishes of the Midwives' Institute were realized in 1902 when the Midwives Act was finally passed into law. Although the 1902 version of the bill was more favorable to the midwife than some of the earlier drafts, it did subject her to substantial medical control by (among other things) creating a medically dominated regulatory board, prohibiting unlicensed practice, and requiring the midwife to send for a doctor if abnormalities in labor were detected. Failure to adhere to the often minutely detailed provisions of the act could result in the loss of certified status.

While enforcement was difficult and uneven, this act, coupled with other developments in perinatal services, set in motion a process which has nearly eliminated independent midwifery in England. The British midwife is now part of an "obstetric team" headed by a physician. Domiciliary confinements have all but disappeared, and there is periodic consideration of a requirement that would make nurses' training mandatory—a move that many feel would make midwives indistinguishable from obstetric nurses. The effect of the licensing law was not immediate. But this law became part of the social environment and had important indirect effects on the occupation. Donnison (1977: 186–87) suggests that the independent practice of midwifery in England began to disappear because of the lack of cooperation by physicians, falling birth rates, the growth of subsidized midwifery services, and the increased popularity of hospital birth. The 1902 Midwives Act was in part a product of these developments, and it contributed to the loss of independence for midwives. For instance, lack of cooperation from physicians would not have had a severe impact on midwives without regulation. With it, midwives were drawn into the hospital and subjected to direct supervision by physicians. The history of state-mandated midwife regulation in America is complicated by the federal/state political structure. Litoff (1978: 56–57) observes: "No two states provided for their midwives in exactly the same way. The laws regulating midwives varied from state to state and the forty-eight separate bureaus of child hygiene worked at cross purposes on a number of occasions." Nevertheless, it is possible to make a few general statements about the changes in the legal status of midwifery in the United States. As in England, the issue of midwife regulation began to emerge around the turn of the century. At least one state (Connecticut) had a midwife licensing law on its books as early as 1893, but more commonly, midwives practiced without state interference or control until the 1920s. The midwife debate reached its height between 1910 and 1920 and took place largely in medical journals and at medical conferences—two arenas of discussion which transcended the political boundaries of the states. In her analysis of the controversy, Kobrin (1966: 353–54) has distinguished four characteristic approaches to midwifery legislation.

1. At one extreme were those who advocated outright abolition of the midwives, with legal prosecution for those who continued to practice.

2. A second group . . . favored eventual abolition, with the existing midwives closely regulated until substitutes could be furnished.

3. A third group was pessimistic about ever abolishing the midwife and thus felt that regulation plus education would elevate the midwife to the relatively safe status she had achieved in England and on the continent.

4. Finally, there were those, especially in the South, who felt

that if, somehow, midwives could be made to wash their hands and use silver nitrate for the babies' eyes, that would, because of a host of economic and cultural reasons, be the most that could be expected.

All parties in this debate professed an interest in public health. The 1921 Sheppard-Towner Maternity and Infancy Protection Act provided funds that allowed several states to institute programs of midwife education and registration. By 1930—one year after the Sheppard-Towner Act expired (chiefly because of strong opposition from the American Medical Association)—all but ten states required their midwives to be registered. Because (unlike England) there were few, if any, midwife associations, much of the legislation generated at this time reflected the views of physicians' organizations anxious to suppress or eliminate the midwife. But even where medical societies were able to secure "favorable" (that is, repressive) legislation, enforcement presented a problem. In Massachusetts, where midwifery was prohibited in 1918, midwives were still attending a sizable number of births as late as 1935. If anything, the Massachusetts experience served to indicate the futility of abolishing midwives, "for illegality did not remove them but only made it impossible to supervise them" (Wertz and Wertz, 1977: 213). The problem of enforcement also suggests that the upsurge in regulatory acts was not solely responsible for the gradual disappearance of the American midwife. In fact, three separate histories of the American midwife locate the reasons for her demise in larger social and cultural changes (see Kobrin, 1966: 362–63; Litoff, 1978: 139–42; Wertz and Wertz, 1977: 215–17). These changes include declining birth rates, restricted immigration (which both prevented new midwives from arriving and reduced the need for them), an increase in the number of hospital beds available for maternity cases, and a growing anxiety about the dangers of birth. However, as in England, it is important to note that regulatory law existed in interaction with these other social developments.

As noted earlier, midwifery was kept from extinction in the United States by the needs of the urban and rural poor. The Maternity Center Association in New York and the Frontier Nursing Service in Kentucky were created to serve the needs of the indigent; their training programs were chiefly responsible for the re-emergence of nurse-midwifery in America (see Rothman, 1982: 63–75). The certified nurse-midwife was given formal recognition by the obstetricians' professional association (American College of Obstetricians and Gynecologists, ACOG) in 1971, and she is now able to practice legally in fifty-one states and jurisdictions. However, this acceptance was bought at the price of independence. Because nurse-midwifery re-emerged in the context of nursing—an occupation created to assist physicians—nurse-midwives inherited a history of control by the medical profession. While some nurse-midwives acknowledge this control, others are struggling for professional autonomy. According to the American Colllege of Nurse-Midwives, "The American nurse-midwife always functions within the framework of a medically directed health service. . . . *She is never an independent practitioner* (ACNM, n.d., emphasis in orginal; see also Runnerstrom, 1968). In contrast, the more independent lay midwife is perceived as an anachronism with limited legality and no effective national organization.

Midwifery and the Law:
Some General Comments

The history of midwife regulation reveals some persistent patterns. Similarities are found in the justification offered for legislation, the process by which proposed legislation became law, and the effects of such legislation.

A concern for public health was always behind the drive for secular systems of midwife regulation. Suggested solutions to the "midwife problem" ranged from virtual elimination of the practitioner to continued unrestricted practice. Of course, implicit in the concern for improving public health is the notion that better methods for optimizing the well-being of the population are available. In this case, the growing science of obstetrics was gaining both public and official acceptance as the safest method of managing birth. Gradually the practice of midwifery was restricted to midwives with demonstrated competence in and allegiance to knowledge developed by physicians.

A crucial element in midwife regulation was the scientific redefinition of the birth experience. Several sources note the changes in birthing care as prime examples of the "medicalization" of life in the twentieth century (see Zola, 1972), but no one has described how this "medicalization" came about. Historical studies show that in the case of birth, medicalization was preceded by "abnormalization." Obstetricians in both England and America made a concerted effort to convince the public that birth was a pathologic condition, not a routine, normal event. Donnison (1977: 38–39) notes that English "men-midwives . . . anxious to establish their own importance in the eyes of the public . . . exaggerated the dangers of childbirth and frightened women into believing that extra-ordinary measures, and therefore male attendance, were more generally necessary than they actually were." Similarly, Kobrin (1966: 353) observes that American obstetricians early in this century "argued again and again that normal pregnancy and parturition are exceptions and that to consider them normal physiologic conditions was a fallacy." An instructional book for expectant mothers published in 1935 warns:

> To consider childbirth as normal and natural is in a sense misleading, as every woman in childbirth is potentially a major surgical case. The risk of an emergency is always present whether with the first baby or the fifth. Therefore, in every maternity case

selection of the doctor is as vital as it would be in a case of pneumonia or appendicitis (Heaton, 1935: 209).

Perhaps the most illustrative of the abnormalization process are the comments of Dr. Joseph DeLee (1920: 39–41) in a passage from his trend-setting article, "The Prophylactic Forceps Operation":

> It always strikes physicians as well as laymen as bizarre, to call labor an abnormal function, a disease, and yet it is decidely a pathologic process. Everything, of course, depends on what we define as normal. If a woman falls on a pitch-fork, and drives the handle through her perineum, we call that pathologic—abnormal, but if a large baby is driven through her pelvic floor, we say that it is natural, and therefore normal. If a baby was to have its head caught in a door very lightly, but enough to cause a cerebral hemorrhage, we would say that is decidedly pathologic, but when a baby's head is crushed against a tight pelvic floor, and a hemorrhage in the brain kills it, we call this normal, at least we say that the function is natural, not pathogenic. [If] the fall on the pitchfork, and the crushing of the door [are] pathogenic [then] in the same sense labor is pathogenic . . . and anything pathogenic is pathologic and abnormal. . . . So frequent are these bad effects, that I have often wondered whether Nature did not deliberately intend women to be used up in the process of reproduction, in a manner analogous to that of the salmon, which dies after spawning.

The "Friedman curve," which defines normal durations for the various stages of labor, is another example of abnormalization. Developed in the late 1950s by Dr. E. A. Friedman, the curve suggests that women whose lengths of labor fall outside a statistical average are abnormal and in need of medical intervention (see Rothman, 1982: 259–60). Parenthetically, I should note that the process of abnormalization and medicalization has occurred in areas other than birth. Before a problem or condition can be placed in the medical bailiwick, the public must be convinced that there is something abnormal about that condition that makes medical attention necessary. The popularity of genetic counseling, for instance, has increased as more couples become convinced that getting pregnant, rather than a normal process, is fraught with the potential for abnormal offspring.

Public acceptance of birth as abnormal can be attributed to two factors. First, the newly enfranchised woman was receptive to modern obstetric technology because it offered further liberation from traditional roles. Second, the self-imposed limitation on the number of births made the expense of a medical birth seem a worthwhile investment. The impressive array of obstetric technology was seen as insurance of a healthy birth.

The consequences of acceptance of this view of birth for midwifery and its regulation were enormous. If birth is accepted as abnormal, then only medical solutions are appropriate. It becomes the duty of the state to replace antiquated methods with more modern approaches.

Another feature of the institutionalization of midwife regulation involves the attitudes of the members of occupations most directly involved. With few exceptions, physicians opposed the registration of midwives on the grounds that legal recognition would enhance the midwife's position, take births away from doctors, and hinder the development of obstetrics. While many doctors regarded assisting in birth as a time-consuming, often messy, and manual task, it was an important way of developing and maintaining a clientele. On the other hand, and for many of the same reasons, midwives favored some type of licensing law, viewing such legislation as a necessary condition for survival.[8] These positions seem consistent with the best interests of the occupations involved, but the effects of regulation turned out differently than either side expected. Instead of establishing midwifery as an independent profession, they placed the midwife in a position of decreased autonomy. The enforcement of midwife legislation posed certain problems. It required collaboration by those least likely to provide it— namely, those who employ the unlicensed midwife. However, when action is taken against a midwife, she receives harsher treatment from a regulatory agency or board than from a court of law. Donnison (1977: 182–83) states that the supervisory and disciplinary powers granted by the 1902 Midwives Act to local authorities and the Central Midwives Board in England were often used vindictively to suspend or expel women from practice for minor infractions. The irony is that regulatory measures are only effective in controlling the certified midwife. It is the court's responsibility to sanction unlicensed practitioners, but courts have proved unwilling to prosecute, partly because of lack of evidence and partly through an unwillingness to deprive anyone of care (see Donnison, 1977: 184).[9]

Of course, the social control exerted by regulation is not limited to disciplinary proceedings. Mandated education for midwives serves as an important means of social control. Donnison (1977: 183) comments on the decrease in penal cases brought before the Central Midwives Board that followed the disappearance of the "bona-fide" midwife in England. Bona-fide midwives were women who had received licenses on the basis of experience rather than through an approved educational program. As this kind of midwife disappeared, the need for the reactive control of penal proceedings diminished and was replaced by the built-in proactive control of socialization that accompanied midwifery training. One form of social control replaced another.

The history of midwifery indicates that health-care occupations are not exclusively shaped by law and technology. Medicine is shaped by the larger culture. Changes in the style of attendance of birth can be traced to changes in the composition of the population and changing attitudes toward technology. The law works in inter-action with these other developments. While earlier discussion has shown that the decline of midwifery was tied to the rise of obstetric science, it is clear that the law accelerated this trend by providing the public with a visible means (a license or certificate) to distin-guish those who were schooled in this new science from those who were not. Well aware of this, medical professionals have pushed certification by educating the public on the benefits of having a cer-tified practitioner, trained in the new techniques, at childbirth. Outlining a nineteenth century plan to "improve the condition of midwives" put forth by the London Obstetrical Society, Aveling (1977a [1872]: 165) notes: "A diploma . . . is offered to those who can show themselves to possess the minimum amount of knowl-edge which an ordinary midwife should have, and it is hoped that the distinction thus offered will induce midwives to seek the in-struction necessary to obtain it." In her narrative concerning Geor-gia's granny midwives, Campbell (1946: 40, emphasis added) com-ments:

> How much of the Old Law is mingled with the New Law in the practice of midwifery by the grannies? Only direct supervision of each delivery would tell. And the public health nurse in Georgia carries too heavy a load for that. She does make home visits to expectant and new mothers. She does what teaching she can in the home and at clinics, *hoping that the mother will come to ex-pect and insist upon the best care the midwife can give.*

The new laws often disrupted traditional relationships important to the midwife. Mongeau *et al.* (1961) state that the decline of the granny midwife in North Carolina can be attributed to disruptions in the traditional midwife-apprentice, midwife-doctor relationships engendered by regulation. In that state, licensing procedures sup-planted long-established training by apprenticeship, and prohibited midwives from using a variety of remedies they once employed un-der the direction of a local physician. It was only a matter of time before the granny midwife—who had no successor nor the sanction of a privileged relationship with the local physician—began to disappear. One old Southern woman recalls (quoted in Wigginton, 1973: 286):

They didn't have t'have a license when they first began, as far back as I can remember. I didn't know of 'em havin' t'have'em until up t'later years. Then they got t'where if they delivered babies, they had t'have a license. And they were finally just completely cut out of th' job at all. Weren't allowed t'do th'job at all.

Legal recognition altered the style of practice by cooptation. Because legal status often brings privileges as well as increased visibility, those who benefit from it are often unwilling to disregard mandated standards. This is apparent in the unwillingness of the American certified nurse-midwife to violate the code of conduct established by her professional organization, and it also holds for licensed lay midwives. An example is provided in Fran Ventre's (1976) account of how an obsolete statute helped her gain legal status as a lay midwife in Maryland. She had been assisting with births illegally, but after receiving the first license issued in her county since 1924 she comments (Ventre, 1976: 114–15):

Ironically enough, since receiving my license I have been free to do very few deliveries. One limiting factor has been the refusal of many obstetricians to provide the medical backup stipulated by the law. To do deliveries without it would risk forfeiture of my license and possible imprisonment. I have not gone underground again because I feel a strong commitment to keeping this license.

It would be misleading to conclude this chapter without recognition of the real benefits licensure offered midwives. Actually, it might be more accurate to say the benefits that licensure offered midwifery, for the advantages of licensure lay in providing public legitimacy for the occupation and in enhancing its image. As technology of medicine extended its dominance over birth, public demand for scientifically trained practitioners increased. Licensure, which allowed midwifery to link itself with medical science, improved the marketability of the profession. But therein lies a dilemma. While licensure improved the image of midwifery, it reduced the independence of individual midwives by requiring midwives to submit to physician authority. Licensure therefore benefited the profession of midwifery while damaging individual professionals. Of course the fates of individual practitioners are inextricably linked with the fate of the profession. Without licensure, midwives faced the prospect of retaining autonomy while being ignored and rejected by the public. This dilemma persists in current struggles over the licensing of midwives.

Lay midwife licensing laws, which have begun to appear in several states, provide more recent examples of the relationship between law and midwifery. In Chapter 3 I look closely at legislation aimed at regulating lay midwives in the states of Arizona, Texas, and California. Examination of these bills and the debate they engendered—in their respective legislatures, among medical professionals, and among the public—reveals the continuation of themes visible in earlier midwife legislation.

Chapter 3

Midwifery in the Legislature: Licensing Laws in Arizona, Texas, and California

The interaction of medicine and law becomes most visible when different kinds of practitioners come before legislative bodies seeking passage of laws favorable to their profession. These cases commonly generate debate between representatives of established medical professions and a group of unorthodox practitioners and their clients. The latter group enters the debate at a disadvantage, however, because cultural faith in the allopathic ideology of "medical experts" weighs heavily in the decisions of legal officials. The struggle of lay midwives to win passage of favorable legislation affords a good example of this process; this chapter considers successful and unsuccessful attempts to establish licensing laws for lay midwives in the states of Arizona, Texas, and California.

The last several years have seen a flurry of legislative activity centered on the licensure of lay midwives. The issue began to appear on the agendas of state legislatures in the late 1970s. Since that time debates over the wisdom of licensure have echoed through statehouse halls and hearing rooms from New Hampshire to California. The nature of these debates varied according to existing state statutes. In some places the argument concerns revisions of laws created earlier in this century; in others the battle is over laws which would legitimize midwifery after a period of legislative prohibition. But the issues here are essentially the same as in earlier laws licensing midwives. These new laws, like those proposed decades ago, are justified by appealing to public health, are concerned with socially accepted definitions of birth, are generally opposed by physicians and supported by midwives, and give control over licensure to nonmidwives. Study of these laws demonstrates that the licensing of paramedicals suits the strategy of the more established medical professions.

When I began my research, the laws governing lay midwives in California, Texas, and Arizona could be described as follows. In California no system of licensure existed, and lay midwives were subject to prosecution for violation of the state's Medical Practice Act. In Texas lay midwives had to register with the county, but were not required to complete educational programs or to demonstrate competency. As a result of an administrative updating of an old law, Arizona maintained a licensing program that required the successful completion of a course of instruction and the passing of a comprehensive examination.

In order to understand what happened in these states it is important to describe the general reawakening of interest in lay midwifery.

The recent concern with the licensing of lay midwives probably seems odd to the casual observer. After all, aren't lay midwives a thing of the past? Why bother to license an archaic practitioner? In fact, legislative concern with lay midwives testifies to the renewed popularity of this practitioner.

As noted earlier, midwives were an important part of perinatal care in the United States until early in this century. Not being "true" medical practitioners, and therefore lacking access to hospitals, midwives officiated primarily at home births. The increasing popularity of hospital birth in this century nearly accomplished their demise, as the proportion of hospital births in the United States grew from 36.9 percent in 1935 to 96 percent in 1960 (see Devitt, 1977; Jacobson, 1956). Laws governing midwives followed developments in medical science, and midwives gradually found themselves legally enjoined from practice in several states. In others they faced restrictions in the kind of women they could engage as clients and in the range of procedures they could employ.

There seemed little dissatisfaction with this state of affairs until the last decade or so. During the 1970s a collective murmuring about medically dominated hospital birth arose, and was accompanied by a small but significant turn toward home birth. The demand for lay midwives increased, in part because home birth became more popular and physicians have been hesitant to participate in home births. Many doctors feel that birth outside the hospital is inherently unsafe (for example, see Pearse, 1979); others feel constrained by threats to their malpractice insurance; there is also pressure from disapproving peers. In truth, most malpractice insurers will not cover a physician who assists at home births, and some physicians have lost their hospital admission privileges through participation in home births. According to the stated policy of one hospital, "Hereafter [December 1, 1976] any physician with OB [obstetrical] privileges at [this hospital] who intentionally participates in a non-emergency 'home delivery' will be viewed as no longer fulfilling the professional expectations of the OB staff of the hospital, and will immediately have OB admitting privileges revoked" (quoted in Annas, 1977: 11).

Table 1 provides evidence of the trend away from hospital births. This table indicates a gradual increase in both the absolute number and the percentage of out-of-hospital births between 1973 and 1977. Between 1973 and 1977 the total number of births increased 6 percent, while nonhospital births showed an increase of 122 percent. In 1978 nonhospital births declined sharply, probably due to a decline in the counterculture movement and a rise in popularity of in-hospital alternative birth centers (see DeVries, 1980;

Table 1. Number and Percentage Distribution of Live Births by Place
of Delivery, United States, 1950, 1955, 1960, 1965, 1970–81

Year	Total Live Births	No. Attended		% Attended	
		In Hospital	Out of Hospital	In Hospital	Out of Hospital
1950	3,554,149	3,125,975	428,174	88.0	12.0
1955	4,047,295	3,818,810	228,485	94.4	5.6
1960	4,257,850	4,114,368	143,482	96.6	3.4
1965	3,760,358	3,660,712	99,646	97.4	2.6
1970	3,731,386	3,708,142	23,244	99.4	0.6
1971	3,555,970	3,523,860	32,110	99.1	0.9
1972	3,258,411	3,233,703	24,708	99.2	0.8
1973	3,136,965	3,114,503	22,462	99.3	0.7
1974	3,159,958	3,133,797	26,161	99.2	0.8
1975	3,144,198	3,103,323	40,875	98.7	1.3
1976	3,167,788	3,123,439	44,349	98.6	1.4
1977	3,326,632	3,276,732	49,900	98.5	1.5
1978	3,333,279	3,300,659	31,350	99.0	1.0
1979	3,494,398	3,460,484	33,914	99.1	0.9
1980	3,612,258	3,576,370	35,888	99.0	1.0
1981	3,629,238	3,591,582	37,656	98.9	1.1

Source: National Center for Health Statistics, *Vital Statistics of the United States, 1977:
Volume 1—Natality,* 1981; National Center for Health Statistics, *Monthly Vital Statistics Report* 32 (9, suppl.): December 29, 1983.

1983; 1984). Since 1978, nonhospital births have once again
climbed steadily.

Further evidence of the discontent with hospitals may be found
in the number of recent publications concerning birthing alternatives. These include periodicals such as *Birth* (formerly *Birth and
the Family Journal*), *Mothering, Newsletter of the Association of
Radical Midwives,* and *The Practicing Midwife,* as well as a variety

of monographs and anthologies (for example, see Lang, 1972; Milinaire, 1974; Hazell, 1976; Sousa, 1976; Stewart and Stewart, 1976;
1977; Arms, 1977; Ward and Ward, 1977; Baldwin, 1979a). A number of associations promoting alternative methods of childbirth
have also been formed in the last few years. These include National
Association of Parents and Professionals for Safe Alternatives in
Childbirth (NAPSAC), Association for Childbirth at Home International (ACHI), the American College of Home Obstetrics (ACHO),
the Association of Radical Midwives (ARM) in Britain, the Midwives
Alliance of North America (MANA), and several state midwifery associations.

Although decisions to give birth outside the hospital are motivated by a variety of concerns, there are some common themes.
Various social movements have encouraged critical review of the
standard physician-attended hospital birth. Also, a growing body of
literature calls attention to the negative, potentially damaging aspects of birth in a hospital.

Both the feminist movement and a general emphasis on the benefits of "naturalness" have encouraged the turn away from hospital
birth. The feminist movement led women to question the treatment they were receiving from society and its institutions; out of
this grew the women's health movement and, specifically, discontent with the medical domination of females by males in obstetrics
and gynecology (see Ruzek, 1978). Our cultural fascination with
"natural foods" and "natural" life-styles, which grew out of the
counterculture of the sixties and seventies and is now widely exploited by advertisers, also prompted a reconsideration of hospital
birth and its heavy dependence on drugs and machines.

Some recent studies of hospital birth criticize its procedures as
dehumanizing, costly, and fraught with the potential for iatrogenic
disease and death. Suzanne Arms' work, *Immaculate Deception*
(1977), perhaps the most influential book for the home birth movement, describes in detail how the hospitals deprive the laboring and
birthing woman of her humanity. She notes that the expectant

mother "is shifted from room to room and rolled from bed to bed; she is examined internally by several attendants she does not know, and poked, stabbed, strapped down and checked out by several more" (p. 109, see also Shaw, 1974). Arms also argues that routine hospital procedures result in assembly-line treatment of mothers and serve to separate parents and children during the crucial period following birth.

Several books that advocate home birth note its economic advantages. The cost of an obstetrician-attended hospital birth free from complications ranges from $2000 to $3000, whereas a lay midwife-attended home birth usually costs $400 to $750. But perhaps most devastating are studies suggesting that birth in hospitals is more dangerous than giving birth at home. Haire (1972) has outlined the potential for disease and injury inherent in modern childbirth techniques (see also Caldeyro-Barcia, 1975). After a study which matched 1046 home births with an equal number of hospital births on the basis of social and medical characteristics, Mehl and his associates (1976) reported no appreciable differences in mortality, but a significantly higher rate of birth injuries to the neonate for the hospital group.

Those who choose to give birth outside the hospital usually cite one or more of the criticisms outlined above as the motivating factor in their decision. And although not all who give birth at home seek the assistance of a lay midwife, it is this group that provides her clientele. Indeed, the midwife's clientele has changed. Those who used midwives earlier in this century were limited by their economic condition or geographic location, while those who currently employ lay midwives often consciously seek them out. Research by myself and others (Hazell, 1974; Ellis et al., 1980; Rubin, 1976; Anderson et al., 1978; Yankauer, 1983: 637) confirms that those who choose to give birth at home do so freely. Generally they are not poor, and many do not live in rural areas. Most are concerned with the spiritual and experiential dimensions of birth, and for them the midwife is the logical choice as attendant. The tradition of midwifery entails a sensitivity to these aspects of the birth process (for example, see Holmes, n.d.; Gaskin, 1978), aspects that are ignored by most physicians, who feel they are superfluous to a healthy birth.

The competition engendered by moderate birth rates and growing numbers of physicians has alarmed medical professionals and organizations. They have reacted with warnings about the dangers of bypassing established medical care, and attacked the character of those who do. A former director of the American College of Obstetricians and Gynecologists (ACOG) has referred to home birth as "in utero child abuse." The past president of the Massachusetts section of ACOG states that home birthers are "kooks, the lunatic fringe, people who have emotional problems they are acting out" (quoted in Annas, 1977). An editorial published in the *Journal of the American Medical Association* provides the following tongue-in-cheek assessment of nonhospital birth (Pearse, 1979):

> Of course, of the mothers who are screened carefully, some of their infants can be delivered at home, and not too many additional babies will die. Only some mothers will have to be rushed through an emergency room to the care of newly telephoned physicians who have never seen the patient. Since only one mother in 8,000 now dies in childbirth in the United States, these mothers and most of their babies will be rescued. What baffles me is why this is considered by some to be a great leap forward in birth care.

A different response by medical professionals has been the attempt to coopt the home birth movement (see DeVries, 1979a; 1980; 1983; 1984). In spite of their harsh condemnation of those who choose home deliveries, physicians and other medical personnel have altered hospital care to make it more attractive to its critics. This more positive reaction—supported by several medical professional organizations—calls for the creation of "family centered maternity and newborn care" in hospitals (ACOG, 1978;

AMA, 1977). In response many hospitals have set up "alternative birth centers" (ABCs). Although these programs vary, most permit a woman who is expected to have a "normal, uncomplicated birth" to labor and deliver in the same bed. They also allow friends and relatives to be present, and permit the infants and their parents to stay together from birth until time of discharge, usually twelve to twenty-four hours after the birth. Many ABCs attempt to recreate the atmosphere of the home with carpeting, hanging plants, pictures, a stereo, overstuffed chairs, and a dining table. Individuals responsible for setting up ABCs readily admit that the programs exist because of consumer pressure. One ABC coordinator told me, "The idea for an alternative birth center came from outside pressure. We felt that an alternative birth center would be a good idea, especially if we could get the people who were delivering at home." The clinical supervisor of an obstetric ward in another hospital in the process of setting up an ABC told me, "I'm sure competition is a major factor in the desire of physicians to open an alternative birth center . . . because they have lost patients. I don't think they have lost many patients yet, but even if you lose one it makes you stand up and think."

In addition to the cooptative arrangements, some medical professionals continue to use peer pressure and legal tactics to prevent home births. A recent case in Nashville, Tennessee, testified to the effectiveness of this pressure. A physician who supported a group of certified nurse-midwives was forced to leave town after the cancellation of his malpractice insurance and the lack of referrals from his colleagues; this *in spite* of congressional hearings in Washington, D.C., to examine if he and the nurse-midwives were victims of illegal restraint of trade (see Committee on Interstate and Foreign Commerce, 1980).[1] Similarly, a Texas midwife reports (Stanwick, 1977): "The one physician who was assisting us was visited by the County Medical Society and informed that if he did not sever all connection with us they would deprive him of hospital privileges and wreck his practice. He was forced to stop offering his services."

Although they have no profession-based control over lay midwives who participate in home births, physicians have used state medical practice acts to prosecute practitioners. In states where the precedent in case law exists, midwives can be charged with practicing medicine without a license; physicians will often initiate prosecution when they feel enough evidence exists. If a midwife happens to be a registered nurse, she can be charged with exceeding her scope as defined in the nurse-practice act.

It is in this climate of criticism, charges, and countercharges that midwife licensing bills have been introduced in several state legislatures (see MAACC, 1980; Sallomi *et al.*, 1981; Cohn *et al.*, 1984). In some cases midwives who feared prosecution have sought a licensing law to enable them to practice. In other cases established medical communities have initiated licensing laws in order to gain more control over these practitioners. In the following sections we will look more closely at specific lay midwife licensing bills in Arizona, Texas, and California, analyzing both the motivations behind their introduction and reasons for their failure or success in gaining passage.

Arizona: Revision of a Permissive Law

Arizona is unique among the states being studied because its midwife licensing law was revised by administrative procedure rather than by direct activity of the legislature. However, this administrative change occurred in the context of threatened legal action and possible legislative revision of the midwifery statute. The administrative process circumvented the more publicly visible legislative route, and allowed the law to be altered by health department bureaucrats with the advice and direction of the medical community.

The first law regulating the practice of midwifery in Arizona was passed in 1957. It is estimated that about one hundred midwives were practicing in the state at that time, chiefly serving poor and minority populations who lived in rural areas or community barrios. In particular, midwives worked among Hispanics and in rural Mormon communities. The law (*Arizona Revised Statutes*, 36-751–36-757) defined a midwife as "any person attending women in childbirth, habitually or for hire," and required all such persons to obtain a license before practicing. A license could be obtained upon payment of the one dollar application fee and demonstration of the ability to meet what were then very loose qualifications for office. These qualifications included:

(a) The ability to read and write [English].

(b) Knowledge of the fundamentals of hygiene.

(c) The ability to recognize abnormal conditions during labor.

(d) Knowledge of the laws of the state concerning the reporting of births, prenatal blood tests, and of the regulations pertaining to midwifery.

Applications had to indicate either the completion of a very minimal course of instruction or a passing grade on a qualifying examination. The law also established regulations defining the "duties and limitations of the practice of midwifery" and mandated penalties for violation of the regulations or for unlicensed practice.

After passage of the 1957 law, approximately 25–30 midwives were licensed; the supervision of this group was assumed by the Bureau of Maternal and Child Health of the Department of Health Services. Enforcement appears to have been minimal, as there is no record of disciplinary actions or convictions for unlicensed practice. Over the years most of these originally licensed midwives ceased practice; the one exception was a group of midwives who worked in a Mormon community located on the Utah border. Between 1959 and 1977 only four midwives were licensed.

In 1976, corresponding with the new popularity of lay midwifery, the Department of Health Services received what they regarded as an "influx" of requests for licensure. It is generally believed that this influx was inspired by publication of a chart that outlined existing state regulations of lay and nurse-midwives. The chart was prepared by an organization known as Home Oriented Maternity Experience (HOME, 1976) and gained wider circulation through publication in various periodicals associated with the alternative birth movement (including *Birth and the Family Journal*, *Mothering*). This chart identified Arizona as one of fourteen states that either licensed or allowed lay midwives to practice. The chair of the Maternal and Child Health Committee of the Arizona Medical Association told me: "Lay midwifery got its start elsewhere and then those groups started to look for places where they could practice legally. They discovered Arizona and started applying to the Department of Health Services for licenses." Several midwives confirmed that they were made aware of the Arizona law by the HOME chart, but I could find no evidence that anyone moved into the state simply to take advantage of the permissive law.

The Department of Health Services responded to this surge in requests for licensure by hiring a certified nurse-midwife to head a task force charged with updating the regulations governing lay midwives. The 1957 law granted the director of the department authority to "provide reasonable and necessary regulations to safeguard the health and safety of the mother and child," and this authority was cited as justification for revising "loose" or "minimal" regulations. The task force was comprised of medical professionals, including representatives of the Maternal and Child Health Committee of the Arizona Medical Association. Proposals for new regulations were solicited from groups such as the Arizona State Nurses Association, the American College of Nurse-Midwives, the Arizona Medical Association, and identifiable groups of consumers and midwives.

While the regulations were being reformulated, the Department of Health Services had to deal with the pending applications for licensure. In an attempt to postpone the issuance of new licenses, applicants were told that the department was out of applications or that the qualifying examination was not prepared. At least one mid-wife responded by hiring an attorney who reminded the department of their obligation to provide applications and offer the exam on a timely basis. Given this legal nudge, the department agreed to offer applications and examinations to the seventeen women who had requested them under the old regulations. Ten of the seventeen were licensed after receiving a grade of 80 percent or better on the examination, which consisted of oral and written sections.

The new regulations were adopted on January 23, 1978. The adoption process requires submission of the revised regulations to the attorney general, who inspects them, signs them, and passes them to the secretary of state for filing. The department was able to expedite this process because a task force member's husband worked in the office of Attorney General (now Governor) Bruce Babbit. The new regulations are considerably more stringent than those they replaced. Each applicant is now required to show evidence of completing a course of instruction with specified content, observe a minimum of ten births, deliver a minimum of fifteen women under the supervision of a licensed practitioner, and pass a qualifying examination that includes written, oral, and practical sections. The regulations also detail the responsibilities of the midwife and the limitations on her practice. Department surveillance of midwives is established by requiring submission of quarterly reports that contain information on each pregnancy.

Since the adoption of the new regulations only a few women have been licensed. By the end of 1978 there were seventeen licensed midwives in Arizona; this included two Mormon midwives licensed before the new regulations, ten midwives who passed the exam while the regulations were being revised, and five midwives licensed under the new regulations. As of July 1981, only seven other midwives had been licensed, bringing the total of licensed midwives to twenty-four, half of whom received their licenses under the old regulations. A major hindrance to potential midwives is the lack of accredited educational programs. While approved instruction is required by the licensing law, the state recognized no educational program at the time of my research. Since then a pilot program was set up at a community college, but it later closed down.

The 1980–81 legislative session saw an attempt to allow unlicensed midwives to practice if they received no compensation for their services. This bill would also have temporarily allowed the issuance of provisional licenses to practicing midwives who had not completed an approved educational course, if they could pass the qualifying examination. The holder of a provisional license would be granted a regular license upon documentation of successful assistance in at least fifteen births. Senate Bill 1336 was authored by a senator whose constituency included a number of Mormon midwives who were dissatisfied with the existing regulations. They objected to the difficulty in obtaining the mandated education and also to the regulation requiring licenses even for those who assisted (only at births of fellow Mormons) without compensation. Given their religious convictions, these midwives were particularly uneasy about continuing their practice in violation of the law. The bill's sponsor admitted being partial to the midwives' cause because of his experience with midwives. His grandmother, a midwife in Texas, had assisted at his own birth.

Senate Bill 1336 passed the senate and made it out of committee in the house, but it died when the session ended without the bill being called for a vote before the house. Although the bill failed to pass, the political maneuvering that surrounded it is instructive. The Arizona Medical Association lobbied strongly against the bill. The author of the bill informed me that the bill had enough votes to pass the house; he suggested that it was never called for a vote because the speaker of the house, who was aware it could well pass, "belonged" to the Arizona Medical Association. The author of the bill also observed that "licensed midwives gave me more opposition [on this bill] than doctors did." He interpreted this opposition as their fear of competition. Finally, it is interesting to note the reaction of the Department of Health Services to the near success of S.B. 1336. As the bill's author told me: "They know legislation is coming if they don't change [the regulations]. They know they will have to work with us." And indeed the department official who supervises the licensed midwives informed me that the regulations will be revised to deal with the predicament of Mormon midwives. I was told by this official: "We will change the rules and regs. We have to do it. If we don't do it, it will be legislated and they would like to change other things. The climate is now antiregulatory and the department regulates everything." She also indicated her fear of legislation that might allow provisional licenses; she felt that people "would come out of the walls" to take advantage of such a clause. As expected, the law granting a one-year grace period for the issuance of provisional licenses did pass in the next legislative season. Fourteen midwives were granted provisional licenses during that year.

The Arizona situation demonstrates the ways in which existing statutes can be tinkered with without the knowledge, input, or consent of consumers or midwives. It is clear that this licensing scheme did not promote the growth of the profession, and that the Department of Health Services succeeded in preventing an "influx" of lay midwives seeking to use the licensing law to become legitimate practitioners. Table 2 indicates that the rate of home births in Arizona is not remarkably different from the national pattern. The presence of licensed midwives has not inflated the number of non-hospital births; in 1978 licensed lay midwives were responsible for only 261 (0.6%) of the 531 births attributed to midwives in Arizona (the rest were delivered by nurse-midwives). Finally, we should also note that legitimation through the revised regulations has not impressed the medical profession. Nearly three years after the adoption of the revised regulations, a spokesperson for the Arizona Medical Association stated (Scott, 1980: 47): "[The association] has not dropped or changed its opposition to lay midwives. Its members hope that new programs of patient education about the availability of birthing rooms will defuse the movement."

Table 2. Hospital and Nonhospital Births in Arizona, 1970–82

Year	Total Births	Number Attended				Type of Attendant at Out-of-Hospital Birth			
		In Hospital		Out of Hospital		Physician		Midwife and Other*	
		No.	%	No.	%	No.	%	No.	%
1970	37,455	36,941	98.6	514	1.4	277	53.9	237	46.1
1971	38,343	37,792	98.6	551	1.4	349	63.3	202	36.7
1972	37,291	36,834	98.8	457	1.2	242	52.9	215	47.1
1973	37,872	37,548	99.1	324	0.9	123	38.0	201	62.0
1974	39,867	39,488	99.0	379	1.0	164	43.3	215	56.7
1975	39,036	38,683	99.1	353	0.9	151	42.8	202	57.2
1976	40,050	39,588	98.8	462	1.2	207	44.8	255	55.2
1977	41,659	41,118	98.7	541	1.3	238	44.0	303	56.0
1978	43,053	42,361	98.4	692	1.6	161	23.3	531	76.7
1979	46,700	45,944	98.4	756	1.6	166	22.0	590	78.0
1980	50,068	49,260	98.4	808	1.6	151	18.7	657	81.3
1981	51,604	50,652	98.2	952	1.8	209	22.0	743	78.0
1982	52,368	51,379	98.1	989	1.9	265	26.8	724	73.2

Source: Arizona Department of Health Services, Department of Family Health Services. Taken from birth certificate data, Phoenix.

* It is likely that the majority of these are midwife-attended births; "other" includes unattended births, and deliveries by fathers, nurses, firemen, paramedics, etc.

Texas: Legislative Attempts to Tighten a Permissive Law

Like Arizona, Texas shares a border with Mexico. But unlike Arizona, there is a great deal of interaction between the Mexican and American cultures along the Texas border. The continued use of the traditional Mexican birth attendant—the *partera*—is just one manifestation of this interaction.[2] *Parteras* and other non-Mexican lay midwives have always figured significantly in the care available to pregnant women in Texas (see Philpott, 1979; Lee and Glaser, 1974; McCallum, 1979; Ortman-Glick, 1978; Streck, n.d.), and, at the time of my research, the state legislature had not yet found it necessary to regulate their practice beyond requiring that they register with the "local registrar" (Texas Department of Health, 1976: Article 4477, Rule 49a; see also Texas Department of Health, n.d.). Table 3 indicates the recent level of activity by midwives in Texas.

Texas possesses a case law that affects the practice of midwifery. After Diana Banti assisted in the birth of a child who subsequently died, a complaint was filed against Ms. Banti alleging that she did "unlawfully treat and offer to treat Julia Valdez, a human being, for a disease and physical disorder, mental and physical, and a physical deformity and injury and to effect a cure thereof." It was further alleged that "she charged therefore and that she did so without having registered a certificate evidencing her right to practice medicine." She was convicted on these charges, but the Court of Criminal Appeals reversed the conviction and established a precedent that separated midwifery from the practice of medicine (*Banti v. State,* 289 S. W. 2d 244):

> It would appear . . . that the legislature of Texas has not defined the practice of medicine so as to include the act of assisting women in parturition or childbirth insofar as the practice of medicine without registering a certificate evidencing the right to so practice is made punishable as an offense. . . . We agree that childbirth is a normal function of womanhood, and that proof that the appellant for a consideration agreed to and did attend Julia Valdez at childbirth does not support the allegation of the complaint that she treated or offered to treat Julia Valdez for a disease, disorder, deformity or injury or effect a cure thereof. Not only has the Legislature failed to include within the definition of "practicing medicine" the branch of medical science

Table 3. Texas Live Births by Type of Attendant, 1977–82

Year	Total Births	Delivered by					
		Physician		Midwife		Other*	
		No.	%	No.	%	No.	%
1977	228,871	221,555	96.8	5,990	2.6	1,326	0.6
1978	242,548	233,059	96.1	7,856	3.2	1,633	0.7
1979	254,263	244,548	96.2	7,143	2.8	2,572	1.0
1980	273,433	264,875	96.8	7,387	2.8	1,171	0.4
1981	281,558	272,494	96.8	7,778	2.8	1,286	0.4
1982	297,683	288,122	96.8	8,109	2.7	1,452	0.5

Source: Texas Department of Health, Austin.
* This category probably includes a number of midwife-assisted deliveries.

which has to do with the care of women during pregnancy and parturition called "obstetrics" but has in a number of statutes recognized practical obstetrics or midwifery as outside the realm of the medical practice act.

The court concluded that as long as midwives did not hold themselves out to be "practitioners of medicine" they could assist in childbirth and charge for their services with no fear of legal action against them.

In 1977 Representative Chris Miller introduced House Bill 1314, "relating to the regulation of the practice of midwifery." The bill was an attempt to provide certification of all midwives who wished to practice, giving responsibility for their education and regulation to the Texas Department of Health. The bill enjoyed little if any support, and it suffered an early death. In 1978, the Texas Board of Medical Examiners asked the attorney general to issue an opinion on the services that midwives may legally provide in Texas. The attorney general responded by reaffirming the legality of midwife assistance in the "normal function" of childbirth and went on to note that "if the performance of an episiotomy or a repair of a laceration of the birth canal by suturing the wound following the delivery of the child is incident to normal childbirth, the midwife may perform the same" (Texas Attorney General Opinion No. H-1293, 1978). The opinion also stated that midwives may not possess or dispense dangerous drugs without the supervision of a physician, nor diagnose disease or obstetrical complications (see Pickens, 1979). Thus, although limits are placed on their practice, Texas midwives have a great degree of autonomy.

This autonomy has troubled the medical community and some legislators, particularly when reports of the mismanagement of births by midwives surface in the press (for example, "Midwife Charged in Baby's Death," *San Antonio Light*, 1979; "Attending Doctors, Lay Midwife Agree: Woman's Death 'Totally Preventable,'" Watson, 1979; "[State Senator] Truan Presses Investigation of Pregnant Woman's Death," Lyon, 1979). Prompted by a concern over poorly trained midwives, Representative Hector Uribe introduced House Bill 635—"a bill to be entitled an act relating to the regulation of lay midwifery, providing penalties"—to the 1979 Texas Legislature. Prior to his election to the legislature, Mr. Uribe was an attorney in Brownsville, a town located near the border in a county with a large percentage of midwife-attended births. In Mr. Uribe's home county (Cameron) nearly 31 percent of all births in 1978 were attended by midwives; in Brownsville during that same year midwives delivered at least half of all children born. Mr. Uribe had also dealt with lay midwifery during his career as an attorney, defending a lay midwife charged with murder and practicing medicine without a license.

In drafting the bill, Representative Uribe sought input from a variety of medical professionals. Particular medical agencies and associations had specific provisions they wanted in the bill. The Department of Health wanted to be able to gather information on the practice of midwifery. The Texas Medical Association (TMA)—

firm in its opinion that midwives offer inferior care—was anxious to ensure that the legislation would in no way sanction or certify midwives. Midwives in Texas had not yet unified, so their input on drafting of the bill was limited. A few midwives did testify when the bill was introduced, but they had little if any impact.

The legal counsel of the TMA drafted a bill for Representative Uribe that made no allowance for certification, registration, or even education.[3] Although Uribe objected to the lack of educational requirements in the bill, he was willing to forego required certification, primarily because a local "licensing" law for Brownsville midwives resulted in a decrease in the number of midwives in the city from seventy-four to ten. He felt that many midwives were driven "underground" by the ordinance, and he did not want this to happen on a statewide level.

The version of the bill introduced into the legislature showed signs of compromise. It created a lay midwifery board, to be appointed by the Texas Board of Health, that would administer a voluntary educational program for midwives. It was hoped that midwives would be cajoled into education by another section of the bill that required them to inform their clients "in oral and written form" of the limitation on their practice and whether or not they had successfully completed the training course. In keeping with the requests of the Department of Health and the TMA, the bill required the "identification" of midwives. In its original form the bill had used the words "registration" and "registry," but in order to placate the TMA these potentially sanction-conferring words were replaced with the more neutral terms "identification" and "roster." The bill also created, for the first time in Texas history, a statutory definition of "normal childbirth" ("the delivery, at or close to term, of a pregnant woman whose physical examination reveals no abnormality or expected complications and who does not exhibit signs or symptoms of hemorrhage, toxemia, infection, abnormal fetus position, or abnormal presentation") and placed statutory limits on the practice of midwifery.

The final version of the bill had wide support and no vocal opposition. The Department of Health was pleased with its authority to gather information on midwifery. The TMA was happy with statutory limits on the practices of midwives. And midwives were satisfied with its voluntary nature. The bill passed both houses of the legislature, but the governor vetoed it. His veto message was short (Clements, 1979):

> This bill would require the Board of Health to appoint a midwifery board which would establish a *voluntary* training course and examination in order to supposedly improve the quality of midwife services. All this would do would allow some midwives to pass themselves off as professionals and this state recognition of midwifery would give credibility to a group that may or may not have credibility. The public would have no way of knowing whether midwives were state sanctioned or not because the whole procedure is "voluntary." No midwife practicing in public would be required to take any course or exam. Although the purposes of the bill are noble, it is questionable if the public would be protected one bit, and I therefore veto House Bill 635.

To some, the veto indicated that the public support given H.B. 635 by the TMA had been undermined by private opposition from this same organization. Representative Uribe was surprised at the governor's action and expressed the feeling that the TMA was responsible for the veto. Although TMA denies this (a TMA lobbyist told me, "We had to convince Hector we were not behind the veto"), comments by TMA spokesmen are strangely echoed in the governor's veto message. Ace Pickens, TMA legal counsel, noted that he was "not entirely in opposition to the bill," but felt it was important to clarify that the educational program could not and would not be construed as certification of lay midwives. He said that the TMA was "fearful that the letter of completion [offered by the educational program] will be used to some extent to indicate certification" (*Odessa American*, 1979). Another TMA official, pointing to his organization's stance against midwifery, claimed that the TMA supports the registration of midwives for the purpose of identification, but remains opposed to licensure. As recently as 1981 the TMA reaffirmed its policy, first formulated in 1977 (Wilcox, 1981): "TMA . . . opposes any action by the State Legislature to expand or endorse lay midwifery by nonmedical personnel."

By the next legislative session (1981) Representative Uribe had become State Senator Uribe, and he introduced a revised version of House Bill 635 to the Senate. Because they bear the mark of political compromise, the revisions made in the new bill, Senate Bill 1093, merit further examination. After the near passage of H.B. 635, midwives began to sense the need for organization, and in May of 1980 a group of them founded the Association of Texas Midwives. Their concern over restrictive legislation is evidenced in the letter they sent to prospective members: they hoped "to secure a continued place for the practice of professional midwifery in the State of Texas" (see also Association of Texas Midwives, 1981). Uribe was anxious to gain their endorsement for his bill, which enabled them to gain a few significant revisions. They were able to restrict the definition of normal childbirth to cases that exhibit "no abnormality or expected complications," excluding the more specific references to "hemorrhage, toxemia, infection, abnormal fetus position or abnormal presentation." They were also able to slightly alter the composition of the lay midwifery board; however, the balance between lay midwives and licensed medical professionals remained even.

Control over the practice of midwifery was tightened by a few revisions intended to satisfy the TMA and the governor. Following the advice of the chairman of TMA's Maternal and Child Health Committee, a section was added requiring that the written disclosure—which lists the limitations on the practice of midwifery and notifies the client whether the midwife has passed the training course—be signed by the client and forwarded to the Department of Health. The chairman had also proposed that a section be added directing midwives to "insist" that their clients seek prenatal care and, if complications arise, "medical care." Such a section was added, but it directed midwives only to "encourage" clients in these directions. Another section was added in an attempt to avoid any appearance of state sanction for midwifery practice: "A lay midwife may not . . . use in connection with his or her name a title, abbreviation, or any designation tending to imply that he or she is a 'registered' lay midwife as opposed to one who has identified himself or herself in compliance with this act." Violation of any section of the law is regarded as a "class C" misdemeanor, punishable by a fine of $200 and thirty days in jail.

Like its predecessor, S.B. 1093 received wide support and little opposition. Uribe's office received letters of support from the Department of Health, the TMA, the Texas Nurses Association, and the Nurse-Midwifery Committee of the Texas Perinatal Association. The Association of Texas Midwives was a little more wary in its support. Their letter reported that "it is the consensus of the Board [of Directors] that we do not object to Senate Bill 1093 in its current form."⁴ In spite of this support, S.B. 1093 died an unnatural death. The bill passed the Senate and cleared the House Health Services Committee, but it died in the House Calendars Committee. Once again Uribe was surprised at the outcome. The house sponsor was on the calendars committee and the senator fully expected that the bill would have no problem reaching the floor. Again the actions of the TMA were suspect. Explaining the failure of the bill, Uribe told a TMA lobbyist: "We see a lot of ghosts, including you guys." The senator's aide told me: "We suspect the docs got to [house sponsor] Wilson and had him kill it quietly." A TMA lobbyist assured me that they were not responsible for the bill's failure: "We are not happy with midwifery as an alternative, but we thought it was a good bill."

The legislative activity in Texas demonstrates an attempt to tighten a permissive law. If either H.B. 635 or S.B. 1093 had passed, Texas midwives would have found themselves faced with clearly defined limits on their practice, limits which did not previously exist. The impetus for this legislation came almost exclusively from its author, and his skill in drafting and willingness to accede to the requests of various organizations produced a bill that was difficult for anyone to oppose. The voluntary nature of the training program outlined in the legislation was the result of a strange coincidence of interests. Senator Uribe and his staff were afraid that mandatory education and certification would drive midwives underground and separate them further from the established medical community. The TMA was afraid that mandatory certification would give a new credibility to midwives. Midwives felt that any mandatory program would be too restrictive.

The failure of the legislation suggests that Uribe's perception of medical opposition may be correct. The TMA is very candid about its opposition to midwifery. The medical lobby is powerful, and while it would damage their image to publicly oppose legislation aimed at improving health services, they are capable of working behind the scenes to defeat bills they regard as threatening. On the other hand, some representatives of the medical establishment indicated that this kind of legislation was desirable; they felt it would gradually destroy midwifery by increasing access to physicians for the traditional clientele of midwives. These clients would note the superiority of physician care and would abandon the untrained midwife. This conclusion seems based on the questionable assumption that midwife care is sought only because access to physicians is blocked by financial or cultural barriers. In fact, many women with ready access to physicians choose midwives in order to avoid "standard medical treatment."

The absence of state legislation has led certain communities to pass local ordinances regulating the practice of midwifery. The city of Brownsville passed a law requiring all midwives to be certified through a city-run program. The cities of El Paso and Laredo considered similar ordinances. The debate over these laws was similar to that described above; their effects will be discussed in the following chapter.

In June 1983, after the data-gathering phase of my research was complete, the Texas legislature passed Senate Bill 238, a lay-midwifery practice act. Once again Senator Uribe was the sponsor, and in most important respects S.B. 238 was identical to S.B. 1093. A lay midwifery board—comprised of three lay midwives, three consumers, an obstetrician, a pediatrician, and a certified nurse midwife—was charged with creating an educational program, a manual, and a test for lay midwives; but most significantly, the training program and examination created by the bill remained voluntary. The bill permitted lay midwives to attend only normal childbirth, which is legally defined for the first time, and prohibited a midwife from using any title that would imply "that he [sic] is a 'registered' or 'certified' lay midwife as opposed to one who has identified himself in compliance with this act."

California: Legislative Attempts to Loosen a Restrictive Law

The legal history of midwifery in California is uneven, marked by overlapping regulations and tempered by various pieces of case law. Midwives were required to register with the state as early as 1917, but it was not until 1937 that a certification program began. Only twelve years later, the licensing program was halted. Midwives holding a license were still allowed to practice, but no new licenses were issued. This situation remained unchanged until 1974, when a perceived shortage of obstetrical care in rural areas prompted legislation enabling certified nurse-midwives to practice. The responsibility for licensing under this new program was placed with the Board of Registered Nursing. The board decided to use the certification standards of the American College of Nurse-Midwives as the licensing criteria, which meant that midwives could practice only under physician supervision. A limited number of training programs and the restrictions inherent in the bill have prevented nurse-midwives from making a significant contribution to maternity care in the state. In 1981 there were only 170 certified nurse-midwives working in California, and (reflecting the distribution of physicians) most of those were located in the bigger metropolitan hospitals.

The legal status of lay midwifery remained hazy until the mid-seventies. Because they intervened only minimally in the birth process, lay midwives felt they were in little danger of arrest for violation of the Medical Practice Act. Some were concerned that compensation for services made them liable for practicing medicine without a license, so attempts were often made to conceal remuneration through systems of barter or by the acceptance of cash only. In March 1974 the worst fears of midwives were realized when, following a year-long undercover operation, three midwives from the Santa Cruz Birth Center were arrested for practicing medicine without a license (see Ruzek, 1978: 57–60). The case made its way to the California Court of Appeals, which ruled, in agreement with the *Banti* decision in Texas, that "pregnancy and childbirth are not diseases but rather normal, physiological functions of women" (*Bowland et al. v. Municipal Court*, 1 Civil 35739). The court continued:

> Therefore, to state that a person practiced or held himself or herself out as practicing a mode of treating a woman in pregnancy or childbirth or the practice of undertaking to assist and treat such a woman does not allege an offense proscribed by section 2141 [of the Business and Professions code, which defines the practice of medicine as treating or diagnosing "the sick or afflicted . . . for any ailment, blemish, deformity, disease, disfigurement, disorder, injury or other mental or physical condition"].

Having clarified that assistance at childbirth was not the practice of medicine, the Court of Appeals ordered the lower court to either amend the complaint against the midwives or dismiss the case.

The midwives' celebration of this victory was shortlived. The attorney general, fearing that the ruling sanctioned midwifery and home birth (see *Her-Self*, 1976), requested a rehearing of the case by the California Supreme Court, which issued its decision on December 6, 1976. Referring to that portion of the statutory definition of the practice of medicine that prohibits the unlicensed from treating any "mental or physical condition," the court stated (*Bowland et al. v. Municipal Court*, 18 Cal. 3d 479, 1976): "We have concluded that normal childbirth, while not a sickness or affliction, is a 'physical condition' within the meaning of . . . section 2141, [and therefore] it is clear that the practice of midwifery without a certificate is prohibited." The case was remanded to the court of origin. The charges against the midwives were eventually dropped, but an important precedent in case law had been established.

In June of 1977, with the support and encouragement of the California Department of Consumer Affairs, Assemblyman Gary Hart introduced Assembly Bill 1896, the Midwifery Practice Act of 1978. This bill, originally drafted by the Department of Consumer Affairs, provided for the training and licensing of non-nurse midwives. It is not surprising that the Department of Consumer Affairs (DCA) was interested in this legislation. Under the administration of Governor Jerry Brown, the DCA, formerly just the institutional home of various licensing boards, adopted a strong consumer advocacy position. One of their priorities was the reassessment of the medical establishment and the monopoly held by medical professionals. To that end several projects were initiated, including the "Health Career Ladder Project," which sought ways to encourage the use of midlevel practitioners (see DCA, 1979), and an extensive study of the ways health is influenced by the current construction of the Medical Practice Act (see Public Affairs Research Group, n.d.; California Board of Medical Quality Assurance, 1982).

In background information papers (DCA, n.d.; DCA, 1977) prepared by the DCA to support A.B. 1896, the agency revealed why it was interested in the bill. First, there was a concern over a lack of obstetrical care. The DCA noted that seventeen of the state's fifty-eight counties had no practicing obstetricians, 27 percent of the state's pregnant women received little or no prenatal care, and only 37 percent of the state's obstetricians were accepting patients with Medi-Cal, California's version of Medicare. Second, the DCA observed that because midwives could provide care more cheaply than physicians, costs for obstetrical services could be reduced by $20 million annually. It was calculated that the state treasury would save $10 million annually. Third, the DCA admitted that the bill was a response to the "growing problem of 'black market' midwives." It was estimated that four hundred lay midwives were practicing illegally in California. In a letter intended to gather support for the bill (Krisman, n.d.), a DCA official suggested that the agency had two choices:

1. Legalize the practice with safeguards to protect the public health and safety, OR
2. Vigorously enforce the current law [i.e., arrest midwives].

This official went on to note that the DCA had chosen the first option.

The original version of the bill, with elaborately detailed training programs and licensing requirements for midwives, was opposed by nearly all associations of medical professionals. Its most formidable opponent was the California Medical Association (CMA). Speaking for the CMA, Dr. Thomas Elmendorf (Anderson, 1978: 5) said the association

is opposing the current legislation on midwifery . . . because we don't think it is in the public interest. We believe that we have made very significant inroads into perinatal mortality and infant mortality . . . and are impacting the statistics that were formerly thought to be so bad for this country. . . . However, we believe . . . that if midwifery is passed and more birthing occurs under less competent supervision . . . our statistics will begin to be reversed.

The California Nursing Association (CNA) was also opposed to the bill, particularly in the revised form that merged nurse-midwives and lay midwives into a single category, "the certified midwife." This proposal troubled the CNA because it would remove jurisdiction over midwives from the Board of Registered Nursing and locate it in a medical licensing board (see Moorhead, 1978). Although lay midwives in California had just formed a state organization, the California Association of Midwives (CAM), no statement on the bill emerged from this group. There seemed a lack of consensus on the merits of licensure among midwives. Some felt it was desirable because it would allow them to abandon the cloak of secrecy and expand their practices; others expressed concern over the possibility of medical dominance (for example, see Ehrlich, 1976).

The bill was effectively killed when it appeared before the Assembly Subcommittee on Health Personnel in January of 1978. The CMA and the CNA had expressed their strong opposition to A.B. 1896, and after some debate it was reduced to a simple directive encouraging the DCA to conduct experimental pilot projects "in order to comprehensively and definitively evaluate the methods by which midwifery training and care may be delivered in California." No money was given to the agency for such experiments. The CMA continued to oppose the bill, although the intensity of its opposition decreased when the bill was neutered in committee. A.B. 1896 eventually passed both houses and was signed into law, but it has not yet led to experimental programs related to midwives.

A second attempt to license lay midwives occurred in April of 1980, with State Senator Barry Keene's introduction of Senate Bill 1829, the Professional Midwifery Practice Act of 1980. Like its predecessor, this bill was drafted by the legal staff of the DCA. Having learned from its earlier defeat, the DCA altered its strategy. In order to curry the favor of the CNA, no mention was made of nurse-midwives, whose supervision was left to the Board of Registered Nursing. The background material prepared in support of S.B. 1829 made no reference to the potential monetary savings afforded by the lower cost of midwifery care. The bill instead focused on the need for midwifery services and the high quality of care offered by midwives. DCA's emphasis on the low cost of midwifery services in A.B. 1896 had backfired; representatives of minorities had assumed that cheaper care meant inferior care and that the state was trying to save money at the expense of the poor.

Like A.B. 1896, the new bill prohibited uncertified practice and limited the practice of professional midwifery to "normal childbirth" under the supervision of a physician. Midwives were to prepare for certification with two years of schooling and a one-year residency, or by a three-year apprenticeship followed by a one-year residency. Upon completion of their training, applicants would be required to pass an examination consisting of written and clinical sections. Responsibility for the certification program would be located in a "Professional Midwifery Examining Committee," which in turn would be under the jurisdiction of the Board of Medical Quality Assurance.

S.B. 1829 gathered more suport than its predecessor. The CNA, no longer concerned about losing control over nurse-midwives, threw its support behind the bill. In addition, the CNA felt that the bill would clarify the scope of midwifery practice, an issue that had been muddled by a recent opinion of the California attorney general, which stated that certified nurse-midwives could not perform episiotomies or suture except under direct physician supervision. What "direct supervision" meant was unclear. The California Association of Midwives also supported the bill. While there was no official association statement in favor of the bill, the CAM sponsored a "Rally for the Midwifery Practice Act of 1980" outside the capitol building on the day the bill was heard in committee. A flyer announcing the rally proclaimed: "Control over women's health care must be returned to women. Legalizing the practice of professional midwives is one way we can do it. We demand an immediate end to harassment of all women health practitioners, including lay midwives." Governor Brown was another source of support for the bill. The governor publicly endorsed the legislation and personally lobbied individual senators.

Opposition to the bill came from physician organizations. In 1979 the CMA's House of Delegates approved a resolution reaffirming its call for births in "obstetrical units of properly accredited and staffed facilities" and "vigorously" opposing all programs encouraging home birth. Joining the CMA in opposition to midwife licensure were the California chapter of the American College of Obstetricians and Gynecologists (ACOG) and the California Association of Obstetricians and Gynecologists (CAOG).

There were isolated instances of opposition from feminist groups. Writing for the Oakland Feminist Women's Health Center, Barbara Raboy (1980) informed the DCA:

> We cannot endorse or support legislation such as S.B. 1829. . . . This is so because S.B. 1829 is the type of legislation that would put many restrictions on midwifes [sic] and put it in the hands of professional medicine, particularly male doctors. . . . I am a bit surprised that the California Medical Association and the local chapter of the American College of Obstetricians and Gynecologists opposed S.B. 1829. If they were thinking clearly, and supported S.B. 1829 they would have total control of women's birthing.

The bill was first heard before the Senate Business and Professions Committee. In his presentation of S.B. 1829 to that committee, Senator Keene stressed the maldistribution of obstetrical care in the state and noted the ability of midwives to remedy that situation. He also observed that midwives could meet the demand by consumers for more family-centered births. Representatives of the CMA, ACOG, and CAOG testified against the bill by noting that it is difficult to distinguish between normal and abnormal birth. Dr. Thomas O'Sullivan, representing CAOG, noted: "It takes a lot of expertise to know which of these babies are going to be hazard. It takes more than two years." Senator Keene offered to meet the objections of the physicians by amending his bill to require closer supervision by physicians, but the physicians stood firm in their opposition. Keene then asked the physicians: "The bottom line is, you've got to be a doctor?" Dr. O'Sullivan replied: "Unfortunately, yes."

The Senate Business and Professions Committee agreed with Dr. O'Sullivan, failing to give the bill the five votes necessary to get it out of committee. As evidence of his continued backing of midwife licensure, Governor Brown met with supporters of S.B. 1829 immediately following its defeat. He pledged his support to similar legislation for the following year and encouraged the group to build a politically active constituency for midwifery. DCA officials were given instructions to help the midwifery proponents.

The DCA, a state agency legally enjoined from lobbying the legislature, realized some steps were needed to counteract the powerful medical lobby if a midwife licensing bill were to arrive on the governor's desk. In 1975–76, the CMA spent more than any other group ($1,353,309) to influence the legislature. In 1977–78 they were the ninth highest spender (Keplinger, 1977; Cooper, 1979). Agency officials decided to create the Midwifery Advisory Council (MAC), whose stated purpose was to advise "California state government on midwifery and childbearing issues" (MAC, n.d.). Thirty thousand dollars was made available to hire two staff persons and to pay traveling expenses for members of Northern and Southern California steering committees. The hidden agenda of the MAC was to politicize the midwifery issue and initiate a grassroots movement capable of putting pressure on legislators. The MAC prepared a slide show on midwifery, arranged to send speakers to community organizations, and periodically issued press releases. It also organized a "Labor Day Picnic and Homebirth Reunion" to attract media attention to midwifery and set up a network of individuals on the basis of legislative district that would allow quick mobilization of "pressure" (by means of phone calls, letters, and telegrams) on particular legislators. The MAC also helped to redraft the bill for submission in the next legislative session.

The stage was set for the third attempt to license lay midwives. The now familiar line was drawn between opponents and proponents. In an editorial, a local newspaper endorsed the licensing of midwives and chastised the medical community for its opposition (*Sacramento Bee*, 1980): "Despite all its talk about childbirth safety, the medical community is not meeting the public's safety needs by insisting that the number of licensed midwives be strictly limited and that those who do practice be kept under the control of doctors." The president of the Northern California Obstetrical and Gynecological Society responded (Berry, 1980):

> Your July 8 editorial encouraging the licensing of lay midwives has left me saddened, dismayed and frustrated. Advocacy for the provision of health care by untrained individuals is untenable. . . . You do not leave the controls of an airliner in the hands of flight attendants, nor can we leave the management of childbirth, the most hazardous trip any of us may ever have to take, to inadequately trained individuals.

In March of 1981, Senator Keene introduced Senate Bill 670, the Midwifery Practice Act of 1981, to the state senate. The bill was scheduled to be heard by the Health and Welfare Committee in April. One significant change had been made from the earlier bills. In order to insure the continued support of the CNA, the Midwifery Examining Committee had been located under the jurisdiction of the Board of Registered Nursing. The California Association of Midwives, several of whose members served on the Midwifery Advisory Council, officially supported the bill, notifying its members of the bill's introduction and encouraging them to contact their legislators. Within the last year several midwives had been arrested for practicing medicine without a license, and many midwives had begun to feel that a licensure law was necessary, if only for protection.

One midwife said, "Every time I do anything, I am risking my neck, my home, my family."

At the hearing, proponents of the legislation focused on the need to protect the health of women and their babies by regulating the 500 to 600 illegal midwives practicing in the state. According to a spokeswoman for CAM, "Our primary concern is the health and safety of mothers and infants." Commenting on the ongoing trials of two midwives, she noted that regulation should not be accomplished through court action; she also emphasized that the current situation separated the clients of lay midwives from the medical system. Once again the opponents of the bill were drawn from professional associations of physicians. The physicians who testified against the bill centered their testimony in three areas: the use of "untrained" practitioners, the difficulty of separating normal from abnormal birth, and the worrisome composition of the Midwifery Examining Committee. One physician noted that lay midwives offered "second-class medical care," and compared their use at birth with using a high school graduate who had a "thirty-month crash course in criminal law to defend someone against a murder charge." Nearly all the physicians pointed to the need for expertise because of the impossibility of distinguishing between "high-risk" and "low-risk" during labor. Several doctors expressed concern that only one obstetrician would be included on the eleven-member Midwifery Examining Committee. The other members would include four midwives—two nurse midwives and two non-nurse midwives—three "public members," a hospital administrator, a pediatrician, and a family practitioner.

The hearing was held in an auditorium that could seat approximately five hundred people. The auditorium was nearly full, and at one point the chair of the committee asked those in favor of the legislation to stand. Almost everyone stood, the majority of them women and children. When the chair asked those opposing the bill to stand, about a dozen people stood, most of whom were middle-aged men. Five votes were needed to move the bill out of committee, and after both sides had given their testimony there was a call for a vote. Some members of the committee were now absent, and others withheld their votes, resulting in a 2–2 tie. The bill was put on call, allowing the absent members and the uncertain members to vote later in the day. Lobbying of those who had not voted continued, but by the end of the day it was clear that the bill was headed for defeat.

California provides an example of attempts to use legislation to loosen the laws that restrict the practice of midwifery. Originally the legislation was sponsored by a state agency interested in promoting consumer causes. Gradually midwives were drawn in to support the various bills presented to the legislature. At times the interests of the state agency and the midwives clashed. Midwives were interested in a licensing law that would allow them autonomy; the DCA was chiefly interested in getting a midwife licensing law on the books. Consequently, the DCA was willing to (and often did) make compromises that midwives felt were too restrictive. The DCA justified its action by reminding midwives that the Brown Administration regarded midwifery favorably, and if no law passed during his tenure it was likely that midwives would suffer in the future. The failure of all three bills introduced in the California legislature is indicative of the political and cultural power of medicine. Their political organization and the general cultural faith in their practice provides medical professionals with a power that marginal medical groups find difficult to overcome.

Licensure and Strategies of Dominance

These recent attempts to regulate midwifery confirm conclusions from earlier regulation and reveal that the strategies used by established medical professions to maintain dominance remain much the same. As with previous legislation, concern for public health is central to all certification plans. In Arizona the law was revised because of a concern that the old regulations, instituted in 1957, were insufficient to guarantee the quality of midwifery services. In Texas, a voluntary training program was proposed to upgrade care and thereby avoid mishaps like those recently reported in the press. In California, the Department of Consumer Affairs drafted a licensing law to control "black market" midwives who practiced with no "safeguards to protect the public health and safety." Each state made an effort to insure that individuals who chose to avoid standard care had the benefit of a midwife who was trained in modern medical technique, and who was ready to call on a physician should any complication arise.

As in earlier midwife legislation, the definition of birth was part of the issue. Where the intent was to tighten permissive laws (as is historically the case with midwife licensure), birth was portrayed as a dangerous event, not a natural process that could be supervised by an informally trained attendant. California, however, provides an interesting contrast in that proponents of the licensing bill, who were interested in loosening a restrictive law, had to persuade officials that birth was in fact a *normal* event. Anisef and Basson (1979: 354–59) have noted that midwifery flourishes where birth is regarded as a "natural, normal physiological process." The near-total hospitalization of birth found in the Western world suggests that physicians have convinced the public that birth is abnormal. Aware of the need to counter this view, the Department of Consumer Affairs in California issued the following statement in support of its bill (DCA, 1977: 2):

> Today's California hospitals and obstetricians are strongly oriented to caring for the abnormal, complicated birth with drugs, technology and other forms of medical intervention. Though these advances in medical science have produced dramatic reductions in infant and maternal mortality rates, drugs and medical intervention are not always necessary to births which are uncomplicated, normal deliveries. According to experts at the

medical schools of the University of California in San Francisco and Los Angeles, most mothers can be screened in the prenatal period into high-risk and low-risk groups, with 90 percent of all mothers generally falling into the low-risk population. . . . Since most births are uncomplicated and normal, alternative birthing practices are safe and reasonable.

The attempt to "demedicalize" birth required counteracting the view that birth is an abnormal event appropriately handled only by trained physicians. Of course, medical professionals defended their proprietary rights by insisting that birth, while it might appear normal to the untrained, is fraught with danger. In his testimony in opposition to the California bill, one physician adduced this specious logic: "If birth isn't a disease, why am I required to have twelve years of specialized education?"

Midwife licensure has been dominated by medical science throughout modern history. As the scientific view of birth gained wide acceptance, laws emerged requiring midwives to abandon their traditional ways and adopt medical techniques. It is significant that the issue of midwife licensure has re-emerged in a period when the medical domination of childbirth is being questioned. As noted in Table 1, home birth is increasing. More importantly, studies of those who choose home birth and employ lay midwives in Arizona (Anderson *et al.,* 1978), Texas (Ortman-Glick, 1978; McCallum, 1979), and California (Hazell, 1974; Rubin, 1976; Ellis *et al.,* 1980) reveal that it is no longer just the poor or minorities who are avoiding hospitals and doctors during pregnancy and childbirth. Yankauer (1983: 637) has noted an upward trend in the educational attainment of women who choose home birth. Nearly half of the women who have midwife-attended out-of-hospital deliveries have thirteen or more years of schooling.

Medical professionals were little concerned as long as they felt that midwives were serving only isolated populations that chose their services because of poverty or cultural preference; midwifery seemed merely a problem of ignorance that would be overcome as the benefits of medicine were more widely known. However, midwifery became a threat to medical professionals when better educated individuals chose to avoid the "benefits" of medicine in favor of the services of midwives. The response to such a threat is enforcement of restrictive laws and the tightening of permissive laws.

In the past, physicians were generally opposed to midwife licensure, while most midwives favored it. These attitudes by and large remain unchanged. In none of the three states studied did midwives oppose the proposed statutes. There was some concern over supervision by the medical profession (see Daniels, 1981a) but most midwives were anxious to obtain the sanction offered by certification. On the other hand, most physicians in the three states wanted to abolish midwifery. Their position on licensure, however, varied according to the social conditions and laws already existing in their states. In California, where non-nurse midwifery ran contrary to case law, medical professionals vigorously opposed certification. In Texas, where traditional birth attendants have a long and continuous history, case law permits unlicensed midwifery. Medical professionals there were willing to endorse a bill that increased government surveillance and limited midwife practice, but did not provide the sanction of certification (or even registration). In Arizona, where midwives had the advantage of an old law in their favor, the state altered the regulations by administrative procedure both to make it more difficult to receive a license and to enhance government control.

All the laws proposed are examples of "hostile licensure." The Texas and Arizona laws place authority over midwives in a committee or agency comprised of a majority of nonmidwives. In California, the proposed Midwifery Examining Committee was dominated by midwives, but that committee was under the jurisdiction of the Board of Registered Nursing. These laws can be considered "hostile" in requiring midwives to obtain the cooperation of physicians in order to practice. For example, S.B. 670 in California stated: "All applicants for certification shall be required to submit upon application for licensure a written plan describing a mechanism for providing to clients continuity of care. The plan shall include a working agreement with a licensed physician and surgeon with current training and practice in obstetrics." Other laws create a dependence on physicians for such things as education or certification of physicial and mental health. These allow disapproving physicians to prevent midwife practice by withholding cooperation. The executive director of the Texas Medical Association commented on an ordinance to regulate midwifery proposed by the city of Laredo (Williston, 1980, emphasis added):

> Any proposed ordinance or statute embracing medical and health care needs physician understanding and support in order to be effective. Physicians at the State level with whom we have conferred feel that there are some real medical shortcomings in the ordinance which is being considered by the City of Laredo. ... The ordinance ... implies that there will be a physician available to care for those who are referred by the lay midwives. *That, of course, is unrealistic.*

In Arizona, would-be midwives find it difficult to realize their career objective because the medical community that administers the midwife program has not established or accredited any schools to provide the mandated training.

The lack of effective organization has prevented midwives from significantly influencing legislation aimed at them. Referring to earlier legislation, Litoff (1978: 107) observes:

> Because midwives were poorly organized, they were not able to help draft the laws and regulations governing their practices. For example, no statements by midwives were made before the 1927 United States subcommittee hearings on the practice of medicine and midwifery in the District of Columbia. In contrast, lengthy testimony was presented by members of the recognized medical profession.

The same was true in the three states studied here. Compared with the medical associations, midwife organizations were poorly organized, pitifully underfinanced, and incapable of achieving a consensus on political issues. When legislators and departments of health sought advice on proposed legislation, medical associations responded immediately, while the associations of midwives spent time and energy trying to organize and seek consensus. When the regulations were being altered in Arizona, there was no midwife association at all, leaving the Department of Health Services to seek the opinions of individual midwives and consumers.

As in most health legislation, consumers had little input. The consumers who did testify at legislative hearings were invariably supporters of midwifery. Midwives were able to mobilize their clients to attend rallies and appear at hearings. Physicians could not, or at least did not, call on their clients in this way. The exceptions here are a few minority spokespeople who expressed concern that the licensing of midwives was a thinly disguised attempt by the establishment to offer cheaper, second-class care to the poor. Midwives felt that these statements were based on a misguided desire to emulate the rich—the same misguided desire that caused the poor to give up breast for bottle feeding.

The examination of midwife legislation reveals the cultural power of medicine. Apart from the political power of their association, medical professionals sustain their dominance in health care through the possession of scientific solutions to illness. A generalized belief in science gives authority to its priests, who are unlikely to condone modes of treatment different from their own. Alternative practitioners are overcome not only by political power but also by public faith in physicians.

There is a certain irony in the drive for licensure by paraprofessional groups. They hope to secure and expand their practice, but receipt of a license often brings restrictions on practice and a consequent decrease in autonomy. Yet the idea of licensure remains seductive. Paramedical groups view the monopolistic benefits granted to physicians by licensure, and assume that similar benefits will accrue to them. Unfortunately, these aspirations rest on a naive view of licensure. Physicians were the first medical practitioners to obtain licensed status, and they were free to define and thereby domi. ate health care. As their political and cultural power has grown, they have become less willing to surrender any authority to ancillary medical professions. In this climate, others who wish to be licensed must be ready to accept control by physicians.

A review of paramedical occupations that have acquired licensed status confirms that "state licensing fortifies medical control" (Larkin, 1981: 16; see also Larkin, 1978; 1983). Although midwives have an autonomous history compared to other paraprofessionals, licensing laws have similar effects on their independence.

Changed social and cultural conditions give modern midwife legislation distinctive features. While earlier regulatory acts in Europe and America sought to control and bring the "benefits" of medicine to a widespread folk practice, the current bills represent attempts to recognize an alternative practice used only by small numbers of people. The supporters of these bills view them as a method to expand the choices available to pregnant women. However, the effect of licensing is more likely only to medicalize the lay midwife. Commenting on the bill to license midwives in California, Roth (n.d.: 2) points out:

> The changes from the original version to the amended version show a major shift toward training and requirements which fit the standard medical model and increased control by the medical profession. What little innovation the concept once had as a piece of legislation has been largely dissipated. . . . [T]his bill contains the crucial features of exclusive licensure. It creates a restrictive monopoly and makes the equivalent activities of all others illegal. It lays on the standard threats of monopoly occupations—not only keeping out the uncertified, but threat-

ening the certified who do not conform to conventional expectations with charges of "unprofessional conduct," which in practice means whatever those currently in power want it to mean. It is the classic tactic to cut off criticism and innovation.

We may conclude that legal recognition for midwives implies restriction. And although the law is limited in its ability to change health-care practice, it helps to create and accelerate conditions that contribute to changing styles of care. Furthermore, legal status alters individual modes of practice, a factor which has a significant impact in aggregate. The following chapter explores the implications of midwife regulation by focusing on the qualitative aspects of births attended by both licensed and unlicensed midwives.

Chapter 4

Midwifery in Action: The Influence of Law on Practice

The avowed purpose of midwife licensure is protection of public health and safety. Hence midwife licensure is most often evaluated in terms of medical outcomes; that is, the extent to which licensing reduces maternal and infant mortality and morbidity. While such evaluations are undeniably useful, they overlook important consequences of licensure not directly measurable in the survival and health of the clientele. These include changes in the composition of the profession and the nature of care offered. This chapter examines the latter consequences, particularly the ways licensing laws influence the practitioner and her encounter with clients.

Most studies of paramedical licensure focus on the negative effects of physician dominance. These effects cannot be ignored, but there are other, perhaps more important, ways in which licensure effects paramedical practice. For example, once licensure is instituted, characteristics of practitioners will change because of changes in educational requirements, recruitment patterns, relationships between practitioners, and the nature of the clientele.

The changes wrought by licensure can be demonstrated by comparison: the midwives in the three states studied present a rough continuum of state and medical control over the occupation. In California, where lay midwifery is prohibited, the state has only reactive control, and medical control is all but nonexistent. In Texas, the registration requirement results in minimal state and medical control. In Arizona, the licensing law provides state control over practitioners and requires limited medical supervision and consultation. I shall expand this continuum by adding a fourth category to our comparison: the licensed, certified nurse-midwife (CNM). There are three reasons for including the CNM. First, licensing laws, which usually require physician supervision and extended periods of education, reflect a desire to push lay midwifery in the direction of nurse-midwifery. Second, although the Arizona law requires licences of midwives, it is too new for changes in recruitment and training to be apparent. Because the state still offers no established educational program, there has been no formalized production of licensed midwives. Most of the currently licensed midwives were practicing before the law was revised; hence they entered the profession with motivations and training similar to midwives in California and Texas. The recruitment and formal training of CNMs, on the other hand, are approximately what we would expect to find under an established licensing law. Finally, the introduction of CNMs into our comparison allows us to observe how midwifery is influenced by location in medical institutions. Most CNMs work in hospital settings under physician supervision. In their survey of nurse-midwifery in the United States, Rooks et al. (1978) collected data on 1,299 CNMs: only five (0.4%) of these were employed in private practice, and only forty-three indicated that they worked in non-hospital settings (3.3%). This provides an interesting contrast to lay midwives in Arizona, Texas, and California, who almost never assist in hospital deliveries. The importance of understanding how a hospital setting influences midwifery is underscored by the desire of many lay midwives to work in hospitals; indeed, proposed licensing laws often include provisions that would give midwives hospital access. For instance, the most recent California bill included a section that prohibited hospitals from discriminating against midwives as a class of practitioners when granting the privilege to admit patients. Further, widespread physician opposition to home birth implies that, if midwives accept supervision by physicians as a condition of licensure, they will be working in hospitals.

Because the hospital-based CNM is employed in a variety of roles, it is necessary to outline these before proceeding in the comparison. While the practice of midwifery is generally associated with birth, CNMs are also capable of providing routine gynecological services and birth-control counseling. In fact, recent studies (Record and Cohen, 1972; Record and Greenlick, 1976; Rooks *et al.*, 1978) show that a CNM brought into a hospital setting is pressed into extraneous clinical and educational duties, leaving her little time for obstetrical care. Those CNMs who do work in maternity wards are often assigned duties similar to those of an obstetrical nurse, acting as little more than an assistant to the physician and a companion to the mother, even though the American College of Nurse-Midwives maintains the CNM is capable of assuming "responsibility for the complete care and management of uncomplicated maternity patients" (*Journal of Nurse-Midwifery*, 1975). The alternative birth center (ABC)—a recent development in maternity care—provides the hospital-based midwife with her greatest degree of autonomy, and there her style of practice can be suitably compared with the practice of lay midwifery.

As indicated in Chapter 3, the ABC attempts to approximate home birth within the hospital. Labor, delivery, and postpartum care are all (ideally) carried out in one "home-like" room in the presence of family and friends, with a minimum of medical interference. Should anything "go wrong," the complete facilities of the hospital are available at a moment's notice. ABC programs are open only to those whose pregnancies are medically defined as "low-risk." If this definition changes at any time during pregnancy or birth, the client is removed from the ABC and given standard hospital care. Although not all ABCs employ midwives, this setting provides the CNM a convenient niche within the hospital bureaucracy.

Because ABC programs segregate a population of low-risk pregnancies, the CNM is provided with "uncomplicated maternity cases" and is able to provide continuous care (that is, prenatal, intrapartum, postpartum) to her clients with a minimum of visible physician supervision. Except for occasional references to CNMs working in other environments, the following discussion will use the CNM employed in the alternative birth center as the main point of comparison with lay midwives in Arizona, Texas, and California.[1]

In order to isolate the differences between licensed and unlicensed midwives that are attributable to licensure, comparisons will be made in four general areas: the nature of the practitioner; the nature of the client; the characteristics of the midwife-client relationship; and the structuring of the birth experience. Although these areas are presented as distinct categories, it should be remembered that they are arbitrary and overlapping distinctions.

The Practitioner

The educational requirements of licensing laws differentiate midwives significantly. Unlicensed midwives, who are not subject to such requirements, usually acquire their training through a combination of self-education and apprenticeship. This training enables them to sustain a naturalistic, noninterventionist view of birth assistance that conflicts with the medically dominant view of birth as an abnormality that usually requires intervention. Most lay practitioners are recruited through experience with the home birth of their children or by their presence at another home birth. In the course of my research I met only one lay midwife who had not had a baby at home. Many home birthers, in fact, have had bad experiences with hospital deliveries. And although health professionals are sometimes relied upon for training in seminars and workshops, the unlicensed midwife's skeptical attitude toward "organized medicine" insulates her from the subtle propagandizing found in formal educational programs.

Training by apprenticeship supports a wholistic approach to birth because the subject is not segmented into areas of study such as physiology, pharmacology, or anatomy. The unlicensed midwife does not reject the knowledge made available by obstetrical science, but she does resist a view of birth which reduces it to nothing more than a scientific process amenable to routinized care. In her book, "Spiritual Midwifery," Gaskin (1978: 11) points out:

> The knowledge that each and every childbirth is a spiritual experience has been forgotten by too many people in the world today, especially in countries with high levels of technology. This book is revolutionary because it is our basic belief that the sacrament of birth belongs to the people and that it should not be usurped by a profit-oriented hospital system.

This view of birth is reflected in attitudes toward training (Merz, 1977: 548): "No matter how it is that a person acquired midwiving techniques, there is an element to being a midwife that cannot be taught. It is a gift, and one that must be shared to truly come to life." The patterns of recruitment and training currently used by unlicensed midwives are supportive of a "spiritual" view of birth, a view which maintains that the body is capable of giving birth with little or no outside intervention. In cases where intervention is required, it is most often a "natural" intervention—for example, to help ease the baby's head out of the birth canal, midwives will use hot oil massages instead of episiotomies; to stimulate labor, midwives give their clients raspberry or cohosh tea rather than pitocin (see Peterson, 1983).

The educational programs mandated by licensing laws affect the type of person who chooses to become a midwife as well as her perception of the birth process. Currently, only CNM educational programs have the formal approval of physician associations, so it is likely that other midwife training programs will seek to emulate them. To become a CNM, an individual must first be a registered nurse and then complete a nationally approved educational program in midwifery. By the time a CNM is ready to practice she has had "a *minimum* of 6 years of specialized training: 4 years in an accredited school of nursing, 1 year or more job experience, and at least 1 year or more of midwifery education" (Brennan and Heilman, 1977: 16–17, emphasis in original). Such educational requirements restrict entry into the profession and begin a process of medical socialization. Only those with the resources necessary to survive a lengthy period of training can hope to achieve the status of CNM.

A recent study of applicants to nurse-midwifery educational programs made the interesting observation that nearly 70 percent had no children (Warpinski and Adams, 1979: 6). This suggests that the majority of CNMs acquire their knowledge of birth only in medical settings under the direction of physicians. Arms (1977: 198–99) comments on the consequences:

> Nursing school, like medical school, teaches that pathology, not the normal is expected. In her education as a nurse, the nurse-midwife is taught to expect anything and everything to go awry in birth, and she has a lusty respect for modern forms of interference which will protect a woman from her own working body. It is a rare nurse who leaves her training unscarred by that emphasis and expectation of disease and disorder. Thus, examined closely in light of her history as a nurse and the harsh reality of her hospital surroundings, the *nurse* takes her place on the growing obstetric team, but the *midwife* has changed and lost her essence in the process. The reason is a simple one. She is no longer the guardian of normal birth and watchful servant of mothers. She is a registered nurse with a post-graduate degree in a specialty called midwifery. And she looks and acts much like the physician authority whom she is licensed to assist. . . . Further,

[she] is trained . . . to defer to the authority of rank. She believes that the physician, not the birthing mother, knows best and holds the power to heal. By training, she sees life as a physican does, full of problems, abnormalities and complications.

In describing her experience with similarly trained British midwives, Comaroff (1977: 126) confirms the observations of Arms. She notes that midwives view pregnancy as a "condition akin to physical illness, suitably treated in terms of medical intervention." A nurse-midwife who works in the nurse-midwifery practice of a New York hospital concludes: "There's too much intervention here. They don't leave people alone. They don't have the patience to wait for nature. There are too many vaginal exams. They use routine IV's with glucose and give routine Pitocin after delivery" (quoted in Arms, 1977: 322). Rothman (1982: 245–48; 1983) also hints at the medical nature of the certified nurse-midwife when she observes that home births "radicalize" CNMs. She points out that nurse-midwives who enter home delivery practice must relearn what constitutes a "normal birth."

In examining the "changing role of the midwife" in Great Britain, Walker (1972) identifies other important changes that have accompanied licensure. She regards the British midwife's loss of independence as a threat to "the continuation of midwifery as such, as distinct from obstetrics" (p. 86). In particular, she sees midwives as "limited practitioners" (Wardwell, 1972) who have been strongly affected by two factors: the concentration on the hospital for maternity care and the trend toward teamwork in health care. While her perspective comes from British data, many of her observations have direct application to American midwifery.

Walker notes that as the use of domiciliary care has declined, midwives have gotten involved with several people other than their clients. In earlier days the midwife dealt primarily with her client; there was little interaction with doctors, supervisors, or other midwives. The modern midwife must interact with all these people as well as social workers, hospital staff, and specialists. This holds true both for hospital-based and the few remaining domiciliary midwives. However, Walker observed a shift in emphasis in the hospital setting, in that the midwife's dealings with a variety of hospital personnel diminished the relationship with her client.

Walker's analysis applies equally well to licensed midwives in America. Even the relatively autonomous CNM who works in a birth center is limited by hospital and medical staff policies, and it is evident that the midwife's intrastaff relationships often impinge upon the client-practitioner relationship. The CNM is not free to provide her services to all who desire them. Written protocols prevent clients with "high-risk" pregnancies from admission to the program. Other policies also influence midwife-client contact. One CNM, for example, expressed displeasure that her "boss" (the head of maternal and fetal medicine in her hospital) would not allow her to accept patients enrolled in a prepaid health service at another hospital. The CNM was anxious to offer an alternative to these individuals, but had no choice but to obey her superior.

Her boss was concerned with problems that might arise when patients required transfer to the regular labor and delivery suite. He was unwilling to have a woman in active labor transported to another hospital (where her medical costs were covered), whereas if she remained at his hospital he feared the difficulty of obtaining proper reimbursement from the prepaid plan.

Protocols also set parameters on the care a CNM may offer. In effect they require the midwife to surrender ultimate responsibility for a pregnancy or birth to a "more skilled" practitioner. Many of the policies contained in ABC protocols were inspired by CNM licensing laws. For instance, the law governing California's CNMs— the California Business and Professional Code (1977: 117–20)— states that the practice of midwifery

does not include the use of any instrument at any childbirth, except such instrument as is necessary in severing the umbilical cord, nor does it include the assisting of childbirth by any artificial, forcible or mechanical means, nor the performance of any version, nor the removal of adherent placenta, nor the administering, prescribing, advising or employing, either before or after childbirth, of any drug, other than a disinfectant or cathartic.

The code states that the certificate to practice midwifery may be revoked for failure to refer to, or summon, a physician for specified conditions during pregnancy, labor, or the lying-in period.

The licensed lay midwife in Arizona faces similar restrictions. State regulations clearly define the boundaries of practice, and a midwife who steps over them is in danger of losing her license. In one case a midwife was sought out by a woman whose previous caesarean section made her ineligible for midwife care. Although the midwife told her she could not legally assist in her birth, the woman was intent on a vaginal delivery and presented herself on the midwife's doorstep when she was in active labor. Recognizing the danger of this situation (to herself and to the mother), the midwife immediately called the director of the midwife licensing program and explained her situation. The midwife was advised to leave the house and call the police. In another case a midwife had her license suspended for using a drug (pitocin) to control postpartum bleeding of a woman who had to be moved from her rural home to a distant hospital. Midwives in Arizona are frustrated by these and similar strictures that prevent them from satisfying the wishes of their clients. There are also some procedures Arizona midwives feel they can safely handle (for example, the use of herbs) that are prohibited by law.

The unlicensed lay midwife faces fewer complexities. They accept the need to limit their practice to "low-risk" pregnancies, but because of their independent position and extralegal status, definitions of risk are more negotiable for them than for licensed midwives. One lay midwife notes (Merz, 1977: 550):

We have no agreement about what constitutes a pregnancy at risk, and therefore not viable for home birth. Each situation is handled individually as a negotiation between parents and midwife. Parents are educated as to possible risks and the limitations of their midwife. Ultimately the decision is theirs. The midwife must then establish for herself whether or not she can take the responsibility for supporting them.

In their study of home birth, Mehl *et al.* (1977: 284) point out that, unlike definitions of risk found in hospital settings, "previous obstetric complications (with the exception of caesarean section) were not used as screening criteria because it was felt that they were iatrogenic to some extent." It is not uncommon for an unlicensed midwife to request her client to see a doctor for some prenatal care, and also to be on call should an emergency arise. The doctor and midwife thus enter into a relationship, but the lack of any bureaucratic framework equalizes their status with regard to the client. Only when it is necessary for the midwife and her client to enter the doctor's "turf" (the hospital) does the hierarchical ordering between the doctor and the midwife become evident.

The relationship of unlicensed midwives with each other serves some important functions. Because they feel a need to learn from each other, and because they share a distinctive and somewhat radical ideology with regard to birth, unlicensed midwives typically work in groups. In some areas these groups maintain contacts with other midwives in larger, informal networks to pass on referrals and to share knowledge. Sensitivity to their collective reputation also leads unlicensed midwife groups to discipline those whose work they regard as sloppy or dangerous. They use peer pressure on errant practitioners to reform or cease practice. The effectiveness of such informal control is difficult to assess. One case uncovered in this study concerned a midwife who was forced from practice because of an increasingly bad reputation among her peers. In this regard unlicensed midwives are similar to physicians, who also use referral networks to rid themselves of incompetent practitioners. In both cases, however, this "local discipline" may drive a practitioner from one area, but does not bar him/her from practice elsewhere. In contrast, licensed midwives lack control networks. Because their authority for training and discipline belongs to state agencies, these midwives do not feel the need to learn from each other or patrol their ranks.

Another difference between the licensed and unlicensed midwife is the nature of their relationship with organized medicine. CNMs have well-established relationships with obstetricians and physicians. Licensed lay midwives in Arizona have established working relationships with medical institutions, despite difficulties in finding supportive physicians. While unlicensed midwives may have informal relationships with certain physicians, these relationships are fragmentary because of the threat of professional sanction (loss of hospital privileges, for example) facing doctors who collaborate. Studies also document that the formal ties between doctor and midwife necessitated by licensure result in the more frequent resort to physician assistance by midwives. Donnison (1977: 185) reports that in Britain, "Ever since the 1902 [licensing] Act had come into operation, the proportion of cases in which midwives had sent for the doctor had been rising steadily." In those American cities which employed licensing, "Midwives, more secure in their licensed status, were calling doctors earlier and oftener" (Kobrin 1966: 356).

The establishment of well-defined relationships with physicians alters the midwife's style of practice. Oakley (1977: 24) comments: "In a home confinement, where [a midwife] must summon a doctor for the repair of an episiotomy, she may be motivated to deliver the baby's head more slowly in order to stretch the perineum gradually and thus avoid the need for an incision." In the case of lay midwives, where physician back-up is not always well-established, and where there is a disinclination to use hospitals, the motivations cited by Oakley result in a style of practice geared to avoiding medical assistance. Interestingly, some techniques employed by lay midwives to avoid medical procedures have influenced physician care. Mehl (1976: 96), in his study of home and hospital birth, reports that "the perineal massage technique used by the midwives to aid in preventing vaginal lacerations during delivery was effective, and, as the physicians adopted this technique, their laceration rate decreased."

Licensed midwifery recruits individuals with motivations different from those of unlicensed midwives. This is probably the most significant indirect effect of licensure. Those who practice midwifery in states where it is prohibited have a strong commitment to their occupation. Yet if midwifery were to be licensed in those states, it would become merely another legitimate career opportunity, a job chosen by an individual because it appears an interesting way to make a living. In his discussion of chiropractors, Roth (1977: 118) states:

> As more and more people enter the field, a greater proportion do so to make a living. They are concerned with holding their own against the competition and with expanding the scope of their practice, if possible. If this means looking more like a doctor and doing things a doctor does, so be it.

These findings apply to midwifery. There may be other intentions, but most CNMs engage in their occupation to "make a living." Being salaried, they are concerned with the efficient use of time, and the client-practitioner interaction becomes part of business. Most of the midwives now licensed in Arizona once practiced illegally, and were drawn to the occupation for reasons similar to unlicensed midwives. How much their orientation can change is illustrated by the Arizona midwife who capitalized on her new status by expanding her practice, staffing it in the fashion of the typical physician practice, and offering regular office appointments. In contrast, "[un-licensed] lay midwives wish to be paid, but they have no desire to make midwifery especially lucrative. Many believe that it should

not just be offered as a commercial service, for midwifery is a calling for dedicated, spiritual women working in concert with like-
minded patients" (Ruzek, 1978: 138; see also Arms, 1977: 195,
251–52). In her "instructions to midwives" Gaskin (1978: 285)
says:

> The spiritual midwife tries to find a way that she can practice
> without charging money, as this makes it easier to keep birthings
> spiritual. Her husband and/or community may assume her sup-
> port. If she is helping ladies for free, she has a better moral posi-
> tion if she needs to talk to a lady about her attitude.

Because they are not interested in "making a living," lay midwives
typically have fewer cases and are freer to spend more time with
their patients during both pregnancy and childbirth (see also Mills,
1977: 52).

Licensure serves to define a jurisdiction for practitioners. Once
defined, those who meet the requirements guard their territory
jealously. Certain CNMs told me that lay midwives should be regarded as no more than "birth attendants" because they cannot offer their clients the complete store of knowledge and techniques
that are a part of midwifery. In Arizona, some licensed midwives
have been diligent in their responsibility to report and thereby prevent the practice of midwifery by unlicensed persons. In that same
state licensed midwives fought a bill that would have loosened the
requirements for entry into the profession.

The restrictions of licensure limit the practice of midwives and
the kinds of clients they are allowed to see. These limitations can reduce the clientele of midwives, particularly when regulations are
newly introduced. Evidence from the city of Brownsville, Texas,
where a training program for midwives was begun in 1976 and certification ordinance introduced in 1977, confirms this observation.
Strict limits on the definition of normal childbirth, coupled with
mandated education and increased surveillance, reduced the number of births with midwife assistance:

In 1974, 66% of all babies in Brownsville were delivered by lay midwives. In 1975, 84% or 2784 were delivered by midwives and 536 were delivered by doctors. In July 12, 1976, the program began and 75% were delivered by lay midwives. . . . In 1977, 66% were delivered by lay midwives and the ordinance #913 was passed on May 2, 1977, and we could then enforce the need for regulation, education, and observation of lay midwives. In 1978, 50% of the deliveries were done by lay midwives (Brownsville Department of Public Health, 1979).

Not unexpectedly, the differences in licensed and unlicensed midwives as practitioners result in characteristic differences in their clientele.

The Client

One characteristic common to clients of both licensed and unlicensed midwives is self-selection. The present structure of maternity care in the United States more or less channels expectant parents toward a standard hospital delivery. It takes an active effort by parents to obtain a midwife-assisted delivery.

This search for an alternative is often rooted in strong feelings of where the responsibility for birth should lie. Parental desire to assume this responsibility varies widely. My own interviews with parents as well as data collected by others (Millinaire, 1974; Nash and Nash, 1979) reveal a range of feelings extending from total reliance upon medical personnel (as in hospital births where the mother is only semiconscious) to a desire for complete responsibility (as in home births where the father "catches" the baby). Hazell (1974: 24) concluded that the home birth couple usually feels that the "primary responsibility for birth" lies with the parents, "not with the doctor or the hospital." Those with such convictions often seek out the lay midwife because "her function is to assist, not to take over responsibility" (p. 37). Lay midwives respect this feeling. One midwife notes that her clients are "people who are taking control of their lives . . . and they're willing to take responsibility for the risks involved." She continues: "I won't let them put those responsibilities off on me. That is what the doctors have done traditionally. They pat the lady on the hand and say, 'Don't worry, dear, I'll take care of everything.' But that is not the traditional role of the midwife" (Anderson, 1978: 1). Those who employ lay midwives to assist in home births are often inclined to accept the consequences of their decision as part of some larger plan. In case of mishap these individuals tend to fall back on fateful explanations rather than faulting themselves for not choosing a hospital birth. The father whose child died five days after a home birth concludes: "We believe that it was the hand of the Lord and we have accepted that. Nobody wanted that baby more than we did. We feel grieved about it, but we are at peace in this" (quoted in King and Saltus, 1978).

When licensure is introduced, part of the parents' responsibility for birthing is transferred to the state. The client often assumes that a licensed midwife is competent because she is certified. On the other hand, when midwives are not licensed, the client must assess the qualifications of the practitioner herself. Licensure actually encourages the client to forego any personal evaluation of the practitioners, even though most clients are not familiar with certification requirements. In Texas, before passage of the most recent law, many midwives took advantage of the registration requirement by advertising themselves as "registered midwives." In turn, many of their clients confused registration with certification. I interviewed several clients who noted that their midwife was registered, and though admitting that they did not know exactly what this implied, most assumed (incorrectly) that it involved some type of training and monitoring. Inclusion of the state as a third party in the relationship between the midwife and her client undoubtedly alters feelings of where responsibility for birth lies.[2]

If licensure moves midwife-assisted birth into the hospital—as it has for the CNM—responsibility for the birth will be shared not only with the state but with physicians. The CNM's client may be more involved in the birth experience than the patient in a standard hospital delivery, but this is still very different from the total responsibility assumed by the mother delivering at home with an unlicensed midwife. Upon entering the ABC, the CNM's client places the ultimate liability for her birth on medical professionals; "responsibility" for the birth is hers only as long as these medical experts define the situation as safe. Should a "regular" hospital delivery be necessary, medical personnel take charge and the parents more or less become bystanders. A proponent of "natural childbirth" comments:

> The mother who goes to the hospital to have her baby is in an impossible situation, really. If a doctor says he's doing something for the safety of her baby, there is nothing she can say. Once she is told a procedure is for her baby, she can offer no argument. If you were in a hospital and your obstetrician said, "Look, we are a little worried about your baby. We want to put you on a fetal heart monitor," what would you say? I don't think a mother really has a choice (quoted in Arms, 1977: 123).

The most responsible parents prepare carefully for birth. According to one doctor: "In our experience, it is usually the parents who are *most informed* . . . who choose a home or home-like birth. Those parents who are *least informed* relinquish themselves to doctors and hospitals without question" (Hosford, 1976: 38, emphasis added). Yet there are subtle distinctions between home-birthers and those using the ABC. Clients of the CNM receive only minimal training in the physiology of birth; instead there is a heavy emphasis on "psychoprophylaxis." Psychoprophylaxis refers to breathing techniques employed during delivery as a substitute for anesthetics. This training is geared for hospital deliveries and emphasizes the division of practitioner and client responsibility. The client is supposed to remain physically and emotionally relaxed so that the practitioner can focus on, and be responsible for, the birth. Those having births at home must learn more about the birth process. Most frequently this knowledge is gained through reading, but occasionally lay midwives organize a class for expectant parents. The classes stress "getting in touch with your body," and encourage self-examinations which allow the mother to determine the progress of labor. Training for CNM-assisted birth tends to downplay this kind of involvement by the mother, recognizing instead the superior knowledge of the practitioner and her colleagues.

When not constrained by poverty or geography, women will choose a birth attendant whose view of birth is consistent with their own. Those choosing a lay midwife view birthing as a "family event" rather than a medical abnormality. The fact that medical backup is arranged in most of these births does not negate this observation. On the contrary, it demonstrates a belief that medical aid will be needed only in case of an emergency. Those who make an informed choice of an unlicensed midwife assume the greatest responsibility, because they deny the state the right to judge the competence of the practitioner. Those who opt for a CNM-assisted birth share their responsibility with the state, which evaluates and certifies the practitioner, and with physicians, who supervise the CNM. The CNM and her patient confirm the idea that birth is abnormal by placing it within the hospital, although the ABC does allow more family participation and diminishes the "medicalization" of birth.

The Practitioner-Client Relationship

Compared to the obstetrician, the midwife establishes closer and more personal relationships with her clients. In their study of CNMs in a hospital setting, Record and Cohen (1972: 358) cite evidence of the client's personal satisfaction with the midwife:

"She thinks of all the little things the doctors don't have time to talk about. There are hundreds of things you don't want to bother your doctor with."

"I admit that I asked questions of [the CNM] that I was shy to ask my doctor, or questions that I thought were too silly to take his time for since he is so busy."

The investigators conclude that "such remarks suggest that either because of individual characteristics, or perhaps because she is a female, or perhaps because as a paramedic she is less removed from [her clients] by professional mystique, the CNM may not only be substituting for the doctor . . . but providing a service that the doctor cannot provide." For many of the same reasons, the lay midwife also creates a personal relationship with her clients, but beyond the general fact that midwives are more approachable than doctors, there are variations in client interactions with licensed and unlicensed practitioners.

The unlicensed midwife cannot offer prenatal care to clients in medical settings such as an office, clinic, or hospital. Usually their care is provided in their own or the client's home. These settings, coupled with the less demanding caseload of unlicensed midwives, create relationships that go beyond concern with the ongoing pregnancy. Furthermore, lay midwives, in keeping with their wholistic view of birth, feel that it is important to know the total person. They believe that emotional problems are a serious obstacle to the smooth progression of birth, and that if the attendant is aware of these potential emotional blocks she will be better able to deal with them. An unlicensed midwife commented in an interview: "Prolonged labor could be because a lady is uptight—outside pressure . . . a fight with her man, fear of becoming a parent, so much more than just physical."

Midwives with legal status can meet clients in what are regarded as more traditional medical environments. Many midwives in Texas and Arizona maintain offices where they see clients for pre- and postnatal care. Those with larger practices maintain offices like those of a physician, with receptionists, appointment schedules, and waiting rooms. The office environment focuses attention on the pregnancy and limits discussion of topics not related to the impending or recent birth.

As expected, relationships between midwives and clients are most specialized in a hospital setting or a doctor's office. Because the majority of CNMs work in one or the other of these locations, their opportunities for interaction with clients are limited. When prenatal care of the CNM's patient takes place in a clinical setting, there is little or no segregation between patients who see a doctor and those who see the midwife. Both groups are routinely processed through a central nursing station for such preliminaries as blood pressure, weight and urine tests, and then must wait to see their respective practitioners. In this context the mother becomes little more than a "maternity patient."[3] Although the CNM's paraprofessional status might make her more approachable, the effects of the clinical setting are unmistakable. The contingencies of appointment schedules and staff responsibilities leave little time for discussion not directly related to the pregnancy. Furthermore, the CNM's large caseload often results in segmented care because she is unable to attend to the needs of all her clients.[4]

Client control of the practitioner also differs between licensed and unlicensed midwives. The CNM is in a bind because she is responsible both to her patient and to her supervisors. A patient entering an ABC finds herself at the lower end of a chain of command since the licensing law stipulates that the CNM's treatment of her is regulated by physician supervisors. If a patient request is not in accord with hospital and/or physician policy, it is often denied. Arizona's licensing law also limits midwives' ability to respond to client requests. Although most of Arizona's licensed midwives are familiar with herbal remedies for conditions of pregnancy and birth, they cannot legally give advice on their use. In contrast, the unlicensed midwife's sole responsibility and ultimate accountability lie with the client, leaving much more room for negotiation between practitioner and client on matters of treatment.[5]

Location also helps determine who controls the pregnancy. The client who enters a hospital is more or less a guest of the practitioner and is less able to direct her care. In general terms, Roth (1972: 430) has noted that in a hospital "control of the patient's treatment is taken out of his hands and information about his treatment hidden from him." "A crucial means of control in the hospital is the strangeness of the setting to the client and the dependence of the client on hospital personnel for orientation to the setting, techniques and routines of the hospital" (Shaw, 1974: 125). On the other hand, if care is given in the client's home, the practitioner becomes the guest of her client and must respect her wishes. Most of those who choose to give birth at home are aware of this. One couple reports (Longbrake and Longbrake, 1976: 158):

> Foremost, and underlying our whole enthusiasm for home-birth, was our desire to be in control of the situation. The setting was familiar and comfortable. We could arrange it to suit *our* needs. Instead of being "intruders" into the medical personnel's world, the midwife and the doctor were our visitors. During the process of labor we were freed from having to respond to new and unfamiliar hospital routines and to adjust ourselves to conform to the behaviorial expectations of others. Rules for institutional convenience and safety were unnecessary.

Ruzek (1978: 132) states: "Thus, unless a woman remains on her own territory, she will not retain the power to control her birthing. The structure of health-care institutions insures that medical definitions of the situation prevail. Lay definitions are legitimate only in lay territory." These varying centers of control are reflected in the roles assumed during birth. Many studies of obstetricians emphasize their role as the "star" of childbirth. CNMs try to avoid this, but they struggle against the environment in which they work. Lay midwives insist that they are just assistants in the birth process.

True to this belief, they do not "deliver" babies, but "catch" them (see Sousa, 1976: 120).

The midwife-client relationship is further affected by the differential recruitment patterns discussed earlier. CNMs are recruited from the ranks of RNs, and their commitment to a long period of training makes it likely that their only experience with birth occurs as an assistant in a medical setting (Warpinski and Adams, 1979). Lay midwives typically enter their careers after a home birth of their own. Established lay midwives are hesitant to take as an apprentice a woman who has not had a baby, because they feel such a midwife cannot be truly empathetic. By making midwifery a legitimate occupational choice for career-minded women (who are less likely to have children) and by requiring lengthy periods of training, midwife licensing laws discourage midwives from having children. Of course, it can be argued that midwives should not have children. One CNM, agreeing with sociologists who see value in neutrality, claimed that a practitioner who had borne a child would lack the objectivity and even harshness needed to snap a laboring woman out of self-pity (see also Holt, 1969).

Licensure affects the economic arrangements between the midwife and her client. Although I found no evidence that licensure drove up the cost of midwifery services, it did serve to formalize fee collection. In California and other states where lay midwifery is prohibited, midwives must be careful about the collection of fees. Payment renders them in technical violation of the Medical Practice Act, which allows a "friend" to help at birth, but not a fee-charging, unlicensed practitioner. For this reason unlicensed midwives are willing to barter and, when paid, often request cash. An unhappy consequence of the unlicensed midwife's strong commitment to her work is that she often receives less than full payment. Because she is not in midwifery to make money, and because her activities are covert, she finds it difficult to press for payment. Her clients are more apt to thank her for the wonderful experience, offer her a gift, and forget the cash. The licensed midwife is more fortunate. In several states she can collect third party (that is, insurance) payments, and the authority and right to practice publicly makes it easier to insist on payment by clients. But although licensure offers an immediate practical benefit to midwives, the formal economic arrangements and the desire to "make midwifery pay" gradually alter the nature of practice.

Finally, the relationship between the unlicensed midwife and her client reflects its illegal nature. In her study of an illegal feminist abortion collective, Bart (1977) notes some positive functions of illegality. She observed that it fostered not only group cohesiveness, but also efficiency, since less time was spent "hassling with licensing agencies and filling out forms." Bart's primary interest lay in intrastaff relationships, but much of what she documents holds true for unlicensed midwifery. The cohesiveness in the collective is similar to the closeness of the unlicensed midwife and her client. The midwife is providing a necessary service that she and the expectant parents believe in and yet that is defined as illegal, allowing for a sense of unification behind a "cause."

As licensure makes midwifery more medical, it is likely that the relationship between clients and their midwives will change in the direction noted by Walker (1972: 91):

> In moving from a home to a hospital environment, the midwife has moved from a culture characterized by personel relations, familiar procedures, active family participation, continuity of care, and a large degree of control over the situation by the mother and her family, to a scientific culture which involves impersonal relations, specialized procedures, a passive role for family members and control by experts.

The Birth Experience

Prospective parents who seek the services of a midwife desire to control the birth experience. However, the presence of any knowledgeable attendant has a great effect on the experience. The very act of requesting assistance from any practitioner is often a tacit acknowledgment of the parents' uncertainty and a recognition of the superior abilities of the attendant. Thus the parental desire for control is effectively modified by the practitioner's definition of the situation, which varies with the practitioner in attendance. The experience of birth is influenced by the degree to which it has become a standardized routine. The experience, the training, and the hospital location of the CNM lead her to streamline her procedures. The ABC supplies written protocols to define "normal" progression through pregnancy and birth. Although these are negotiable to a certain extent, the definitions present an idealized frame of reference. Because any variation is regarded as abnormal, this routine view of birth anticipates intervention (see Nash and Nash, 1979). Approximately 25–30 percent of those who begin labor in an ABC are in fact removed because of some complication (DeVries, 1980). Theoretically, if the patients do not agree with the proposed treatment, they are free to refuse care and leave the hospital, but they seldom do. As Linck (1973) observed in reference to extent of dilation, "Eight centimeters is not the time to fight."[6]

On the other hand, the lay midwife consciously avoids treating birth in a routine fashion. After describing some elements of a "typical" birth, a lay midwife noted (Merz, 1977: 551): "Here I must stop with my description of repeated rituals, because there is no repetition from birth to birth. Each birth is a unique process that cannot be duplicated." One result of this approach is a lower rate of transfer to the hospital than found in ABCs. Mehl et al. (1977: 284) report that the lay midwives involved in their study hospitalized only 17 percent of their cases, compared to the 25–30 percent in an ABC as mentioned above.

It is not surprising that licensure pressures lay midwives toward standardization. A licensed midwife in Arizona, for instance, is prohibited from attending a woman over thirty-five years of age, with no allowance made for factors such as the health of the mother, number of previous pregnancies, or obstetric history. Furthermore, the training requirements and medical supervision that accompany licensing laws push midwives toward routinized birth. Altered recruitment patterns also provide midwife trainees who are more likely to accept medical definitions of birth. In addition, the expanded practice that often accompanies legitimation fosters standardization as an expeditious method of dealing with a large number of clients.

The dependence upon breathing techniques in labor and delivery ("psychoprophylaxis") also threatens parental control over birth. These techniques are often considered a suitable substitute for anesthesia or analgesics, but as Margaret Mead has commented:

> It should be pointed out that natural childbirth, the very inappropriate name for forms of delivery in which women undergo extensive training so that they can cooperate consciously with the delivery of the child, is a male invention meant to counteract practices of complete anesthesia, which are also male inventions (quoted in Arms, 1977: 178–79).

ABCs typically encourage the mother to employ these techniques to "get outside of the situation." In effect, then, there is little difference between this and the use of drugs; both function to remove the mother from the experience and allow the practitioner to dominate (see Oakley, 1979: 628–31). Lay midwives also employ breathing techniques, but in a less structured way and with a different emphasis. It is their contention that the breathing helps the laboring woman *focus* on her situation and allow her to "go with the flow":

> We don't practice breathing techniques during pregnancy because we feel that if you practice in a certain way, you might tend to be a little rigid when it comes to the actual experience of childbirth. We work out breathing techniques in the here-and-now at the birthing (Gaskin, 1978: 84).

If licensure results in midwifery becoming a hospital-based practice, midwife and client will unquestionably surrender a degree of their autonomy to the institution. This will likely include use of the more rigid breathing techniques—convenient for the institution because they make for an efficient and quiet operation—as well as other routines necessary to deal with a number of birthing women in a central location. Indeed, the organizational demands often require the "pacing" of deliveries. A fixed amount of available space coupled with an unpredictable number of patients often necessitates speeding up or slowing down the normal progress of birth. Rosengren and Devault (1963: 282) suggest that the pacing of births is also related to professional status:

> As one resident put it, "our average length of delivery is about 50 minutes, and the Pros is about 40 minutes." Thus, the "correct" tempo becomes a matter of status competition and a measure of professional adeptness. The use of forceps is also a means by which the tempo is maintained in the delivery room, and they are so often used that the procedure is regarded as normal.

Such constraints are not found in the home. Ruzek (1978: 138) points out that lay midwives operate on a different time frame than the professional:

> Rather than viewing midwifery as a full-time occupation, a job, or a task to be completed as quickly as possible, lay midwives look forward to births as meaningful, spiritual life-events to experience and enjoy. The long hours spent with laboring women are rewarding and satisfying because of the "birth energy": They are not draining, as are long hours worked in a frenetic hospital delivery service.

Note that Ruzek is discussing individuals who choose midwifery for reasons other than simply "making a living." As midwifery is legitimated through licensure, we can expect more practitioners who regard it as nothing more than a "full-time occupation, a job, or a task to be completed as quickly as possible." Thus midwife-assisted birth will come to look more like medically directed hospital birth. The creation of the ABC is partial evidence that the medical profession is aware of the benefits of a home environment. But even though the ABC allows greater freedom, it is still an enclave within the larger hospital. The coordinator of one ABC involved in my study told me, "It may not be hospital in here [the ABC] but as soon as you step out that door it is . . . and you cannot forget that." The laboring woman must leave her home, travel to the hospital, and be processed through admissions before she can take advantage of the "home-like" environs. Even inside the ABC, hospital influences are pervasive. For example, hospital staff, frequently unknown to the mother before her arrival, are responsible for monitoring the course of labor, nor is it uncommon for the ABC to be within hearing distance of other hospital patients. Family involvement in birth can also be restricted by age limits on observers. In her assessment of ABCs, Jordan (1978: 87) comments:

> Hospital birthing rooms, in spite of a bit of interior decorating to make them more homelike, are no improvement over the labor and delivery room in regard to the territory issue. The woman still gives birth in an unfamiliar environment, attended by unfamiliar people, a guest on somebody else's turf with few rights and fewer resources. While more flexibility is allowed in such things as position during labor, real decision-making power remains with medical personnel. In important ways the woman still does not own the birth. One could characterize the introduction of birthing rooms as a token demedicalization and a fairly superficial response to public demands for change.

Some features of birth at home cannot be duplicated in a midwife-assisted ABC birth. Lay midwives and others advocating home birth cite cases where labor has slowed and even stopped because of unfamiliar surroundings or the intrusion of strangers. The home environment permits alternatives for stimulating labor that would not be workable in an ABC. Sexual stimulation, for example, is sometimes helpful in speeding a slow labor, but use of this technique is unlikely in an ABC, where the couple cannot be certain they will not be interrupted.

Summary: Licensure and the Practice of Midwifery

Most studies of licensure focus on quantitative outcomes. They measure the way licensure alters the accuracy and efficacy of services offered clients (White, 1979; Sullivan and Beeman, 1983). I have looked instead at the qualitative effects, in particular how licensure works to change the nature of the practitioner, the client, and the relationship between the two. Several previous studies have discussed how professionalization and increased bureaucratic control change health care (Daniels, 1969; Engel, 1969; Freidson, 1970; Goode, 1960; Goss, 1963), but few have examined how these variables literally create a "medical" encounter.

A few general points remain. First, state certification does not ensure medical endorsement. Although licensure laws mandate medical supervision for midwives, the medical profession remains reluctant to accept practitioners from other than traditional medical fields. CNMs have gained a degree of medical acceptance (see *Journal of Nurse-Midwifery*, 1975) because they are drawn from the ranks of nurses, an ancillary medical occupation. Having no such tradition, lay midwives—both licensed and unlicensed—find it difficult to obtain physician support. In Arizona and Texas, where lay midwives practice legally, they often find support only among physicians who are marginal to the medical community (for example, osteopaths, or doctors near retirement), and therefore relatively immune from reprisals from their peers. This lack of medical support is harmful only to the degree that midwives need it to provide adequate care. The compromises required to win medical endorsement would undoubtedly refashion lay midwifery in the mold of nurse-midwifery.

Second, licensure laws are only partly successful in limiting unlicensed practice or unauthorized procedures. The imprecise nature of physiological processes allows the midwife to adjust some facts to fit the regulations. In Arizona, for example, because the birth of twins is often not predicted by physicians, their delivery by a licensed midwife does not bring disciplinary action, though it is prohibited and the midwife might have known about it in advance. Similarly, the length of labor or the time elapsed since rupture of membranes are easily altered to fall within mandated guidelines. However, Arizona midwives are disciplined for knowingly violating the regulations. The fear of suspension or revocation of their licenses prevents them from stepping too far beyond their legal mandate. One midwife told me that although she felt competent to perform some prohibited procedures, she felt a responsibility to uphold the Arizona law as an example to other states that might be leaning toward licensure.

It is difficult to judge the extent of unlicensed practice in Arizona. A licensure law on the books drives unlicensed practitioners further "underground" because their actions are now clearly defined as illegal and incur specific penalties. One unlicensed Arizona midwife was issued a "cease and desist" order at the request of a licensed midwife, but she apparently ceased practice for only a short period and is now back at work.

These observations highlight the essential irony of licensure. Midwives who work where midwifery is prohibited and no licensing law exists, have a type of autonomy that is denied midwives working with the "benefit" of licensure. When midwifery is illegal, midwife and client become coconspirators unwilling to report or provide evidence against each other. This fact, coupled with the private nature of home birth, gives the unlicensed midwife a great deal of freedom in her practice. The more formal relationships that licensed midwives have with their clients force them to stick closely to the legal definition of practice. In this sense, midwives who are allowed to practice openly face more restrictions in their practice than midwives who are legally prohibited from practicing.

But there is a price paid for freedom. Working without a license puts a strain on midwives: they cannot openly advertise, and are often unable to accompany their clients to the hospital when complications arise. Many unlicensed midwives also admit to a nagging fear of facing legal action through some unavoidable mishap at a birth. A number of recent cases against midwives have fueled these fears. The California Association of Midwives compiled a list of fifteen midwives who were either formally charged or investigated between 1980 and 1983 (*CAM Newsletter,* 1983). In response, some midwives are quitting their practices, and others are returning to school for training in more legitimate health occupations as registered nurses, physician assistants, certified nurse-midwives, or nurse practitioners. We shall explore disciplinary proceedings and legal actions against midwives in the next chapter. As might be expected, licensing laws influence these proceedings, altering both their formal and informal characteristics.

Chapter 5

Midwifery on Trial: Violations of Regulatory Law by Midwives

On the evening of November 30, 1979, officers from California's Madera County sheriff's department, an investigator from the California Board of Medical Quality Assurance, and representatives from the local media descended on the home of Rosalie Tarpening, a licensed physical therapist and unlicensed lay midwife. As the reporters looked on, the sheriff's deputies arrested Tarpening, charging her with murder and the practice of medicine without a license; they cited her involvement in the birth of Gabriel Villa, an infant who was apparently stillborn. Before leading her away in handcuffs, the deputies ransacked her next-door office for evidence that could be used at her trial. She could not afford to post a bond for the $100,000 bail, and was placed in jail. One week later the bail was reduced to $25,000 and Tarpening was able to post a bond and win her release. The pretrial procedures in this case stretched out for nearly two years, and it was not until August 1981 that she went to trial for practicing medicine without a license, the murder charges having been dropped after preliminary hearings.

In Arizona, a licensed lay midwife went to her mailbox and discovered a letter from the Department of Health Services. The letter informed her that her license was being suspended for one month because she used a drug, pitocin, to control a mother's postpartum bleeding. She had used pitocin once before and had been warned about violating the regulation that prohibits midwives from administering drugs. Upon learning that she used this drug a second time the department decided to take disciplinary action.

These two instances of midwives in legal trouble offer a graphic example of the way licensing affects midwives. Where no licensing law exists, the actions of midwives are judged in the same way as the actions of any citizen. When a licensing law is in place, however, midwives are set apart as a distinct group of practitioners and their actions are judged on the basis of a legal code that defines acceptable and unacceptable behavior.

An Uneasy Truce: Midwives in the Courts

When she spoke in favor of licensing on behalf of the California Association of Midwives at the most recent legislative hearings on licensure in California, lay midwife Patricia Ternahan cited the cases of two sister midwives who were prosecuted for the unlawful practice of medicine, and commented that "this is not the way to regulate midwifery." Ternahan called attention to the fact that in the absence of licensing laws, legal action becomes the only method for the regulation of midwives. This situation makes for an "uneasy truce" between the medical community and the midwives (see King, 1981). That is, lay midwives are free to practice with a minimum of harassment as long as none of their cases comes to the attention of medical professionals. Because her clients are unlikely to inform the authorities, a midwife becomes susceptible to legal action only when she transfers a mother or baby to a hospital and the attending physician feels that the case was improperly handled.

Physicians may file charges against midwives to protect themselves as professionals or to protect their profession. A formal complaint serves to officially lay responsibility at the feet of the midwife rather than the doctor. Many physicians also regard legal complaints as a way to discourage competition.

Legal actions against midwives in states without licensure laws have several distinct characteristics. First, legal actions are most frequently initiated by physicians. Clients of the unlicensed midwife are aware of her legal status and have usually accepted full responsibility for the outcome of the birth; hence they are unlikely to use the legal system to retaliate, even when the outcome is less than desirable. These same clients are often unwilling to testify against their midwife if she is prosecuted. Second, when midwives are tried in courts of law their cases draw public attention through media coverage and the publications of midwife organizations and other groups promoting alternative birth. Third, midwives who have been arrested generally receive wide support from sister midwives and their sympathizers. Midwives are particularly sensitive to the possibility of an unfavorable decision that will set a damaging legal precedent, and their organizations frequently offer support to the accused through defense funds and fund-raising events. Finally, there appears to be a hesitancy on the part of the courts to penalize unlicensed midwives and thereby foreclose this option in maternal care. Three cases against unlicensed midwives are illustrative.

In June of 1978, lay midwife Marianne Doshi assisted Christine and Robert Gannage with the birth of their daughter. The pregnancy and labor had progressed normally, but the baby girl was born pallid and apparently lifeless as a result of a true knot in the umbilical cord. The midwife attempted to resuscitate the baby, and with the help of local paramedics transported her to the nearest hospital where she was put on life support systems. From there the infant was transferred to a neonatal intensive care unit at a larger hospital in a metropolitan area 250 miles away. Five days after the birth the child died. The coroner declared that the death had been caused by asphyxiation, "at the hands of another." As is typical in cases of this type, charges against the midwife were instigated by a physician. Two days after the birth Dr. John Mahnke, chief of obstetrics at a local hospital, contacted the sheriff's department and the California Board of Medical Quality Assurance. Subsequently, a grand jury was convened by the district attorney to investigate the matter. Although the Gannages were granted immunity from child-abuse charges for their testimony, their comments before the grand jury attest to a desire to protect their midwife. Christine Gannage told that body (Stern, 1978: 18): "Everybody has been very concerned about the injustice done here. I don't believe that Marianne did any injustice. She gave me more care than I ever received from any cold, unfeeling obstetrician." Robert Gannage later told reporters (King and Saltus, 1978): "For the state to say we feel grieved about [the death of our child] and want to prosecute, to me that is a great injustice. They are losing sight of reality."

Two years earlier, the district attorney in the same county had attempted unsuccessfully to prosecute another midwife for an infant death. The Doshi case offered a second—perhaps stronger —case for the prosecution. The D.A.'s investigators told the director of the county health department, "This time we've really got the goods on them." Sergeant John Hastie, a sheriff's detective who investigated the case, claimed that "this is gonna be the shot heard 'round the world'" (King and Saltus, 1978). On July 7, 1978, Marianne Doshi was arrested and charged with murder and practicing medicine without a license. The second-degree murder charge was made possible by a law that allows the perpetrator of a misdemeanor to be charged with a felony if any of the victims of the misdemeanor are injured. In this case the death of a child during the commission of a misdemeanor (practicing medicine without a license) served as adequate cause for the elevated charge.

Reports of Doshi's arrest and trial were given wide coverage in the media (King and Saltus, 1978; Stern, 1978; Petit, 1978; *The San Francisco Chronicle,* 1978a; 1978b; Schrag, 1978; Hurst, 1978). Publicity and support for her cause were provided by several organizations committed to alternative birth, including the California Association of Midwives, the Association for Childbirth at Home International, and the Feminist Women's Health Center in Los Angeles.

It is inaccurate to speak of a trial in this case, for the charges against Doshi were dismissed on a pretrial motion. The judge was Richard C. Kirkpatrick, a conservative Superior Court judge appointed by Ronald Reagan. His comments reflected hesitancy to make a judgment that denied alternatives to traditional medical care (Burns, 1978):

> I really feel that we have a segment of our society that wants to choose an alternative to what the California Medical Association, or the medical profession, wants to provide as far as the birth of children goes. And I think these people probably have the right under our constitution. . . . I really have a feeling that these people should be able to make their own options to this thing. I have a great deal of sympathy for the Gannages in this case, and I certainly hope that the case is not carried out any further. I think it would be a tragic thing. . . . I hope that the medical profession has enough maturity at this point, and I really think it is that, to say there are alternative ways. I am really sincere when I say that somehow I hope that they will work with the representatives, and with the people that want to exercise this alternative for themselves, to be closer to their children and have their children at home. . . . I am convinced . . . that had that child died in the hospital, or at home under a doctor's care, that we would have a thousand doctors lined up between here and Los Angeles willing to testify that the doctor provided medical treatment according to the standard of care. I think that this was a circumstance that

happened, and it is very unfortunate; but I think, from reading the medical testimony, it is something that just could not have been prevented.

As expected, the medical community was not happy with Kirk-patrick's ruling. Dr. Mahnke, the originator of the charges against Doshi, was "disappointed. I think a crime was committed and I think it should have gone to trial to at least evaluate it" (quoted in Hurst, 1978). Dr. John Miller, chairman of the state chapter of the American College of Obstetricians and Gynecologists, made it clear that the judge was not going to tell members of the medical community how to run their affairs: "The difficulty I find with the judge's decision is that these people are totally unlicensed. They are just a group of people, some with no qualification, whose only experience in some cases is having watched five or six people give birth. They have no comprehension of the complications." He continued by stating that if the judge was suggesting that the medical community should work with unqualified people, "then I think he is totally out of his mind" (quoted in *The San Francisco Chronicle*, 1978a).

The ruling in the Doshi case gave California's unlicensed midwives a feeling of freedom in their practices. This feeling was shattered one year later with the arrest of Rosalie Tarpening for murder and the unlawful practice of medicine. The arrest, described at the beginning of this chapter, came as a result of Tarpening's assistance at the birth of Gabriel Villa, the child of two illegal immigrants from Mexico. Although the nine-hour labor at the Tarpening home was uneventful, it was immediately apparent that something was wrong when the child was born. Gabriel made a grunting sound at birth, but it appeared that he was not breathing. Tarpening suctioned the baby, massaged him, and held his body under hot and cold running water, all with no visible effect. She advised the mother's relatives to take the infant to the hospital while she attended to the mother.

Gabriel was taken to Madera Community Hospital where an

electrocardiogram showed an erratic heartbeat. Attempts by physicians to resuscitate the child failed, however, and he was declared dead. Upon hearing that a lay midwife had been involved in the delivery, the medical community took an interest in the case. An autopsy was performed and the coroner reported that the immediate cause of death was "aspiration of amniotic fluid and subarachnoid hemorrhage." The coroner's report continued: "Baby died as the result of negligence on the part of the person who delivered it." Armed with this evidence, and at the request of local physicians, the county sheriff arrested Tarpening.

The arrest and pretrial proceedings were carried in the local media (Hunter, 1980; Hendrix, 1980; *Woodland Daily Democrat,* 1980; *Sacramento Bee,* 1981a; 1981b) and widely discussed in newsletters and magazines of organizations involved in this issue (*NAPSAC News,* 1980a; 1980b; 1981b; *CAM Newsletter,* 1980; Baldwin, 1980; Bowers, 1981). All accounts of Tarpening's legal troubles in the newsletters included solicitations for funds to cover the costs of her defense. Midwives in California were particularly anxious to aid Tarpening because they feared the effects of an unfavorable ruling on their own practices. The California Association of Midwives issued the following "official statement" (*CAM Newsletter,* 1980: 6):

We, the California Association of Midwives, are outraged at the arrest and indictment of Rosalie Tarpening because of her involvement in this birth. We believe that parents should have the right to informed choices of alternative birth settings and care. Present data and studies indicate that planned home birth is a safe and responsible alternative. We believe that state interference in the parents' choice of birth is a violation of our human and constitutional rights. We believe that this type of harassment of parents and birth attendants is indicative of medical and governmental restrictions on freedom of choice in health care and the freedom of communities to develop appropriate systems of health care for themselves. . . . The arrest of one of our members, Rosalie Tarpening, is an inappropriate response to a complex social issue. The medical community and government officials should consider how to assist in making chosen out-of-hospital birth safer, rather than how to suppress it. . . . *The California Association of Midwives wholeheartedly supports Rosalie Tarpening* and our members have agreed to do everything in our power as an organization and as individuals to secure the funds needed to provide Rosalie a fair and adequate defense. WE INVITE YOU TO JOIN IN OUR EFFORTS!!

The founder and director of Informed Homebirth, Rahima Baldwin, specified in her newsletter why she felt it important for all midwives to support Tarpening, regardless of the facts of the case. She felt support for Tarpening should not be contingent upon judging her a "good midwife" (Baldwin, 1980):

What does it mean to be a "good midwife"? Good by whose standards? Since we don't have electronic fetal heart monitors, we can never be "good" by certain (obstetrician's) standards. It is our judging one another that perpetuates our being and feeling judged, results in malpractice suits, and keeps our health care system functioning the way it is today. Can we not recognize that it is adherence to the viewpoint of a good or bad practitioner and a good or bad birth that has led to compulsory hospitalization and domination by the medical profession? We . . . know just by looking at the situation and by looking within, that charging anyone with . . . murder for having or helping parents to have their baby born at home is an affront to all of our rights and freedom of choice. I would like to urge us all to unite and show our support of Rosalie Tarpening, who is in no way separate from ourselves and the issues which concern each of us deeply.

Interestingly, this nonjudgmental support makes midwives more like doctors, who are likewise quick to "cover" for one of their number regardless of the circumstance. There has been some debate among midwives about this problem (see Daniels, 1981b; Ehrlich, 1981).

The preliminary hearings in Tarpening's case offer an interesting example of the conflict of traditional and nontraditional medicine in the courtroom. When Tarpening's lawyer was asked if she thought the issue in this case was home birth, she replied (Hendrix, 1980): "Don't you think it is? When was the last time you saw a doctor tried for a tragedy in a hospital? But the minute there's not a doctor involved, they dash right ahead. It would never be a murder charge, or a homicide, if it were a doctor." The D.A. and his deputy who tried the case, Paul Avent, did not feel that home birth was on trial. Avent was quoted as saying (Anderson, 1980: 5), "We don't believe the home birth issue is an issue here." Commenting on the outpouring of support for Tarpening from various organizations, Avent told a reporter, "I'm a little dismayed, they are probably more interested in Mrs. Tarpening's plight than in the plight of the family [of the dead child]" (Hunter, 1980: 68).

The preliminary hearing began with a parade of witnesses for the prosecution. Most were "medical experts" who testified that Gabriel Villa had been born alive and had died because of the mismanagement of the delivery. There was consensus among these experts that if the delivery had occurred in a hospital, Gabriel would have lived.

The defense's opportunity to call witnesses came in November 1980. Tarpening and her supporters assumed the defense would contend that the child had been born dead and that death would have been inevitable in home or hospital. The fact that witnesses for the defense included two outspoken critics of traditional medicine—Dr. Robert Mendelson and Dr. William Matviuw—lent credence to this assumption. After the defense established that Gabriel's death was unpreventable, these two would argue that the real issue was the desire of medical professionals to protect their turf. But after conferring with her witnesses, Tarpening's lawyer chose an entirely different strategy. She called as her only witness Dr. Edith Potter, a renowned infant pathologist who had authored several books and numerous articles on the pathology of the fetus and the infant. In a lengthy and dramatic cross-examination, Dr. Potter and the defense attorney proved to the court that the infant *had* been born alive, and that it died as a result of overly aggressive attempts at resuscitation at the hospital (see Bowers, 1981).

The defense strategy succeeded in having the murder charge dropped. The prosecution's expert witnesses had contended that the autopsy provided evidence that the child died from a lack of oxygen. The defense attorney called on a higher level of medical expertise (one of Dr. Potter's books was referred to authoritatively in the coroner's report that accused Tarpening) to refute this testimony and protect her client. Thus, ironically, traditional scientific medicine was used to defend nontraditional medical practice. Although the murder charge was dropped, Tarpening still faced trial for practicing medicine without a license. A guilty verdict was handed down nearly two years after the death of the Villa infant. Tarpening was sentenced to two years probation and had her license to practice physical therapy suspended for six months.

A final example of legal action against unlicensed midwives is provided by the arrest and trial of Delia Burns. Dee Burns came to the attention of the authorities following a maternal death at a birth she attended. As usual, charges were initiated by local physicians, not by the husband of the dead woman. At the trial he told reporters that he did not blame the midwife for his wife's death. Speaking about the midwife, he added: "She was a friend, she has always been a friend, and I hope she still is" (*The San Francisco Chronicle,* 1981).

Unlike the cases discussed earlier, the coroner's report absolved Burns of any responsibility for the mother's death, but the following investigation resulted in three counts of practicing medicine without a license. At her trial in Municipal Court, which occurred before the Tarpening trial was complete, Burns became the first midwife in recent history to be found guilty and sentenced. The judge ruled that the midwife was to spend thirty days in jail and three years on probation. One of her attorneys proclaimed (*The San Francisco Chronicle,* 1981): "Dee is being made an example. The established medical forces in this state don't want midwives around. They do not want midwives licensed, because they don't want the competiton."

At this point Burns was ready to give up and accept her sentence. The difficult experience of having one of "her mothers" die, coupled with the investigation and trial, had exhausted her physically and emotionally. However, her sister midwives, while concerned about her well-being, were even more concerned about the implications of the conviction. They explained how the conviction would harm the rest of California's six hundred illegal midwives, and convinced Burns to appeal her case and at the same time to seek clemency from the governor. Neither effort succeeded, and when required to begin serving her time, Burns disappeared (*CAM Newsletter,* 1983).

In this climate of increased arrests and apparently less lenient courts, midwives have begun to prepare against the threat of legal action. At a recent California Association of Midwives meeting, a lawyer explained the legalities of arrest procedure and the steps that could be taken to defend against conviction (see *CAM Newsletter,* 1981: 2–3). The attorney reminded the midwives of a fact made apparent by earlier cases: that the most effective means of preventing conviction is collective action aimed at convincing legal officials that midwifery is a safe and desirable alternative to standard medical care.

Disciplining Licensed Midwives

When a licensed midwife is believed to violate her legally defined scope of practice, the case is referred to a regulatory board for review rather than to a court of law. Disciplinary action is typically confined to suspension or revocation of her license. This administrative disciplinary action has certain extralegal characteristics which are different from court actions against unlicensed midwives. Proceedings are not publicized in the media or in alternative birth organization newsletters. There is little support for the accused midwife from her sister midwives or concerned organizations. Outcomes of legal action are also likely to be different. Unlike a court, an administrative agency reviewing a licensing violation is provided with a range of penalties specific to the offense, making disciplinary action against the midwife more likely. Of course, legal actions against both licensed and unlicensed midwives do share some elements in common, the most notable being the unwillingness of the midwife's client to report violations of the law or to testify against her midwife. As is true with unlicensed midwives, accusations are made by someone other than the client.

Since Arizona revised its law in 1978, two midwives have been subjects of administrative proceedings. One had her license revoked; the second had her license suspended for one month and, as a consequence of a second incident, revoked. In the first case the midwife had an unavoidable infant death followed by a second infant death in a breech birth. The law prohibits midwives from assisting in diagnosed breech births. In cases where the breech is undiagnosed, midwives must seek medical assistance as soon as it is evident. Because the midwife did not consult with a physician, the Arizona Department of Health Services (DOHS) decided her license should be taken away. The midwife, who had taken the licensing exam before the revised regulations took effect, was given a chance to take the new exam, but could not pass it.

The second midwife, whose license suspension was described in the introduction to this chapter, faced permanent loss of her license because of her involvement in a birth in which the child was born dead. The father was a chiropractor who practiced acupuncture, and he was officiating at the birth when the midwife arrived. The midwife was told that there had been no fetal movements for quite some time, which led her to suspect that the baby was dead. When she could not hear any fetal heart tones her suspicions were confirmed. She did not, however, call immediately for medical assistance as the law prescribes, preferring to let the parents experience the event in privacy. This neglect of legal duty was sufficient ground for the DOHS to revoke her license. With passage of the most recent law that established a one-year period when provisional licenses were granted, this midwife was able to regain her right to practice.

In all these incidents midwives were brought to the attention of the authorities by physicians or other medical personnel, not by the affected client. The administrator of the licensing program said that practically all investigations of midwives have begun with the receipt of letters of complaint from physicians and hospitals. She observed that the clients of midwives seldom bring complaints. Referring to her most recent case, she noted, "Even when we brought revocation hearings, the couple who lost their baby testified in behalf of the midwife." In another case the administrator questioned the practice of a midwife and received an "irate letter" from one of her clients.

Aside from surveillance by medical personnel, midwives are required to file detailed reports with the DOHS for every birth they attend. In normal births some facts can be altered to protect midwives who might be exceeding their statutory authority, but midwives are hesitant to alter facts on cases that are referred to physicians because it might endanger the health of their clients and because these cases are more thoroughly scrutinized. Thus the judgments and actions of midwives are readily available for review at any time. This reporting procedure is a routine part of most lay midwife licensing laws.

What is most striking about the Arizona cases is their lack of publicity. Media coverage was minimal, but more importantly, midwife organizations and alternative birth groups did not rally to the support of the accused. Their literature and newsletters did not even mention the hearings. Similarly, two unlicensed Arizona midwives who were issued "cease and desist orders" by the attorney general received neither support nor publicity for their cause. Apparently, when licensing laws are in effect, it is assumed that individual midwives are responsible for complying with the regulations. Those who fail to comply, for whatever reason, are left to their own resources. Licensure, then, removes the actions of midwives from the public realm, thereby eliminating potential public scrutiny and support. Lack of support at least partly explains why every attempt to suspend or remove a midwife's license in Arizona has proved successful.[1]

It should be noted that midwives licensed in another area of medicine (in some form of therapy or as an RN, for example), and who work in jurisdictions without midwifery licensing laws, may be subject to review for their actions as midwives by their licensing boards. Such was the case with Tarpening, who lost her license to practice physical therapy. Such was also true for Joann Ruiz, a registered nurse in California. The Ruiz case reveals that public support can be effective in preventing licensing boards from taking punitive action. This incident began in October of 1977, when Ruiz sent one of her clients to the hospital for assistance in removing an adherent placenta. As a precaution against excessive bleeding, the midwife administered a drug to the mother before transfer. The attending physician was irate when he learned that a lay midwife had administered a prescription drug. When he discovered that the attending midwife was also a registered nurse he reported her to the Board of Registered Nursing for violation of the Nurse Practice Act. The subsequent hearings were well publicized, and supporters of Ruiz picketed the nursing board office. The mother refused to testify against her midwife, even though threatened with contempt charges, so the board eventually dropped its investigation because of lack of evidence (see Bathen, 1978; 1979).

In a similar case in Massachusetts a registered nurse had her license suspended for one year for participating in home births. The

Board of Registered Nursing there found Janet Leigh guilty of "deceit" for falsely representing herself as a "nurse-midwife." Leigh claims she has never advertised herself as a nurse-midwife. It is her opinion that the board's jurisdiction is limited to her activities as a nurse and that they have no control over her private practice as a lay midwife. She is currently appealing her suspension in the courts (Knox, 1984).

These cases suggest that unlicensed midwives who become credentialed in another health occupation might be increasing rather than reducing their liability. Once they have completed the training and are licensed in the legitimate occupation, they have merely accumulated one more thing to lose. While such a strategy can provide legitimacy—RN's who are lay midwives in California have been allowed to work under standardized procedures that establish formal, working relations with physicians—it serves to add another layer of surveillance over practice.

Licensure and Legal Action

We can now examine legal actions against midwives a little more deeply. Perhaps most important, clients of either unlicensed or licensed midwives are unlikely to bring charges against their midwife, and are likely to support her should charges be brought by someone else. This solidarity is most likely the result of enthusiasm for home birth. Home birth, though a growing trend, is still nontraditional, and those who choose it have strong feelings about it. Home birth couples are typically promoters of self-care and are wary of the encroachment of medicine into all areas of life. These feelings help explain why parents are hesitant to blame the midwife and unwilling to jeopardize the larger "movement" by filing a complaint.

Physicians, who are aware of this reluctance, feel obligated to notify the authorities about illegal practices, usually citing a human-

itarian interest in the rights of the unborn. In reference to the trial
of Marianne Doshi for the death of the Gannage baby, Dr. Kent
Ueland, chief of maternal-fetal medicine at the Stanford School of
Medicine, stated (King and Saltus, 1978): "I'm glad that someone
has finally done something about this. . . . The mother and father are
willing to take the risk. But it is unfair to the baby. . . . You should
give the baby some say." Countless physicians have echoed this argument in one form or another, describing parents who give birth
at home as "selfish," more interested in their own experience than
their child's health. Legal precedents favor the physicians' viewpoint, concluding that the rights of the child should indeed be considered when deciding where and how birth should occur. In 1978,
the Court of Appeals for the Seventh Circuit in Illinois ruled that
the constitutional right to privacy does not guarantee parents the
right to decide "by whom or by what method" their child will be
born (Stern, 1978: 19). In another relevant decision, *Roe v. Wade*,
the United States Supreme Court declared that in the third trimes-
ter of gestation, "the state's interest in the rights of the unborn
child supersedes the woman's privacy right" (Stern, 1978: 19).
When the rights of the unborn child are thus considered, they focus
concern on the safest method of assisting in birth, and it is here that
the cultural power of medicine is most strongly felt.

Physicians have generally declared that birth outside a recognized medical facility and assisted by "lesser trained" personnel is
dangerous both to mother and infant. Courts and legislatures usually accept this "expert" assessment by medical professionals. To
support their argument about the increased risk of extra-hospital
birth, physicians frequently refer to a study by the American College of Obstetricians and Gynecologists (ACOG) as proof that infant death in home births was two to five times greater than in hospital birth. This frequently quoted but seldom cited study claims to
have gathered information from "48 state departments of health"
(Pearse, 1980).[2] Actually, the data are questionable. Only eleven
departments of health had data available on infant mortality, and

the category of nonhospital births in all of them included planned and unplanned deliveries (that is, births occurring by accident outside the hospital). Despite lack of careful inquiry into this issue the claim to scientific objectivity gives physicians' declarations unquestioned authority.

The supporters of home birth recognize the prestige given to scientific methodology, and beyond the extra-medical benefits they believe accompany home birth they have begun to defend the practice on medical and scientific grounds. Several scientific studies indicate that birth at home is as safe, if not safer, than hospital birth for a preselected group of healthy women (Mehl et al., 1976; 1977; Burnett et al., 1980). Commenting on this trend, Jordan (1978: 88) notes that the "homebirth movement"

speaks the medical language of outcome statistics. We find that, at least in the public arena, the comfort of the woman, financial considerations, humanization of birth, deepening of the couple and family relationship through the joint experience, taking responsibility for one's own life and limb rather than delegating it to professionals and institutions, the spiritual production of birth, and all other citable advantages of homebirth, are subordinated to discussions of medical safety. The strongest argument which the homebirth movement can advance (and does advance) in this country, is the statistical argument which shows that home-birth outcome is in no way inferior to hospital outcome. I would suggest that the reason why all methods of birthing which have gained any currency in this society take as their paramount justification the criterion of medical safety, is the undiminished presence of the medical definition of the event. The details of obstetric practices may change in response to societal pressures. What shows no sign of changing is a deep consensus, shared by all of us, that at least for us, the justification for any way of doing birth must include as its most fundamental concern the issue of medical safety for mother and child.

This "undiminished presence of the medical definition of the event" is what motivates advocates of home birth and lay midwives to use physicians to defend their practices in the courts. In summary, the most remarkable difference between legal actions taken against licensed and unlicensed midwives is the lack of publicity and support for licensed midwives facing loss of their license. The actions of administrative agencies—not nearly as spectacular as court proceedings—do not attract the press. Such a situation favors the established medical profession (or those who control it) rather than the public interest because disciplinary actions are unavailable for public review. Midwife groups and alternative birth organizations, who are quick to rush to the aid of an unlicensed midwife, give little support to licensed midwives accused of improper activity. It appears that when an unlicensed midwife is charged, the issue becomes nothing less than the right to freedom of choice in health care. Referring to the trial of Rosalie Tarpening in the CAM newsletter, a sister midwife stated (Ehrlich, 1981: 4):

> I have realized that the issue is not actually whether Rosalie did or did not "do right" in this birth. Her arrest and trial are part of a concerted effort to eliminate home birth and to eliminate midwives and to eliminate all but the standard of technological care in birth. It is part of an enormous national, and world-wide, power struggle.

Yet when a licensed midwife is accused, freedom of choice is not an issue (other midwives are licensed to practice). Instead, the question becomes the competence of the midwife or her willingness to stick to the regulations. The larger question of whether the competency standards and regulations are fair never surfaces.

The punishment faced by licensed and unlicensed midwives for illegal activity also varies. Licensed midwives face loss of their license to practice while unlicensed midwives face incarceration and/or fines. The fact that few unlicensed midwives have been sen-

tenced to jail suggests that court officials feel the available punish-
ments are overly severe. It is significant that, in the cases discussed
here, the murder charges were dropped while charges of practicing
medicine without a license were successfully prosecuted. In Arizona, where the licensing law tailors penalties for offenses, there is
less reluctance to take punitive action.

Further evidence that courts are more lenient than regulatory
agencies comes from the case of Elizabeth Leggett, a registered
nurse practicing lay midwifery in Tennessee. That state licenses
certified nurse-midwives, restricting practice to RN's with post-
graduate training. State law also allows the unregulated practice of
lay midwifery. Because she was a nurse, Leggett had her license revoked by the Tennessee Board of Nursing for delivering babies
without the credentials of a nurse-midwife. Leggett appealed this
decision in the courts claiming she had the right to practice because of the state's permissive lay midwife law. The court agreed
with Leggett, overturning the board's decision (see Evenson, 1982:
327). Courts in Florida have also protected the right of unlicensed
midwives to practice, constraining the state's Department of Health
and Rehabilitative Services from enforcing legislative guidelines
which are vague and unlawful (see Evenson, 1982: 328).

Attempts to use the court as a regulatory instrument in states
which have no licensing law have potentially negative consequences. Although the courts have proven lenient in many cases,
the costs associated with any legal action are high. To the extent
that physicians are hostile, unlicensed midwives become less willing to refer their complicated cases. Some physicians recognize
this. One California obstetrician has noted (quoted in Divoky,
1981): "The more communications we have with lay midwives, the
better for the patient. We want them to call, and call early, if there
is a problem. Patient care is the point." However, those who speak
for physicians and their associations in states without licensing laws
apparently feel that patient care can be enhanced by severing communication with midwives and driving them out of business.

Chapter 6

Conclusion: Birth, Medicine, and the Law

The fields of law and medicine have much in common. Their practitioners are regarded as professionals and receive the benefits of that status. Both occupations have attained a measure of freedom from outside sources of control; they regulate themselves through their own professional organizations. Perhaps most important, medicine and law are characterized by extensive technical bodies of knowledge, the mastery of which provides authority to the professional.

However, the right of lawyers and physicians to the claim of "neutral" and "scientific" authority has long been questioned, though not by the public. Sociologists and others have demystified medical and legal institutions by exposing the social forces that influence them. Justice Oliver Wendell Holmes debunked the pretensions of law in 1881:

> The life of the law has not been logic: It has been experience. The felt necessities of the time, the prevalent moral and political theories, intuitions of public policy, avowed or unconscious, even the prejudices judges share with their fellow men, have a good deal more to do than the syllogism in determining the rules by which men should be governed (quoted in Lerner, 1943: 51–52).

Here and elsewhere (Holmes, 1897) Justice Holmes was concerned with demonstrating that the law is not a body of logically consistent principles, but rather that the law is subject to a variety of social influences which reshape and recast legal principles. The science of medicine can be evaluated in a similar fashion. In fact, it is not unreasonable to apply a slightly altered version of Holmes' statement to medical science: "The felt necessities of the time, the prevalent moral and political theories, . . . even the prejudices doctors share with their fellow men, have a good deal more to do than science in determining the nature of medical practice." As Springer (1973: 294) notes, medicine has expended its efforts according to the concern of society at large: "Great exertions of time and energy have been made and large infusions of dollars have been required to alleviate particular illnesses. Medicine has responded to articulated felt needs." Springer's observations are confirmed by studies that demonstrate the political nature of medical research (Chubin and Studer, 1978; Krause, 1977). Far from being objective, medical decisions are influenced by "felt necessities," "intuitions," and "prejudices."

If we are to explore the relationship between medicine and law, we must examine the social forces behind the facade of scientific objectivity. That is my intent in this concluding chapter. With midwife licensure as the case in point, I will examine the ways licensure affects the regulated profession, the field of medicine, and the larger society.

Licensure and Dominance

My study has shown that state sanction to practice does not bring autonomy to midwives, but rather formalizes the dominance of physicians over them. This conclusion confirms the cultural power of scientific medicine and its primary agents, physicians. William White (1979) has provided a study of the licensure of clinical laboratory personnel that, rather interestingly, fails to take account of this cultural power. White (1979: 119–20) offers three models of support for licensure:

(1) the public interest model, in which consumers or their
agents seek licensure in order to improve the quality of services,
(2) the acquired model, in which occupational elites or rank-
and-file members of an occupation seek to use licensure to increase their incomes, and
(3) the bureaucratic model, in which bureaucrats support licensure in order to increase their agency budgets and improve
their own career opportunities.

White concludes that the bureaucratic model most accurately
applies to the subjects of his study, although he grants that most
laboratory workers (the "acquired model") supported licensure
also. White's conclusions are insightful, but limited. For example,
White (1979: 122) notes that physicians, reluctant to share their
power, have "consistently opposed licensure [of clinical laboratory
personnel]," but he does not consider the ways in which licensure
is won at the expense of independence.

In his studies of allied health occupations in Great Britain, Larkin
(1983) suggests that the dominance of scientific medicine is not affected by paramedical licensure. Larkin (1981: 16, 25–26) observes:

Many para-medical groups have achieved state registration in the
post-war period, and prominent members of those professions
have considered such developments to be a kind of "professional
emergence." It [is here] argued that, in the longer historical perspective, such changes were conclusive steps in a logic of subor-
dination. . . . Para-medical innovation may add to the division of
labor, but rarely alters it. . . . Limited recognition is no more the
end of dominance than imperial withdrawal is the remoulding of
international economic relationships.

Although midwifery has different, more autonomous roots than
the occupations Larkin studied, his conclusions are applicable.
Where midwives have been licensed, they have suffered an increase

in surveillance and control by physicians. Licensing laws proposed for lay midwives would have similar consequences. In her study of health licensing in seven countries, Roemer (1973: 258–59) confirms the loss of independence:

> Midwifery, like nursing, shows the same pattern of close supervision of education by the licensing agency or a closely related agency. . . . Continual upgrading of educational requirements for midwives is tending toward a fusion of the professions of nursing and midwifery. . . . All statutes are meticulous in specifying the duties and functions of midwives and their responsibility to summon a physician in abnormal or difficult cases.

Given the fact that licensure works against the autonomy of these paramedical professions, it is important to explore how physicians deflect challenges to their dominance. Their cultural prestige is probably the most important factor, but they derive their formidable political power from well-established professional organizations that defend their interests anywhere that policy decisions are made. By way of contrast, paramedical groups are weakly financed, less thoroughly organized, and often suffer from internal division. In their study of attempts by optometrists to gain favorable legal recognition, Begun and Lippincott (1980: 91) observe that "internal segmentation in optometry [has reduced] its political effectiveness." On the other hand, the cultural power of physicians is continually reinforced. Almost daily the electronic and printed media carry stories about the advances of scientific medicine in the "war" against disease and illness. And although scientific medicine has its critics (for example, Illich, 1976; Mendelsohn, 1979), the marketing of medicine through the media serves to sanctify physicians as the priests of scientific medicine (see Montgomery, 1982). In his ethnography of power relations on a Health Systems Council, Hanson (1980) describes how the cultural power granted to physicians results in provider (that is, physician) control of what is supposed to be a consumer-oriented agency. Hanson (1980: 172) concludes:

In significant ways "provider mystique"—characterized by consumer dependency on providers and a provider attitude which conveys the idea that physicians and other medical professionals know what is best for consumers—is carried into council meetings for consumers and providers. . . . Since consumers are generally socialized to respect the prestige, knowledge and power of the medical profession, the stage is already set for providers to dominate discussion and control the meetings. The mystique supplies the predominant definition of the situation at council meetings.

The cultural authority of physicians also gives their testimony before legislative bodies the status of "expert advice," thereby enhancing their influence over legislation.

As paramedicals—including midwives, optometrists, radiographers, and nurse-practitioners—have sought scientific respectability through licensure, physicians have invoked their power to insure that these new occupations remain subordinate. Licensing laws are typically written in a way that requires paramedicals to gain the cooperation of physicians. And often physicians fail to cooperate, claiming medical or legal problems prohibit consort with the lesser trained. For instance, physicians have expressed a reluctance to work with a midwife because they cannot be certain of the midwife's competence and are fearful of malpractice suits if they assume responsibility for her actions (see Wilcox, 1981; Scott, 1980).

A more subtle way that physicians assert and maintain dominance over paramedicals is through their exclusive authority to diagnose patients. All midwife licensing laws, for instance, stipulate that midwives can attend only women expected to have a "normal" or trouble-free pregnancy and delivery. Unfortunately for midwives, the definition of "normal" is left to physicians, who can restrict it to a highly select group of women. Oakley (1980: 22) suggests that it is in the interest of physicians to classify *all* pregnancies as "abnormal":

The doctor views reproduction as a potentially problematic condition, reserving the label "normal" as a purely retrospective term. Every pregnancy and labour is treated as though it is, or could be abnormal, and the weight of the obstetrician's medical education acts against his/her achievement of work satisfaction in the treatment of unproblematic reproduction. The consequence of this attitude is of course that "normal" reproduction becomes an anachronistic category:

[Physician]: Interesting, very interesting, most unusual.
[Registrant]: You mean it was a normal delivery?
[Physician]: Yes—pushed the baby out herself!

The equation of "normal" with "unusual" illustrates the medical rationale, for if this equation did not hold, obstetricians would presumably have no valid role in managing reproduction.

Evidence from alternative birth centers verifies the reluctance of physicians to judge pregnancies "normal." By definition, women in these programs have been classified as "low-risk" pregnancies, but from 30 to nearly 50 percent are removed before birth because of the diagnosis of some "abnormality" (see DeVries, 1980). The power to diagnose, given exclusively to physicians, allows wide control over potential competitors.

Some organizations interested in promoting the independent practice of midwifery recognize the dangers in licensure. Commenting on a recent midwife licensing law in the state of Washington—a law passed with the help of midwifery advocates (see Evenson, 1982)—the executive director of the National Association of Parents and Professionals for Safe Alternatives in Childbirth (NAPSAC) stated (Stewart, 1981: 21):

The new bill just passed firmly reinstates [control of midwives in the Medical Licensure Board], which is why the doctors and nurses endorsed it. . . . Considering the openly stated opposition of doctors and nurses in Washington State to the idea of "the free practice of midwifery," one can only hope that the new bill, which has also been lauded by some midwives there, will increase and not decrease the availability of midwifery services. From NAPSAC's official standpoint, we cannot support this bill, nor any bill that would place physicians in any authority over midwives. Medical doctors can rightfully regulate themselves, but there is no way they can regulate other competing professions without an unavoidable conflict of interest. In the end, it is the public who suffers the degradation of health care services that inevitably results from such a conflict.

Several studies of licensed health occupations reveal that licensing does little to control quality of care, restricts the supply of practitioners, reduces their productivity and competition, and interferes with their geographic mobility (see Begun and Lippincott, 1980: 59). After their review of health-care regulations, the editors of the *Iowa Law Review* (1972: 1162) conclude:

> While the consumer naturally assumes that the public regulatory system is working to protect his interest, the reality of the situation is that the public regulatory system is so closely entwined with the private regulatory system that the public interest has been distorted for the benefit of private interests. The result is both an inadequate assurance of the quality of health-care personnel who perform needed services as well as an inadequate supply of such personnel.[1]

Dominance over medical care also creates some problems for physicians. Ultimate authority by implication gives physicians full *responsibility* for health. This increases the likelihood of malpractice actions by disgruntled patients who for one reason or another were not successfully treated. By way of contrast, paramedical personnel, who are given only limited authority in medical care, are very rarely the subjects of malpractice actions. Physicians are also more likely to be sued because their imposing authority leads to formal relationships with their patients. Paramedicals, on the other hand, tend to establish closer relationships with their clients. An individual is less likely to sue a friend than an institution.

Law and Medicine in Society

Although the influence of physicians on the licensing of paramedicals has been immense, physicians have not freely wielded the law as a tool of dominance. Laws do alter the practice of medicine. Similarly, developments in society have forced physicians and other medical practitioners to change their ways.

It is difficult to generalize about the relationship between law and the practice of midwifery. Earlier discussion pointed to the differences between licensed and unlicensed practitioners. We can conclude that as her practice is legalized—that is, subjected to regulation and licensure—the lay midwife will begin to approximate her certified counterpart. Licensing bills introduced in the California and Texas legislatures (which evolved from less to more medical control and supervision), restrictive revisions in the Arizona law, and current attitudes toward home birth among medical professionals (see Pearse, 1979) suggest that licensure will push the lay midwife toward more medical training and direct medical supervision. These changes will bring individuals with a different set of motivations into lay midwifery, alter client-practitioner relationships, and significantly influence the nature of the lay midwife-attended birth. These facts and the examples of past midwife licensure indicate that the law will continue to change the nature of this occupation.

It appears that law, however, is incapable of immediately altering traditional relationships. Aubert (1966), in his study of the Norwegian Housemaid Law, has shown the difficulty of legislating long-standing arrangements between individuals. In this case a law attempting to define the working conditions of housemaids was unable to penetrate the privacy of individual homes or change the relationships between housewives and their maids. Similarly, midwife licensure has not wholly disrupted established patterns of care related to childbirth. In many areas, prevailing traditions make a license inconsequential. This is particularly true for midwives working in rural areas among poor and minority populations, where enforcement of licensing laws is notably lax.

But if its immediate impacts are limited, law has proven to be an important element in shaping midwifery. Licensing sanctions a particular group of practitioners. Established medical professionals are restricted to interacting with licensed midwives, and the public gradually accepts the "benefits" of retaining certified practitioners. Cut off from the mainstream, the uncertified midwife faces a decreasing clientele and eventually drops from sight. Midwives who are already licensed begin to alter their practices in order to comply with the law. One Arizona midwife informed me that she had changed some of her earlier practices, even though she believed the changes were detrimental to her clients: "Before [being subject to] the regs I used to use cayenne to control [post partum] bleeding and I never had to transport a woman [for that problem]. Now that I can't use herbs I have had to transport women for bleeding and occasionally they even need to be transfused." Although many would question the wisdom of using cayenne as an antihemorrhagic agent, this midwife's change in practice demonstrates the effect of law.

Licensure also affects the midwife's clientele. Several clients in Texas and Arizona told me that they would not employ a midwife if they lived in California, where lay midwives practice illegally. This demonstrates the effect of state sanction, and such changes in clientele undoubtedly influence the midwife-client relationship and (consequently) alter the nature of midwifery.

Neither medicine nor law is independent of the social conditions that surround them. Indeed, both respond to the "felt necessities of the time" (Roth, 1977: 122–24). It has been suggested that a complete understanding of change in medicine requires the exploration of how medical and nonmedical movements interact. Consider midwifery. The methods of attending birth have been attacked or supported by a number of social movements with broader concerns (see DeVries, 1981: 1085–87). The movement of birth into the hospital and the subsequent decline of midwifery earlier in this century are in part traceable to the collective efforts of women suffragists who spread the gospel of hospital birth and "twilight sleep" (see Wertz and Wertz, 1977: 132–77). Similarly, the gradual shift of birth back to the home and the growing demand for midwives (licensed and unlicensed) are linked to diffuse social currents in contemporary society. The revolt by women against traditional sex roles—and in particular, the dominance of obstetrics by men—increased the demand for home birth and midwifery (see Ruzek, 1978; Scully, 1980). A general interest in "natural" life styles led to criticism of the technological interference in the natural process of birth, and it also renewed interest in the noninterventionist techniques of midwifery. Finally, the interest in self-fulfillment, which earned the seventies the title of the "Me decade," created a concern with the experiential dimension of birth (see Lasch, 1978; Yankelovich, 1981). Birth was no longer a necessary evil to be endured by those who wanted children. It was now relished as an important life experience, an experience marked by growth, achievement, and personal satisfaction. Midwives were sought out because they were sensitive to this dimension of birth.[2]

These social movements have accompanied (and encouraged) movements for change *within* medicine, contributing toward a slow "humanization" of medical care (Howard *et al.,* 1977). Renee Fox (1977) has suggested the possibility of a decline in medical dominance and a "demedicalization" of society. Reforms of this type within the medical establishment demonstrate the direct influence of larger social movements. Thus alternative birth centers in hospitals were created to appeal to new consumer interests and to deflect interest in home birth.

On the whole, the law follows more than it initiates change. However, as we have seen, the ability of law to sanction practitioners can gradually alter the structural conditions of medical practice. Laws generally prove most effective when their mandates conform to the cultural conceptions of the public. In this case, the desire of midwives and other paramedicals to gain the benefits of scientific medicine makes them willing to adhere to the law, even though adherence can detract from the special, nonmedical aspects of their practices.

Medical Hegemony and the Law

W. F. Cottrell (1940: 36) called our attention to the "tremendous interrelationship between technological and social facts" in his study of railroading. The law is one of the more important social facts that interacts with technology. Hurst (1950: 10) has suggested that much of the influence in this relationship flows from technology to law: "The law has almost always been acted upon by, or has responded to technological change, rather than controlled it. The relation between law and technical change was full of color and tension. But in almost every case, the scientist or the inventor took the initiative." Hurst's observations remain accurate. The segmentation of knowledge characteristic of our time, and the subsequent spawning of specializations, have created enclaves of knowledge that are (or are assumed to be) beyond the understanding of the nonspecialist. This creates a dependency within legal institutions on testimony offered by specialists. Such "legal dependency" is especially apparent in matters related to medicine. Several observers have noted that the power of medicine stems largely from its monopoly of knowledge (see Freidson, 1970: 108–10; Yedida, 1980).

The hegemony of medicine is supported by several legal opinions. In their report on the United States Supreme Court, Woodward and Armstrong (1979: 182–89, 229–40) detail the reliance of the justices on medical opinion in the *Roe v. Wade* abortion decision. Woodward and Armstrong (p. 182, emphasis added) claim that the author of the majority opinion, Harry Blackmun (former general counsel to the Mayo Clinic), "wanted an opinion that the medical community would accept, one that would free physicians to exercise their *professional judgment*." More pertinent to the present study is the decision in *Fitzgerald v. Porter Memorial Hospital* (523 F.2d 716, 7th Cir. 1975), which held that parents' interest ir having the father present in the hospital delivery room during birth was insufficient to invalidate hospital regulations preventing such access. In justifying this decision, Justice John Paul Stevens (now of the United States Supreme Court) stated that there were "valid medical reasons" for prohibiting fathers from access. He felt it undesirable to impose an "inflexible rule on all hospitals" that would substitute the court's judgment for the *"professional judgement"* (my emphasis) of hospital staff. Stevens also made reference to several medical articles that supported his contention that valid medical reasons underlay hospital rules. In his note on the decision, Newman (1976: 1305) asserts that "Judge Stevens bowed too easily to those persons within the medical profession who voiced objections to [natural childbirth] procedures." Newman cites evidence introduced by advocates of alternative birth methods that suggests there are no valid medical reasons for the exclusion of the father from the delivery room.

The judicial deference to the "professional judgment" of physicians in these and other legal opinions is significant, because the same deference has shaped legislation on midwifery. The advice of physicians has contributed to the failure of many midwife laws, and controlled those that do gain passage.

The supporters of midwifery and home birth, aware of the hegemony of medicine, have begun to employ the criteria of scientific medicine in defense of their cause (see Mehl *et al,* 1976; 1977; Mehl, 1977; Hazell, 1974; Epstein and McCartney, 1975). This new tactic is interesting in light of Goode's (1960: 904) observation that "rival professions are not willing to put their claims to the test, partly because to do so suggests that there is still higher authority than they." Yet the cultural power of scientific medicine is such that health practitioners seeking legitimacy have no choice (see

Jordan, 1978: 88). Some midwives, however, remain hesitant to use scientific criteria, claiming that midwifery is an art. As Goode (1960: 904) suggests: "Art is not testable."

It is more than slightly ironic that the proponents of midwifery and home birth defend their position with data on rates of mortality and morbidity among mothers and infants. To do so suggests that quantity (was a positive medical outcome achieved?) is more important than quality (was the experience enriching for its participants?). Home birth advocates, after all, often point out that exclusive concern with "quantity" dehumanizes care. Recent studies have shown that the "humanization" of maternity care (to the extent that it has occurred) has come about not through a stress on statistical outcomes, but through a focus on qualitative aspects of the experience. For example, Klaus and Kennell's (1976; 1981) innovative work on parent-child bonding has led to changes in obstetric routines once thought essential (that is, medically necessary) for the safety of mother and child. If Klaus and Kennell had not gone outside standard medical practice, they would never have concluded that the practice of separating infants and their parents to prevent infection was damaging to the process of attachment between a newborn and its mother and father. The dangers of maximizing medical outcomes are recognized by Zola (1972: 502–3):

> Nor does it really matter if . . . we were guaranteed six more inches of height, thirty more years of life, or drugs to expand our potentialities and potencies; we should still be able to ask: What do six more inches matter, in what kind of environment will the thirty additional years be spent, or who will decide what potentialities or potencies will be expanded and what curbed?

The Dilemma of Licensure

The issue of midwife licensure remains a dilemma. It is commonly argued that certification is necessary for public protection, but at least one group of lay midwives has observed (Carson *et al.*, 1977: 519):

A license isn't really a guarantee of expertise: Anyone graduated from medical school can legally deliver babies, even if they've had the experience of only three or four deliveries. Yet we, with much more experience, are barred legally. . . . Medical licensing diminishes any accountability to people, the "consumer," in favor of accountability to a licensing board.

For the most part, certification eliminates consumer evaluation of medical practitioners. The typical client simply accepts a state-issued license to practice as a judge of ability. Where such licensing systems do not exist, as with California's lay midwives, this responsibility remains with the client. Recognizing this, certain advocates of lay midwifery have proposed alternative means of regulation. Allen Solares' (n.d.[a]; n.d.[b]; 1983) proposed "Health Responsibility System" is perhaps the most well-thought out. He says that systems of regulation must seek a balance between consumer self-determination, competition, and consumer protection. To achieve this balance he suggests assessing health practitioners on the "degree of hazard" their practices pose to the public. Once assessed, the least restrictive degree of regulation that is consistent with safety should be applied. Solares envisions that a number of health practices that are noninvasive—including midwifery—could be regulated through a voluntary certification program that is controlled by consumers and that provides the information necessary to make an informed choice of practitioners. The weakness in Solares' system lies in the determination of "degree of hazard." We can expect that the medical professions would exert themselves to show that all alternative health practices are hazardous to the public.

Midwives in some areas with no licensing laws have begun systems of self-regulation, thereby imitating the history of the medical profession. In Massachusetts, where lay midwifery is prohibited by a legal decision that defines assistance at birth as the practice of medicine, lay midwives are formulating a peer review program.

This voluntary program would allow a committee of midwives to review the credentials and performance of individual midwives. An "Initial Peer Review Form" distributed by the Massachusetts Midwives Association (MMA) asks for information on a midwife's training, statistics from the births she has attended, details of a plan for medical backup, as well as a discussion of her "role at birth" and her "strengths and weaknesses as a midwife." A midwife who successfully completes this review can claim certification by the MMA. The issue of peer review came up in California following complaints about a specific midwife. After receiving a letter of complaint, the Steering Committee of the California Association of Midwives appointed several midwives to review both the midwife and the birth in question. A description of the review was published in the *CAM Newsletter* (Rosenberger, 1983) and that description generated a debate on peer review in the next several newsletters. Some midwives supported peer review as a way of forestalling action by state agencies and as a necessary device to insure competency. Others saw peer review as potentially divisive and expressed a reluctance to pass judgment on another midwife. The editor of the newsletter summed up the issue by quoting the minutes from a meeting of midwives in the San Francisco area. The consensus of that meeting was that midwives "need" both peer review and some type of standards (*CAM Newsletter,* 1984: 13).

Although midwives recognize the need for regulation of their practice, the dilemmas inherent in the regulation of health care discourage concerted action in that direction. The problem of licensure for midwives is perhaps best summarized by a lay midwife (Ehrlich, 1976: 126):

Certification of nonmedical midwives is something of a paradox. While responsibility for quality care must be assumed by its practitioners, much of the value of lay midwives is that they are *non*medical attendants who approach birth as a natural process. They have learned to midwive by midwiving, not by seeking degrees. Midwifery is an art as well as a science. Intuition and sensitivity are prime requirements of a good midwife. How can a woman be trained in and measured for these subtly elusive qualities? Requirements for licenses and credentials, while meant to safeguard the consumer, often become bureaucratic roadblocks to practice. Also, institutionalizing professionals leaves the consumer out of the process of evaluating care. The likelihood of midwifery falling into this trap is especially high since medicine sees birth as its domain, and would regulate all birth attendants.

This study of midwifery licensure has demonstrated that legal recognition of a medical occupation may prove unfavorable both to the occupation and the public. On the other hand, the ability of law to control alternative forms of care is limited. In fact, even if lay midwifery falls "into the trap" of legal recognition, there is comfort in the knowledge that law has been unable to exterminate alternative forms of care when people really want them.

Appendix:
On Researching Midwifery

Data for this study were gathered from a variety of sources—
including historical documents, interviews, and observation—over
a three-and-a-half-year period from 1978 to 1981. Research sites included the halls of state capital buildings and hospitals; the offices
of doctors, midwives, and bureaucrats; the homes of midwives, doctors, and consumers; and informal settings such as automobiles, air-
planes, restaurants, and various libraries.

Historical Data Sources
Qualitative studies on current phenomena have been notoriously
disinclined to consider historical data. Most qualitative research has
been undertaken by sociologists with an allegiance to the symbolic
interactionist perspective. That is, they are interested in how individuals create, exchange, and sustain social definitions, and therefore they tend to focus only on the immediate context of a given interaction. Past interactions and historical processes that affect
social interaction are often neglected in this approach.

My own research required a consideration of historical influences. The history of midwifery and the rise of medical science are
crucial to understanding current midwife legislation.

Data on midwives were obtained from a variety of secondary
sources. The recent concern with the role of women in society
spawned several histories of midwifery. Along with more general

works (for example, Litoff, 1978), there are studies that focus on the plight of women as health workers (Ehrenreich and English, 1973) and on the changing experience of women as patients (Rich, 1976). Historical studies that deal more generally with medicine were another source. Data on midwifery were gleaned from histories of the medical profession (Stevens, 1971; Starr, 1982) as well as from accounts of medical practice in a given locale (Peterson, 1947). A final source of secondary data was the mass media. Midwifery makes "good copy," so that articles from newspapers and magazines and tapes of radio and television broadcasts provided valuable information on issues related to midwives.

I obtained useful primary historical data from archives and private documents; in addition, state departments of health provided statistics regarding the number of midwives and the distribution of births. Archives and legislative libraries in the various states provided useful background information on specific pieces of legislation and case law. Included here were items such as early drafts of bills, analyses of legislation by the staffs of legislative committees, and records of cases heard in state courts. Private documents were obtained from individuals and organizations who played key legislative roles. I found state departments of health, legislators, state medical associations, and midwife organizations extraordinarily helpful in allowing me access to personal correspondence, intrastaff memos, never-published press releases, and notes from personal files.

A final source of historical data—periodicals issued by specific organizations—is a mixture of primary and secondary data. When a magazine published by a state medical association includes an article on lay midwives, that article is a secondary data source because it gives information through the eyes and interpretation of its author, but it is also a primary data source because the publisher deemed it relevant for the audience of the periodical. Hence it reveals something about his or her motives and the organization's position on the issue. I have used several articles that are informative in their own right, but might be seen as propaganda because of their inclusion in a periodical or newsletter of a midwife association or medical organization. The same holds true for various pieces of information found in an organization's files. For instance, the "midwifery" file at one state medical association contained newspaper clippings regarding mishaps at midwife-attended births. The clippings gave me valuable secondary information about the incidents, but were also a source of primary information about legislative strategy and attitudes towards midwifery.

Interviews

Interviews proved the best means of gathering certain kinds of information. For instance, legislators and lobbyists provided information related to licensing bills and legislative maneuvering not available from any other source. Similarly, interviews with midwives, consumers, and physicians supplied me with data on events I was unable to witness.

I interviewed a wide range of people, including midwives, consumers, physicians, hospital administrators, legislators, lobbyists, legislative aides, and bureaucrats. Because of the duration of the research and my involvement in other projects, it is impossible to come up with an accurate count of the interviews relevant to this study. There were well over one hundred, as well as hundreds of less formal discussions. In fact, it is difficult to separate the formal from the informal. Do two to three pages of notes from a discussion with a client waiting to see a midwife count as a formal interview? Does one page from an interview with a physician reluctant to speak about midwives? How about a two-sentence summary of a discussion with a woman on an airplane whose daughter had a home birth?

I have also used information from interviews conducted for another study. During the course of this research I received a small grant to study alternative birth centers. For that study I visited ABCs at twenty-five hospitals, interviewing consumers, administrators, physicians, and midwives. It is my impression that qualitative researchers often inflate the number of "interviews" by including the most casual of conversations. This improves the appearance of their methodology, but rather than yield to inflationary pressure, I will leave my numbers imprecise.

The more casual interviews were a consequence of "hanging out" with midwives and working in a few bureaucratic positions (I will describe these in the following section). The structured interviews were conducted with a schedule that guided the conversation but allowed open-ended responses. The schedules evolved out of my earlier research in California; as new issues were discovered, they were added to the schedule, and old ones discarded or revised. Depending on circumstance, interviews were recorded electronically or by hand. The results were transcribed or summarized, making them available for future analysis.

Observation

A third data-gathering technique employed in this study was observation. At times this entailed participant observation; in other instances I was simply a researcher-observer. I was a participant observer when I assisted in the deliveries of my three children, when I assisted at a friend's home birth, and when I participated as an advisor and consultant to public agencies. My eldest daughter was born in the hospital with the assistance of a certified nurse-midwife, and my son and younger daughter were born at home with the assistance of lay midwives. These experiences provided valuable insights into the nature of midwife-assisted birth.

Other first-hand information emerged as a consequence of my employment at government agencies interested in midwifery. These appointments included membership on the perinatal subcommittee of the Golden Empire Health Systems Agency, which is located in Sacramento; membership on the steering committee of the Midwifery Advisory Council, which was designed to provide advice on legislation to the California Department of Consumer Affairs; and a consultant position with the same state agency. The agency, while technically prohibited from lobbying, was a strong proponent of licensure, and during my tenure there I observed their strategies to secure passage for a licensure bill. Quite early I decided against assuming the guise of a midwife or an apprentice midwife, even though such a strategy was the only way I could directly observe the conduct of midwives during births. At one point a group of midwives did ask me to consider apprenticing with them. Although jobs for Ph.D. sociologists are hard to come by, and although it would have been interesting to become one of very few male lay midwives, I did not feel I could be honest in my apprenticeship. Had I accepted the invitation, it would have been more for the chance to gather data than out of desire to become a midwife.

The ethical issues associated with disguised research have been discussed by sociologists (Davis, 1961; Lofland, 1961; Roth, 1962; Erikson, 1967) in an unsatisfactory attempt to arrive at some universally applicable principle. Roth (1962) suggests that because the field researcher is often uncertain where his work will lead, it is impossible to separate secret from nonsecret research. Using Roth's ideas as a springboard, Erikson (1967) concludes that it is unethical for social scientists to deliberately misrepresent themselves or the nature of their research. In the end, the decision to adopt or reject disguised observation must be made by the individual researcher in the context of the intended research. In my case, I felt that the experience of my children's births coupled with intensive questioning of midwives and their clients made any such deception unnecessary.

I did considerable observation in my role as researcher. Schatzman and Strauss (1973: 59–63) note that there are several levels at which observation can occur, ranging from "watching from outside" to "participation with a hidden identity." Much of my observing falls in the middle of this continuum, an area which they label "limited interaction." I made my role as a researcher clear at the outset, whereupon I observed midwives in their interactions with clients, attended both childbirth education classes and midwife training sessions, and generally observed the routine activities of midwives.

I recorded data with techniques explicated by Douglas (1976), Schatzman and Strauss (1973), and Lofland (1971). The method involved recording detailed field notes as well as theoretical insights that emerge during observation. Field notes were transcribed or summarized to make them compatible with data from interviews.

The Ends of Research

Why do research? The most cynical response to this question links the pursuit of research with self-interest. Successful research helps to secure employment, tenure, grants, prestige, and might even earn the researcher some pocket money in royalties. Whether they are employed by academic institutions, the government, or private business, sociologists gain prestige from the articles and books that grow out of their research. A somewhat less cynical observer might suggest that researchers derive a more benign personal satisfaction from their work, namely the pure enjoyment of research and discovery. While the motivation is still personal, it is not quite as crass. An idealist would argue that the researcher's aims are altruistic, motivated by the desire to help others and to improve the human condition by promoting a better understanding of the world around us. In reality the motives of any one researcher are some combination of the above. Although few researchers would confess to self-interest as their primary motivation, a certain amount of self-interest is needed to keep one going when the hours grow long and the work tedious.

This mix of motivations suggests the importance of values in the practice of research. The meaning researchers find in their work is related to their values. For the self-interested, research is a means of accomplishing personal goals. For the ideologue, research is a way of promoting ideology. Thus, the Marxist sees class struggle reflected in all of society's institutions, and the more conservative functional-ist sees society as a smoothly operating machine. Historically, the social sciences downplayed (ignored, some would say) the effect of values on research, claiming that researchers could leave their val-ues behind when they were working. Within the last few decades, sociologists and other social scientists recognized that values and people are inseparable and now encourage researchers to identify their values, so readers can evaluate reported results in the context of the researcher's value system.

Earlier in this book I suggested that I had "unconventional senti-mentalities." The unconventional sentimentality that leads me to desire a future for midwifery is not a value itself but the outcome of a larger value system based in a Christian world view. I believe that it is my responsibility to promote love and justice among people. Reflecting my belief, I have tried to identify injustice in the provi-sion of medical services to encourage a more equitable system of health care. Of course, I would enjoy the rewards that accompany a successful book, but my main hope is that my effort helps to give us a medical system that offers true health *care*.

Epilogue:
The Trap of Legal
Recognition

This book was, and remains, something of a curiosity. Reviewers of the first edition were, for the most part, bemused. They found the data interesting, accurately reported, even compelling, but they did not know what to do with my conclusions. My argument—that for midwives the cost of legal recognition would almost certainly be the end of a distinctive profession of midwifery—followed logically from the data, but many readers wanted to believe the data were anomalous. Surely, in other states at other times, midwifery would benefit from licensure.

Reviewers were left wondering if I was a friend or a foe of midwives. I often asked myself the same question. My goal, then as now, was to secure a place for a truly independent profession of midwifery. Unfortunately, my study of the most common avenue to professional independence, licensure, convinced me that it would not foster autonomous midwifery in this country. In the absence of other paths to legitimate practice, I had no choice but to recommend that midwives avoid licensure and look for new and creative ways to establish their profession (DeVries, 1986).

My discussion of "commonsense" understandings of medical licensure in chapter 1 anticipated the confused response of reviewers.

Physician reviewers, using "public common sense," assumed that licensure was an unalloyed good and recoiled at my suggestion that
the public might be better served if midwives remained unlicensed
(see, e.g., Russell, 1987). They failed to appreciate how licensure
primarily served the interest of the dominant profession and how
it removed choice, hindered communication, and diminished the
quality of care.[1] Sociologists and midwives, employing their own
version of common sense, could not understand my insistence that
licensure would *not* benefit midwives in their competitive struggle
with physicians. In their view, licensure is an effective tool in the
contest between professions.

The publication of the second edition of this book gives me the
welcome opportunity to revisit my analysis. Few social scientists
have the luxury of testing their analyses against time, checking the
relevance of their findings in a changed world. Have the events of
the past ten years supported or disproved my earlier conclusions
about the impact of licensure on midwifery? Have new facts come
to light? Have more recent studies challenged my explanations?

In 1984, when I finished the first edition of this book, I was not
optimistic about the future of licensed midwifery in the United
States. Midwives here were caught in a true dilemma: legitimacy
could be gained only by sacrificing the distinctiveness of their profession. Lacking the political power to shape and secure favorable
legislation, midwives were at the whim of others. I suspected that
all new attempts to create permissive laws would be met by organized opposition from the medical lobby. And if, over the objections
of medical lobbyists, a licensing bill managed to become law, I was
convinced that the details of its implementation would complicate
the lives of practicing midwives and would, ironically, discourage
growth of the profession.

I made these pessimistic predictions just over ten years ago. In
the intervening decade our health care delivery system has changed
in ways no one expected. How have American midwives fared since
the mid-1980s? In order to answer this question we must consider

the condition of midwifery on several levels: its overall health, measured in terms of its size and participation in health care and medicine; developments in licensing; the treatment of midwives in the courts; and the "changing nature" of midwifery.

Health of the Profession

There are many ways to measure the vitality of an occupational group. The most obvious is a survey of its growth: an expanding profession is a healthy profession. In the case of midwives, however, the task of counting is complicated. Widely varying definitions of midwifery make it nearly impossible to get a precise count of midwives. Does a woman certified as a nurse-midwife but practicing as a nurse "count" as a midwife? What about a traditional midwife who attends only one or two births per year? Should she be included in our census?

In spite of these definitional problems, the number of practicing midwives is periodically tallied. Because there is a standardized legal definition of certified nurse-midwifery and because CNMs have uniform training requirements, it is easier to count nurse-midwives than it is to (find and) count traditional midwives. In 1982, the American College of Nurse-Midwives estimated that 2,500 CNMs were working in the United States; ten years later that number had grown to approximately 4,000 (see ACNM, 1993; National Commission on Nurse-Midwifery Education, 1993).

When it comes to traditional midwives, the best we can do is an estimate. Given the great variation in state laws and differences of opinion about who counts as a traditional midwife, all tallies of traditional midwives must be viewed with skepticism. The Midwives Alliance of North America (MANA) has long recognized the need for more accurate counts of practicing midwives. In 1989 they took a step in this direction with the creation of the North American Registry of Midwives (NARM). However, the primary purpose of the

NARM is not simply to provide a list of all active midwives. It is an effort to raise the credibility of midwifery, and, as such, all NARM-registered midwives must pass an examination intended to establish a minimum level of competency. Hence the NARM is a subset of all practicing midwives. In 1991, two members of a task force created by the Minnesota Department of Health surveyed all 50 states and found approximately 2,000 traditional midwives in practice (Barroso and Coffey, 1991). Others claim the number may be as high as 6,000 (Korte, 1995). Because these numbers are unreliable, and because there are no earlier estimates, it is impossible to speak meaningfully about growth or decline in the number of traditional midwives.

No matter how one counts, or who one counts, the growth of midwifery has been far from explosive. Added educational programs (National Commission on Nurse-Midwifery Education, 1993) have allowed the number of nurse-midwives to expand, nearly doubling in ten years; but the total is below the expectations of the ACNM. A few years ago they coined the slogan, "10,000 [nurse-midwives] by [the year] 2000." It is unlikely that number will be achieved. We gain some perspective on the growth of midwifery by contrasting it with growth in the number of specialists in obstetrics and gynecology: in 1980 there were 26,305 obstetrician/gynecologists in the United States; by 1992 that number had grown to 35,273 (Roback *et al.*, 1993).

But sheer numbers is only one way to assess midwives' success. Another, perhaps better, method is to examine their contribution to the health care system or, more specifically, the number of births they attend. Here again we find the role of midwives expanding while their overall contribution remains small. In 1980 midwives attended 1.7 percent of the nation's births; by 1992 that number had grown to 4.9 percent (National Center for Health Statistics, 1994; see also DeClercq, 1992). Significant growth, yes, but midwives remain underused. Following the numbers reported above, midwives represent about 15 percent of the obstetric workforce, and yet they attend less than 5 percent of the births. Perhaps it is premature to expect midwives to be significant players in American health care. Before midwifery can be widely accepted, it must be proven in the crucible of research. After a heavy dose of criticism and discrediting earlier in the century (see Devitt, 1979a; Litoff, 1986), it will take some time before midwives can establish themselves as necessary members of a health care team. How is midwifery treated in the world of medical and public health research? Is the profession creating a scientific foundation for practice? Is it gaining credibility?

In the past decade, evaluations of midwife care began to appear more regularly in the pages of medical journals. A series of articles appearing in the 1980s assessed the quality of care by midwives at home births (Burnett *et al.*, 1980; Hinds *et al.*, 1985, Schramm *et al.*, 1987). The conclusions of these articles were nearly identical: planned home births with trained attendants posed no special risk for mothers and babies, while unplanned home births and untrained attendants brought poor results. In a widely cited study published in the *New England Journal of Medicine*, Rooks and her colleagues (1989) verified the safety of nurse-midwife-attended births in birth centers. Further research in the 1990s supported the safety of out-of-hospital births (see, e.g., Durand, 1992; Tew, 1990). Research also emphasized the value of midwives for reducing unnecessary interventions. Both traditional midwives and nurse-midwives were credited for cutting the rate of Caesarean sections (Sakala, 1993; Butler *et al.*, 1993). Goer (1995) has collected a number of research articles that question current obstetric practices and recommend midwife care as the safest and least expensive approach to birth.

Why hasn't this small but well-placed body of scientific evidence helped midwifery prosper? The answer to this question lies in a closer look at the research itself, considering where and how it was done and the reaction it provoked. Much of the work emphasizing the value of midwives is done in health maintenance organizations (HMOs) and other managed care settings, a fact that underscores the importance of financial incentives for the future of midwifery. Midwives are popular in HMOs and government programs, environments where costs must be controlled. Because they are more often cared for in medicaid programs and HMOs, black, Hispanic, and Native American women are far more likely to have a midwife-attended birth than are white women (Parker, 1994). It ought to be enough to show that midwives generate high levels of satisfaction, promote confidence in their clients, and improve outreach to underserved communities. But it is not. Midwives are allowed to flourish to the extent that they improve the bottom line.

Furthermore, supportive research is not often done by midwives themselves. We learn of the value of midwifery from epidemiologists, physicians, and social scientists. Midwifery suffers when other professions develop and expand its knowledge base. As long as the expertise of midwives is founded in knowledge developed by others, they will be a subordinate profession. In other parts of the world, where midwives have more autonomy, they claim control over a body of knowledge unique to midwifery (see DeVries and Barroso, 1996).

Finally, the response of physicians to this body of research is instructive. Their instinctive reaction is to protect the current system. In his editorial review of an article on the safety of out-of-hospital births in Missouri, the executive director of the American College of Obstetricians and Gynecologists, Warren Pearse (1987), reluctantly agrees that home birth can be safe, but he insists there is no reason to develop a system to serve the few women who choose this option. He fails to consider the documented advantages of midwives and home birth in terms of cost, accessibility, satisfaction, and the reduction of unneeded interventions. Ignoring research demonstrating how midwives save money, Pearse illogically argues that it would be prohibitively expensive to develop a system that licenses and regulates midwives.

Measured in terms of its growth and presence in health care, the situation of nurse-midwives is improving very gradually: their numbers are growing, educational programs are expanding, and they are attending more births. The future seems less bright for traditional midwives. Their contribution to maternity care is small and is seldom recognized. Although several states have considered midwife legislation over the past ten years and although MANA is making an effort to standardize credentialing procedures, the legal status of traditional midwives remains uneven and problematic. We turn next to a detailed review of recent legislation regulating the practices of midwives. Our focus in the following section is on the varied laws governing traditional midwifery, not on the (more or less) uniform rules for nurse-midwives.

Midwifery in the Legislature

Among the many conclusions generated by my review of midwife legislation in the first edition, two stand out: 1) midwives themselves have little control over proposed and enacted laws; and 2) what appears to be legislation favorable to midwives often turns out to be more restrictive than the laws replaced. Over the past ten years several new pieces of legislation concerning traditional midwifery have been introduced in statehouses across the country. Do any of these differ dramatically from the laws I evaluated ten years ago?

We begin with a review of the legal status of traditional midwifery. Just after the first edition of this book was published, Wolfson (1986) reported that lay midwifery was clearly legal in 11 states, clearly illegal in 10 states, and "effectively illegal" in 12 states; the other 17 states had a variety of old and ambiguous laws. One year later, Butter and Kay surveyed a variety of state agencies and came to a slightly different conclusion: "As of July, 1987, 10 states have prohibitory laws, five states have grandmother clauses authorizing

practicing midwives under repealed statutes, five states have enabling laws which are not used, and 10 states explicitly permit lay
midwives to practice. In the 21 remaining states, the legal status of
midwives is unclear" (1988: 1161). Using yet another classification
scheme, Korte (1995: 57) gave the following report of the legal status of traditional midwives in 1995: 14 states "legal by licensure,
certification or registration"; 11 states "legal through judicial interpretation or statutory inference"; 7 states "not legally defined but
not prohibited"; 8 states "legal by statute but licensure unavailable";
and 10 states "prohibited through statutory restriction or judicial
interpretation."

Two things become evident when we compare these reports.
First, traditional midwives have gained some ground in the recognition of their practice, moving from 11 (or 10) "clearly legal" states in
the mid-1980s to 14 in the mid-1990s. Second, the differing totals
and the different ways of counting used by the researchers reveal
significant confusion over the definition of legal and illegal. This
second observation should cause us to rethink our first. Have traditional midwives actually gained ground? The difficulty in distinguishing legal and illegal, permitted and unpermitted, reminds us
that there is a difference between "law on the books" and "law in
action." Before we celebrate the expanding role of traditional midwives, we must explore this distinction further.

The three surveys summarized above relied on reports from
official agencies: departments of health, state licensing boards, and
the like. They represent surveys of laws on the books, the official
view of the legal status of midwives. Barroso and Coffey (1991) surveyed traditional midwives practicing in each of the 50 states, asking them to describe the laws governing their practices. Their report gives us a view of midwifery laws in action, the way laws are
experienced by working midwives. They report 14 states where traditional midwifery is clearly legal, 31 "gray" states where the practice
is undefined, and 16 states where traditional midwifery is clearly

illegal. If you are counting, you will notice that there is something suspicious about their numbers: somehow they arrived at a total of 61 states! The reason for the inflated total is that several states were counted in both the "clearly legal" and the "clearly illegal" categories. In these states, the laws allow for licensing, but licenses are difficult or impossible to obtain, hence many midwives there choose to work illegally. In Arizona, for example, where Barroso and Coffey counted 40 traditional midwives, 25 are licensed and 15 are working without a license; of the 41 traditional midwives working in Arkansas, 20 remain unlicensed. What appears to be an advance in the recognition of traditional midwifery is not regarded as such by many practicing midwives.

The state of New York provides a recent example of "favorable" legislation that works against the interests of midwives. Korte (1995) considers New York a state where traditional midwifery is "legal by statute, but licensure unavailable." In June 1992 the New York legislature passed a bill that unifies nurse- and lay midwifery, acknowledging the legitimacy of different approaches to midwifery training. The bill established a 15-member board of midwifery charged with setting standards for education and practice.

Traditional midwives worked hard for the passage of the bill, but by early 1994 several of these same midwives felt betrayed. The midwifery board, set up in the Department of Education, included several nurse-midwives but no traditional midwives, creating doubts that less-medical, home-based practices would be protected in the new regulations. Two years after the law was passed, the mechanism to allow traditional midwives to obtain licenses was still not in place, but the prohibition on unlicensed midwifery was being enforced with a new rigor. In 1993 and 1994 several midwives were investigated by the Department of Education's Office of Professional Discipline. This heightened scrutiny caused several midwives to voluntarily stop practicing. The codirector of New York Friends of Midwives reported that four midwives in the Albany area stopped attending births for fear of being charged with practicing medicine without a license. "They are laying low," she said. After an investigation in October 1993, a midwife in eastern Long Island signed an agreement to stop attending births until she was licensed. She told a reporter, "I was working on this law day and night, I feel like I got sold out" (Karlin, 1994). Korte (1995) describes more severe actions against two upstate midwives: in 1994 Julia Kessler and Karen Pardini, with a total of 32 years' experience and 2,500 births (with no infant deaths) between them, were charged with practicing both midwifery and medicine without a license. Midwives who once practiced freely in the margins of an old law, are in clear violation of the new law.

One of the older licensing laws for traditional midwives, and one that is considered "friendly" toward midwifery, is found in the state of Washington. Passed in the early 1980s, the Washington law offers licenses to graduates of a state-accredited three-year educational program. Lay (i.e., unlicensed) midwives are allowed to practice if they do not advertise or charge for their services, a rule that allows friends or members of religious groups to assist each other at birth without fear of prosecution. How have midwives fared in this favorable environment? In 1989 two faculty members of the Seattle Midwifery School complained, "formidable barriers . . . stand in the way of full practice . . . for state licensed midwives: lack of (affordable) malpractice insurance, inability to obtain hospital privileges, incomplete reimbursement from third party payers and excessive restrictions on the scope of practice" (Myers and Myers-Ciecko, 1989). Three years later, Baldwin *et al.* published the results of their study of the professional relationships of Washington's midwives, concluding, "Only certified nurse midwives have forged mutually satisfying relationships with the physician community. . . . Licensed midwives, despite their status as licensed birth attendants, have been dissatisfied with their consulting relationships with physicians" (1992: 262, 264). Many midwives choose to remain outside the law. A study of unlicensed midwives in Washington state revealed that several are, in fact, practicing illegally, charging for their services (Myers *et al.*, 1990). As I noted earlier, "state certification does not ensure medical endorsement" (115). Even though the state has acted in their favor, licensed midwives in Washington are limited by the unwillingness of the medical community to incorporate them fully. Situations like these in New York and Washington demonstrate the need for more uniform and more credible licensing legislation, legislation that will allow midwives to become a legitimate and recognizable part of our health system. At their best, current models of licensure allow a minimum number of midwives to survive, meeting the needs of a small group of women seeking to give birth outside the hospital. In response to uneven and confused local legislation, several state organizations of traditional midwives have initiated programs of self-certification (see DeVries, 1986; Butter and Kay, 1990), but these have done little to promote the profession or shape legislation. In whatever form, licensure as it exists today has decidedly not brought the benefits of midwifery to a larger group of women.

Several advocates of midwifery have stepped forward with plans for the promotion and regulation of midwifery:

1. Writing in a well-known alternative birth periodical, the *NAPSAC News*, Mehl Madrona and Mehl Madrona (1993) angered a number of traditional midwives when they argued that even the "good" licensing laws were inadequate, failing to advance midwifery in America. After a lengthy analysis of the current condition of midwifery in the United States and elsewhere, they insist that traditional midwives will remain marginal unless they jettison apprentice-based education in favor of rigorous formal education programs. They derive many of their suggestions for reform from their study of Dutch maternity care.

2. In 1994 the Women's Institute for Childbearing Policy (WICP) issued a position paper, "Childbearing Policy within a National Health Program," calling for a "primary maternity care

system" that is centered on midwife care delivered in birth centers and homes. They suggest extending existing education and licensure programs (WICP, 1994).

3. The Midwifery Communication and Accountability Project (MCAP), founded in 1990, is seeking to make state regulation of midwifery uniform through the use of "Model State Legislation" (MCAP, n.d.).

4. As noted above, MANA established a registry exam, designed to "determine whether entry level knowledge has been achieved, and assist in fostering reciprocity between local jurisdictions" (MANA, n.d.).

5. MANA and the ACNM cooperated in the "Interorganizational Workgroup" (IWG), developing guidelines for midwifery certification in the United States. The guidelines allow for two types of midwives: the "certified midwife," credentialed through the MANA system, and the certified nurse-midwife, approved under ACNM guidelines (see WICP, 1994: 66–68; Burst, 1995; Rooks and Carr, 1995).

The number and diversity of suggestions for the regulation of midwifery coming from advocates of midwifery does not bode well for the future of the profession. Continued disagreement among midwives and their supporters—I saw the same thing in the early eighties—makes difficult the kind of coordinated and innovative effort needed to effect change. In an environment where midwifery faces persistent and strong opposition from physicians (see, e.g., Giacoia, 1991), factionalism among midwives extinguishes any hope of meaningful reform. Tjaden observes that "without state licensure, lay midwives have no true professional autonomy" (1987: 42). Unfortunately, it is also true that *with* the sort of licensure traditional midwives have experienced in the United States, created in the context of disagreements between midwives and power imbalances with the medical profession, there is no true professional autonomy either.

Midwives in the Courts

Where there are no clear regulations governing the practice of midwifery, an "uneasy truce" between midwives and the medical community continues: midwives are free to practice until they attract the attention of medical professionals. If a client of a midwife comes to the attention of a physician and the physician believes something improper was done, then the law is invoked as a regulatory mechanism and courts become the arena of regulation.

Over the past ten years, stories of this sort of regulation, many of them dramatic, have accumulated. Korte (1995) recounts the story of a Missouri midwife whose office was ransacked by seven law enforcement officers (wearing bullet-proof vests). They removed all her computer disks and destroyed her files and other materials. She was charged with eight felonies and several misdemeanors for practicing medicine without a license. The charges were eventually dropped in exchange for a five year probation period. Mitford (1992: 221–40) describes similar incidents in California, and the homepage of *Midwifery Today* on the World Wide Web, a new medium for generating support for midwifery, includes an appeal for help for an Indiana midwife in legal trouble for practicing medicine without a license.

These cases and cases described by Hafner-Eaton and Pearce (1994) and DeClercq (1994) follow the pattern of legal actions against midwives reviewed in chapter 5: they are initiated by physicians; they draw media attention; courts are unwilling to levy too heavy a penalty; and the midwives involved receive support from sister midwives and clients.

A pair of recent cases, however, indicates that the character of legal actions against midwives might be changing. In late 1994 a Michigan couple whose baby died three weeks after it was born sued the two traditional midwives who attended the birth. The couple, who chose to give birth in the midwives' clinic, claimed that the supervising midwife failed to recognize an emergency and waited too long before calling the hospital. The case is remarkable because it is the parents (not physicians) who are bringing charges in the form of a civil (not criminal) suit for monetary damages. The father of the dead child acknowledges that "the midwife experience was beautiful," but goes on to comment, "she [the midwife] way overstepped her bounds" (Niemiec, 1994: 3A). It is worth noting that the birth took place in a clinical setting where the midwife-client relationship tends to be formalized. In the clinic the client is just that, a client, not a "coconspirator" in the resistance to American obstetrics. When midwifery becomes established, it often adopts the form of clinical medicine, including more routinized relationships with clients. When the relationship between midwives and clients becomes more formal, legal actions like this—unheard of in the 1970s—become more common.

A second case reflects an expansion of the use of law as a tool of regulation. In this situation, described by Korte (1995: 56–57), three CNMs faced felony charges in association with an emergency breech birth (assisting at a breech birth is outside the permitted scope of practice for nurse-midwives) at a birthing center. One of the three was handcuffed and jailed. Although the charges were later dropped, the use of law to control the practices of midwives already regulated by licensing laws represents a major departure from earlier custom, and suggests a new level of scrutiny and control by physicians.

The "Changing" Nature of Midwifery

Although midwifery has not blossomed in the United States, it has been a persistent presence in American maternity care. What are the results of its proximity to medicine? The model of care represented by midwives has the power to change medical practice, but the medical setting also exerts pressure on midwifery, encouraging accommodation to the American way of birth. There are several ways midwifery has influenced obstetric practice over the past two decades. The enormous popularity of LDRs (combined labor, delivery, and recovery rooms) can be credited to midwives and their supporters in the alternative birth movement (see Mathews and Zadak, 1991). The pioneers of parent-infant bonding research, Drs. Klaus and Kennell (1976) acknowledge lay midwives and home birth as their inspiration. Although obstetricians were able to control the implementation of "bonding," they were pushed to change their practices by the presence of an alternative form of maternity care (see DeVries, 1984). More recently, Pel and Heres (1995: 95 – 105), studying obstetrics in the Netherlands, demonstrated the power of midwives to alter care given by individual obstetricians. Their research showed that, controlling for "risk" factors, obstetricians who work with midwives have lower rates of intervention.

But midwifery is also changed by medicine. When midwifery enters the world of obstetric technology, it runs the risk of having obstetric knowledge replace midwife knowledge. Barroso and I observed this in our survey of fetoscope use by CNMs (1996). We found that the fetoscope, a simple mechanical tool for finding fetal heart tones, is now rarely used by CNMs. The preferred tool is a "doptone," a device that uses sonar technology to make the task of finding heart tones easier. This seems an innocent development, but some midwives argue that valuable knowledge, unique to midwifery, is lost when the doptone is traded for the fetoscope. For example, a midwife using a fetoscope is able to find the point where the heart tones are the clearest and loudest, allowing the precise position of the child to be identified. With an amplified doptone, subtleties in the heartbeat are impossible to notice. Furthermore, the fetoscope brings the midwife much closer to the woman, allowing the caregiver to assess level of relaxation, skin tone, and overall condition.

Considering that medicine is supported by both structural arrangements and cultural ideas, the "corruption" of midwifery by medicine seems much more likely than its opposite. Lacking power and authority, midwifery must adapt to succeed. An "adapted" midwifery, using the tools and techniques of medicine, has little to offer obstetrics. It is significant that the research demonstrating the potential of midwives to reduce obstetrical intervention (Pel and Heres, 1995) was done in the Netherlands. Dutch midwives remain outside of medical control and thus offer an independent perspective on maternity care. Pel and Heres (1195: 104) comment, "[because] midwives show patience and stimulate confidence, as opposed to physicians who act faster and anticipate pathologic events, the reduction in anxiety might explain the decreasing effect of the employment of midwives on the rate of obstetrical interventions."

The challenge for midwives is to find a way to practice that preserves the unique body of knowledge and method that is theirs. For some midwives this involves remaining outside the world of medicine; this is the choice made by many traditional midwives. Other midwives choose to subvert the medical setting. Nurse-midwives report a variety of techniques for getting around restrictive hospital and physicians policies: smuggling lubricants for perineal massage into "sterile" delivery rooms, removing monitors so laboring women can walk around, speeding labor with warm baths or massage rather than oxytocin, violating rules that limit food intake (DeVries and Barroso, 1996). If midwifery is to be an agent of change rather than the subject of change, this sort of resistance and subversion is necessary.

The Last Word

Checking my work against empirical reality is only one way of assessing its quality. Another measure of a book's merit, one that we professional researchers sometimes find more important, is its reception by colleagues, its place in the body of recognized knowledge. For many of us "How did they like it?" becomes a more important question than "Was it true?"

Before closing this book for a second time, I must take note of the work of several other scholars who have joined the study of midwives since 1985. For the most part, their scholarship confirms and extends my research.

In their book *Labor Pains*, Sullivan and Weitz explored many of the same issues covered in *Regulating Birth*. They looked at midwifery in the United States, England, and New Zealand and came to conclusions nearly identical to mine, observing that "the rise of all modern midwifery . . . [might] be a false labor" (1988: 214). Where they disagree with my analysis (109–11; 205–6), it is often the result of their oversimplification of my arguments: they ignore my emphasis on the way law interacts with other social forces, suggesting that I saw licensure as the only operative factor in midwifery's demise.

More interesting for the future of my work and the future of midwifery are studies that explore the role of culture in the decline of midwifery. Davis-Floyd's (1992) important study of birth as an American rite of passage illustrates how cultural values sustain American obstetrics. She deconstructs our American birth practices, calling attention to the need we have as a culture to affirm our values at the transitional time of birth. She reminds us that we live in a culture that values, among other things, technology, the control of nature, and patriarchy. We should expect our birthing rooms to be dominated by men and technological devices that impose their timing and regulation on the natural process of birth.

Borst's (1988, 1989, 1995) careful historical studies of Wisconsin midwives give further evidence of the cultural roots of birth practices. Her research challenges the simplistic notion that physician resistance led to the extinction of midwifery. She shows that as immigrant women assimilated, the culture that supported midwifery disappeared, and along with it the midwives: "In the end midwifery, practiced by immigrant, working class women, remained rooted in the cultural life of traditional ethnic communities. When these communities began to assimilate and adopt American ideas, there was no place for the midwife" (1989: 48).

In his study of the rise of man-midwifery in England, Wilson (1995) adds his voice to those emphasizing the role of culture in the fading fortunes of female midwives. He observes that "male practitioners were turned into midwives not by their own desire, but through the choices of women. . . . the making of man-midwifery was the work of women" (192). His conclusions, which challenge conventional histories of midwifery, rest on an analysis of the role of "fashion" in shaping medical practice: "Fashion was in general the symbolic reflection of a new culture of class; in the world of women, for which childbirth was so crucial, fashion dictated the need for the man-midwife. . . . fashion offered a bridge by which those of intermediate or ambiguous status could symbolically climb the ranks" (191).

For the most part, the first edition of this book focused on the structures that constrained midwives. If culture was part of the analysis, it was as a dependent variable: I showed how political and legal structures influenced the culture of midwifery, how the structural setting of care shaped the culture of the midwife-client relationship. But the work of Davis-Floyd, Borst, and Wilson, and my own work in the Netherlands (DeVries, 1996) shows culture to be an important independent variable, promoting or discouraging midwifery.

"Cultural analysis" of birth is at once liberating and depressing. Liberating because it offers the knowledge we need to transform birth practices; depressing because the transformation requires changing deeply held values. Consider, in conclusion, an illustration. Martin (1987) presents a discussion of the metaphors we use to talk about birth, showing how these words—*reproduction, labor, progress*—reflect an industrial, capitalist mentality. True, and a bit disheartening when one realizes how our birth practices are tied to deeply ingrained economic ideas. But there is the hint of liberation here as well: it is freeing to learn that not all Western cultures use these same metaphors. The Dutch, for example, use different images when speaking of birth. Reproduction is *voortplanting*, literally "forward planting," an agricultural metaphor. When a Dutch woman is in labor, she is *aan het bevallen*, "in the act of birthing." Labor pains are *weeën*, the same word found in *heimwee*, homesickness, or more literally, the "aching" (*weeën*) for home. And the Dutch, you will recall, still use midwives and support birth at home.

In the preface I pointed out that twenty years ago we members of the alternative birth movement were full of hope, convinced we could change American obstetrics, convinced by the "rightness" of our quest. The intervening years have been discouraging, but, oddly (naively?), I am convinced that the changes we sought are inevitable. More and more the wisdom of midwifery is confirmed by epidemiology, and, more important, social and historical research is providing new understandings of the forces that prevent the wisdom of midwifery from being realized. The reestablishment of independent midwives in the United Kingdom and Canada and the use of nurse-midwives by managed care organizations in the United States are preparing the cultural soil needed to sustain a new obstetric system, a system that is characterized by love and justice, a system that makes prudent use of our resources, a system that supports women, babies, families.

Notes

Preface

1. See Goer (1995) for a review of the literature on the safety of midwife-attended birth and home birth.
2. Dutch is one of the few, if not the only, European language with a separate word, "*gezin,*" for the nuclear family. Other languages have only the more general word, "family," which must be qualified to refer to the smaller family group of mother, father and children.
3. See Pott-Buter (1993) for a discussion of the unique status of Dutch women.

Chapter 1

1. For a review of medical licensure, see Roemer (1980).
2. Serber (1975) provides evidence of a similar relationship between regulator and regulated in his study of insurance regulation (see also Nader and Serber, 1976).
3. Issues like these are seldom studied because they fall in cracks between specialty areas. The lack of communication between scholars in different areas of study is a sad fact of academic life. There are several reasons for it. First, there has been a proliferation of "scholarly material" in the form of articles, monographs, research notes, and so forth that makes it difficult to keep current in one specialty, let alone others. Second, academic reputations are built within specialty areas, not in general disciplines. Once a reputation is built, its possesser becomes an "expert" who is unwilling to become a novice elsewhere. Finally, there is little support for research that does not fall in a specific area. Most granting agencies solicit proposals only within limited areas. These proposals are in turn reviewed by experts who reinforce a system that discourages broader investigations. Such confined

academic interests have harmful consequences. Because scholars do not communicate with each other, work is needlessly repeated, valuable insights are lost, and some problems simply remain unexplored.

4. Allopathy is defined as "treatment of disease by remedies that produce effects different from or opposite to those produced by the disease." Allopathy finds its roots in an empirical philosophy of medicine. Markle and Peterson (1980: 154) outline the tenets of this approach to medicine: "The empirical tradition stresses the mechanistic nature of the organism and the foreign nature of disease. Viewing the patient as a complex machine (e.g., the heart as a pump), the physician treats localized symptoms and repairs or excises defective parts. Illness is an external imposition on the patient. Sickness is combated with drugs, and little emphasis is placed on nutrition. . . . In the empirical tradition the decisive factor in treatment is the physician himself, while the role of the patient in treating his or her own disease is downplayed." For an examination of alternative medical traditions and the manner in which allopathic practice came to dominate Western medicine, see Coulter (1973), Starr (1982), Brown (1979).

5. See also Annas (1977).

6. The ambiguity of lay midwife licensing laws leads to different conclusions regarding its legality in various states. The National Center for Health Statistics (1979: 162, 475) reports that lay midwives can practice in twenty-seven states and jurisdictions, twelve of which no longer implement their licensing laws. The Health Resources Administration (1977: 75–78) reports that nineteen states and jurisdictions have licensing laws for lay midwives, while three states permit practice without a license. Evenson (1982) reports that sixteen states prohibit lay midwifery, seventeen have licensing or registration laws, and seventeen have no law that specifically allows or prohibits the practice (see also Cohn et al., 1984). Of course, some of the variation in these numbers reflects changes in regulations over the years, but much of the confusion is the result of the lack of clarity in the existing laws.

Chapter 2

1. Because my main interest is in presenting only enough information to make it possible to investigate the history of midwife regulation, the following is a brief and incomplete summary of the midwife's history. For more detailed accounts see Forbes (1966), Donnison (1977), Donegan (1978), Litoff (1978), Kobrin (1966), Oakley (1976), Roush (1979), Wertz

and Wertz (1977). Shorter (1982: 35–176) provides a less sympathetic history of midwifery. Some interesting primary sources dealing with the nineteenth century midwife have recently been republished; see Aveling (1977a [1872]; 1977b [1882]), Hersey (1974 [1836]), Rosenberg and Smith-Rosenberg (1974).

2. In 1960, midwives were responsible for only 2.0 percent of the nation's births, and by 1974 this number was reduced to just 0.3 percent. Although this trend appears to be reversing—in 1980 midwives attended 1.7 percent of the nation's births, and in 1981 they attended 1.9 percent—midwives are primary attendants at only a fraction of all births in the United States (National Center for Health Statistics, 1979: 161; 1982; 1983; see also Jacobson, 1956; Devitt, 1977; 1979a; Litoff, 1978).

3. The term "suppression" is in quotes because although the church had the power to discipline uncertified midwives, patterns of enforcement varied and the uncertified practice of midwifery remained fairly widespread (see Donnison, 1977: 7).

4. For a feminist interpretation of the relation between witchcraft and midwifery, see Ehrenreich and English (1973).

5. Note the use of the term "medical monopoly." Donnison assumes that midwifery licensure prevented a medical monopoly; evidence here and in later chapters suggests that it created a medical monopoly instead.

6. It has been suggested that in the early 1800s licenses were obtained from the church purely for the pretense of the official authority they conferred (Donnison, 1977: 22).

7. It is interesting to speculate on the outcomes of this early municipal regulation on the current status of midwifery. Although in all industrialized countries the midwife is under the supervision of physicians, she appears to have greater independence in those countries where municipal regulation came early. It is possible that early regulation allowed midwifery to grow with the obstetric specialty, rather than in opposition to it as in Britain and the United States, where the lack of regulation sent midwives and obstetricians on separate courses.

8. Litoff (1980) has reminded me that "we do not know how early twentieth-century American midwives felt about midwife licensing." However, she goes on to state, "In contrast, during the 1940s, 1950s, and 1960s, nurse-midwives worked long and hard to obtain legal recognition. In return for public acceptance and legal recognition, they lost a fair degree of autonomy."

9. Ramsey (1977) points to some similar reasons for the difficulty of repressing all types of illegal healers in nineteenth century France.

Chapter 3

1. The CNMs this physician was supporting were seeking permission to do deliveries in a hospital; had they been doing home births we could have expected a similar or even harsher reaction by the doctor's colleagues (see *NAPSAC News,* 1981a).

2. See Jordan (1978) and Buss (1980) for descriptions of the practice of *parteras.*

3. In the original version of the TMA proposal there was a general endorsement of basic educational programs, but that section was crossed out on the copy found in Mr. Uribe's files.

4. During this same legislative session the Medical Practice Act was being rewritten under the provisions of a sunset act — an act which forces periodic review of the state law — and a few midwives expressed concern that the TMA would use that occasion to create law prohibiting the practice of midwifery. The TMA was certainly committed to maintaining and perhaps expanding the authority of physicians. A spokesman for the organization is quoted ("Doctor Warns against Review of State Board," *El Paso Times,* September 23, 1979): "If continued, the Board of Medical Examiners may be altered drastically. . . . There could be consumer members of the BME. . . . Consumerism could go rampant. . . . With the Board of Medical Examiners up for review and modification, the entire Texas Medical Practice Act could be up for grabs. And I mean grabs, rivalling the Cimarron Land Rush — in this instance a grab for turf — by every paramedical outfit you can think of, all of whom would like to practice medicine." And in fact legislative approval of the new Medical Practice Act was denied in the regular session because of a dispute over a clause allowing optometrists to use diagnostic drugs.

Chapter 4

1. The development of the alternative birth center allows for the construction of an imaginary continuum to describe the birth experiences available to the individual. The continuum extends from standard hospital births on the one hand to home birth on the other, with the ABC located somewhere between. Although this conceptualization might appear simplistic, it has great utility. For example, consider the many views on the dangers associated with birth. Those endorsing hospital birth cite the dangers of

ABCs, and feel that home birth represents an unacceptable risk. On the other hand, those espousing home birth view the ABC as a questionable compromise, and feel the intense medicalization of birth in a "pure" hospital setting is hazardous to both mother and child. Indeed, many of those choosing home birth describe a previously unsatisfactory experience in hospital birth (see also Arms 1977: chapter 5; Mehl *et al.*, 1976; 1977; Annas, 1978). And those involved in ABCs feel there are definite risks associated with both home *and* hospital births (see Brennan and Heilman, 1977: 48-51). Further, the likelihood of intervention in the birth process is practically nonexistent at a home birth and increases steadily as one approaches a "pure" hospital delivery (Mehl *et al.*, 1976; 1977). Conversely, the responsibility of the parent(s) for "getting the child born" is near zero in a standard hospital birth and almost total in a home birth. Since the majority of midwives involved in this study do not participate in the "pure" hospital birth, that end of the continuum will not be given much consideration. However, the points mentioned here will be elucidated by the comparison between the CNM and the lay midwife. More information concerning the standard obstetric birth may be found in the following sources: Danziger (1978); Kovit (1972); Macintyre (1977); Nash and Nash (1979); Oakley (1976; 1979); Rothman (1977; 1982); Shaw (1974). For more detailed information on the alternative birth center see DeVries (1979a; 1979b; 1980; 1983; 1984).

2. Gill and Horobin (1972) offer a more thorough analysis of the role played by the state in doctor-patient interaction.

3. See Shaw (1974: 39-58) for a more complete description of prenatal care given in several contexts.

4. The desire to have continuous care provided by one practitioner has proved an important factor in the decision to give birth at home in Britain (Goldthorpe and Richman, 1974).

5. In his study of lawyers and their clients, Rosenthal (1974) suggests that client participation results in more favorable outcome.

6. When a woman's cervix is dilated ten centimeters she is in the final stages of labor, ready to push her baby out. Linck is implying that in the middle of labor a woman's choice is limited.

Chapter 5

1. The woman who ran Arizona's licensing program told me it was important to have *no* unsuccessful suspension or revocation hearings: "If we

[initiate] proceedings and nothing happens, [the midwives] will have nothing to worry about."

2. The study is referred to by innumerable physicians, but not once have I been able to locate a reference to its place in publication.

Chapter 6

1. For similar statements see Hodgson (1977), Forgotson *et al.* (1970), and Forgotson and Cook (1967).

2. These social trends have caused some established midwives in Britain to question their role in birth. In 1976 a group of student midwives in Britain formed the Association of Radical Midwives (ARM) because they were "disappointed by the content of their courses, the treatment of the women they served and the role to which they were expected to adapt" (Thomas, 1978; see also ARM, 1978). Since that time their numbers have expanded, and they are active in trying to maintain a degree of independence for British midwives.

Epilogue

1. Russell (1987) claims the mortality rate for home birth is 50-100 times greater than for hospital birth! He fails to cite a source for this incredible statistic. See Tew (1990) for a detailed analysis of the safety of home birth.

References

ACNM (American College of Nurse-Midwives)
n.d.   *What Is a Nurse-Midwife?* Washington, D.C.: The American College of Nurse-Midwives.
1984   Personal communication to author, June 12.
1993   *Facts: Nurse-Midwives Historically Key Answer to Maternal Healthcare Problem.* Washington, D.C.: The American College of Nurse-Midwives.

ACOG (American College of Obstetricians and Gynecologists)
1978   *The Development of Family Centered Maternity/Newborn Care in Hospitals.* Chicago: ACOG.

Adamson, G., and D. Gare
1980   "Home or Hospital Births?" *JAMA* 243: 1732-36.

Akers, Ronald
1968   "The Professional Association and the Legal Regulation of Practice." *Law and Society Review* 2: 463-82.

Akers, Ronald, and R. Hawkins, eds.
1975   *Law and Control in Society.* Englewood Cliffs, N.J.: Prentice-Hall.

AMA (American Medical Association)
1977   "Statement on Parent and Newborn Interaction." Chicago: AMA.

Anderson, Barbara
1980   "Tarpening Preliminary Hearing Is Delayed Again: New Date— April 7." *Madera* (California) *Tribune* March 24: 1-2.

Anderson, Jim
1978   "Midwife." *The Sacramento Bee* February 26: Scene 1, 5.

Anderson, S., E. Bauwens, and E. Warner
    1978   "The Choice of Home Birth in a Metropolitan County in Ari-
            zona." *JOGN Nursing* March/April: 41 - 45.
Anisef, Paul, and P. Basson
    1979   "The Institutionalization of a Profession." *Sociology of Work
            and Occupations* 6 (3): 353 - 372.
Annas, George
    1977   "Medicolegal Aspects of Homebirth and Alternative Hospital
            Birth Methods." Paper presented at the meeting of the Ameri-
            can Public Health Association, Washington, D.C.
    1978   "Homebirth: Autonomy vs. Safety." *Hastings Center Report* 8:
            19 - 20.
Arizona State Legislature
    c.1958 *Arizona Revised Statutes*, 36-751 - 36-757. Vol. 2A, St. Paul,
            Minn.: West Pub. Co., 288 - 91.
ARM (Association of Radical Midwives)
    1978   "Why Radical?" *Association of Radical Midwives Newsletter*
            (June): 3.
    1979   "Marianne Doshi Tried and Acquitted of Murder." *Association
            of Radical Midwives Newsletter* 4: 3, 15.
Arms, Suzanne
    1977   *Immaculate Deception*. New York: Bantam.
Arney, William R.
    1982   *Power and the Profession of Obstetrics*. Chicago: University of
            Chicago Press.
Association of Texas Midwives
    1981   *Newsletter* 1: 1-6. Hawkins, Tex.: Association of Texas Mid-
            wives.
Aubert, Wilhelm
    1966   "Some Social Functions of Legislation." *Acta Sociologica* 10:
            99 - 110.
Austin Lay Midwives Association
    n.d.   "What This Is All About . . ." Austin, Tex.
Aveling, J. H.
    1977a   *English Midwives, Their History and Prospects*. New York:
    (1872) AMS Press.

1977b   *The Chamberlens and the Midwifery Forceps.* New York: AMS
(1882)   Press.
Baldwin, L., H. Hutchinson, and R. Rosenblatt
1992   "Professional Relationships between Midwives and Physicians:
         Collaboration or Conflict?" *American Journal of Public
         Health* 82 (2): 262–64.
Baldwin, Rahima
1979a   *Special Delivery: The Complete Guide to Informed Home-
         birth.* Millbrae, Calif.: Les Femmes.
1979b   "An Update on Midwifery Training." *Mothering* 12 (Summer):
         51–54.
1980   "A Call for Unity and Support." *Special Delivery* 3 (2): 3.
Banta, H. D., and S. B. Thacker
1979   "Assessing the Costs and Benefits of Electronic Fetal Monitor-
         ing." *Obstetrical and Gynecological Survey* 34 (8, Supple-
         ment): 627–42.
Baquet, Dean, and Jane Fritsch
1995   "New York's Public Hospitals Fail, and Babies Are the Victims."
         The New York Times March 5–7.
Barroso, Rebeca, and Melissa Coffey
1991   "Legal Status of Traditional Midwives—United States." Unpub-
         lished.
Bart, Pauline B.
1977   "Seizing the Means of Reproduction: An Illegal Feminist Abor-
         tion Collective—How and Why It Worked." Paper presented at
         the American Sociological Association Meetings.
Bathen, Sigrid
1978   "Home Births." *The Sacramento Bee* March 13: B1.
1979   "Nurse-Midwives Caught in a Web of Medical Politics." *The
         Sacramento Bee* March 25: A3.
Bayes, Majorie
1968   "Maternity Care in the World." Pp. 117–26 in *Report of a
         Macy Conference: The Midwife in the United States.* New
         York: Josiah Macy, Jr. Foundation.
Becker, H. S.
1964   *The Other Side.* New York: Free Press.

Becker, H., and B. Geer
    1957   "Participant Observation and Interviewing: A Comparison."
            Human Organization 16 (3): 28-32.
Beeman, Ruth, and W. K. Carlile
    n.d.   "One Year's Experience with Home Births and Licensed
            Midwives." Tempe: Arizona Department of Health Services.
Begun, J., and R. Lippincott
    1980   "The Politics of Professional Control: The Case of Optometry."
            Pp. 56-104 in J. Roth., *Research in the Sociology of Health
            Care, Volume 1.* Greenwich, Conn.: JAI Press.
Berlant, J. K.
    1975   *Profession and Monopoly.* Berkeley: University of California
            Press.
Berry, B. J.
    1980   "The Risks of Lay Midwifery." *The Sacramento Bee* Septem-
            ber 29.
Blumer, H.
    1956   "Sociological Analysis and the Variable." *American Sociologi-
            cal Review* 21: 683-90.
BMQA (Board of Medical Quality Assurance, California)
    1982   *Proposal for Revision of Section 2052 of the Medical Practice
            Act.* Sacramento, Calif.: BMQA.
Bohannan, Paul
    1965   "The Differing Realms of Law." In L. Nader, ed., *The Ethnog-
            raphy of Law.* Supplement to *American Anthropologist* 67
            (part 2): 33-42.
Bohannan, Paul, and K. Huckleberry
    1967   "Institutions of Divorce, Family and the Law." *Law and Society
            Review* 1: 81-102.
Borst, Charlotte
    1988   "The Training and Practice of Midwives: A Wisconsin Study."
            Bulletin of the History of Medicine 62 (4): 606-27.
    1989   "Wisconsin's Midwives as Working Women: Immigrant Mid-
            wives and the Limits of a Traditional Occupation, 1870-1920."
            Journal of American Ethnic History 8 (2): 24-59.
    1995   *Catching Babies: The Professionalization of Childbirth,
            1870-1920.* Cambridge, Mass.: Harvard University Press.

Bowers, John
    1981   "Homebirth on Trial." *Mothering* 19 (Spring): 69–77.
Brennan, Barbara, and Joan Heilmann
    1977   *The Complete Book of Midwifery.* New York: E. P. Dutton.
Brown, E. R.
    1979   *Rockefeller Medicine Men.* Berkeley: University of California Press.
Brownsville (Texas) Department of Public Health
    1977   Memo of Record. Unpublished.
Burnett, C. A., J. Jones, J. Rooks, C. Chen, C. Tyler, and C. A. Miller
    1980   "Home Delivery and Neonatal Mortality in North Carolina." *JAMA* 244 (24): 2741–45.
Burns, Micheal
    1978   *Partial Transcript of 995 Motion to Set Aside Indictment.* Unpublished: Merit Reporting, San Luis Obispo, Calif.
Burst, H. V.
    1995   "An Update on the Credentialing of Midwives by the ACNM." *Journal of Nurse-Midwifery* 40 (3): 290–96.
Buss, F. L.
    1980   *La Patera: Story of a Midwife.* Ann Arbor: University of Michigan Press.
Butler, J., B. Abrams, J. Parker, J. Roberts, and R. Laros
    1993   "Supportive Nurse-Midwife Care Is Associated with a Reduced Incidence of Cesarean Section." *American Journal of Obstetrics and Gynecology* 168 (5): 1407–13.
Butter, I. H., and B. J. Kay
    1988   "State Laws and the Practice of Midwifery." *American Journal of Public Health* 78 (9): 1161–69.
    1990   "Self-Certification in Lay Midwives' Organizations: A Vehicle for Professional Autonomy." *Social Science and Medicine* 30 (12): 1329–39.
Caldeyro-Barcia, Roberto
    1975   "Some Consequences of Obstetrical Interference." *Birth and the Family Journal* 2: 34–38.
California Board of Medical Quality Assurance
    1982   "Proposal for Revision of F. 2052 of the Medical Practice Act." Report, Sacramento, November 1.

CAM (California Association of Midwives) *Newsletter*
  1980   "Midwifery Hits the Courts Again." *CAM Newsletter* March 21:
          5-6.
  1981   "Northern California Minutes." *CAM Newsletter* April 21: 2-3.
  1983   "Midwives and Other Outlaws." *CAM Newsletter* September 7.
  1984   "Peer Reviews." *CAM Newsletter* Spring: 12-13.
Campbell, Donald, and H. L. Ross
  1968   "The Connecticut Crackdown on Speeding: Time Series Data
          in Quasi-experimental Analysis." *Law and Society Review* 3:
          33-54.
Campbell, Marie
  1946   *Folks Do Get Born.* New York: Rin2ehart and Company.
Carlson, Rick J.
  1970   "Health Manpower Licensing and Emerging Institutional Re-
          sponsibility for Quality of Care." *Law and Contemporary
          Problems* 35: 849-78.
Carson, M., S. Felton, S. Gloyd, S. Leuhers, M. Mansfield, J. Mertz, S. Meyers,
and S. Rivard
  1977   "A Working Lay Midwife Home Birth Program in Seattle, Wash-
          ington: A Collective Approach." Pp. 507-44 in D. Stewart and
          L. Stewart, eds., *21st Century Obstetrics Now!* Chapel Hill,
          N.C.: NAPSAC.
CBS (Centraal Bureau voor de Statistiek)
  1992   *Geborenen naar aard verloskundige hulp en plaats van ge-
          boorte, 1992* (Births by source of obstetric assistance and
          place of delivery, 1992). Voorburg, the Netherlands: CBS.
Chambliss, William
  1964   "A Sociological Analysis of the Law of Vagrancy." *Social Prob-
          lems* 12: 67-77.
Chard, Tim, and M. Richards, eds.
  1977   *Benefits and Hazards of the New Obstetrics.* Philadelphia:
          J. B. Lippincott.
Chubin, D., and K. Studer
  1978   "The Politics of Cancer." *Theory and Society* 6: 55-74.
Clements, William P.
  1979   "Proclamation by the Governor of the State of Texas, No. 41-
          1738." June 13.

Cohen, H. S., and L. Miike
    1973   *Developments in Health Manpower Licensure*. Department of Health, Education and Welfare. Publication No. (HPA) 74-3101.
Cohn, Sarah, Nancy Cuddihy, Nancy Kraus, and Sally Tom
    1984   "Legislation and Nurse-Midwifery Practice in the USA." *Journal of Nurse-Midwifery* 29 (2): 55-174.
Colombotos, John
    1969   "Physicians and Medicare: A Before-After Study of the Effects of Legislation on Attitudes." *American Sociological Review* 34: 318-32.
Comaroff, Jean
    1977   "Conflicting Paradigms of Pregnancy: Meaning Ambiguity in Antenatal Encounters." Pp. 115-34 in A. Davis and G. Horobin, eds., *Medical Encounters*. New York: St. Martin's Press.
Committee on Interstate and Foreign Commerce
    1980   *Nurse-Midwifery: Consumers' Freedom of Choice* ("The Gore Hearings"). Serial No. 96-236. Washington, D.C.: U.S. Government Printing Office.
Cook, Thomas, and D. T. Campbell
    1979   *Quasi-Experimentation: Design and Analysis Issues for Field Settings*. Chicago: Rand McNally.
Cooper, Claire
    1979   "Report Says Public Utilities, Businesses Spent Most for Lobbying." *The Sacramento Bee* September 21.
Cottrell, W. F.
    1940   *The Railroader*. Palo Alto, Calif.: Stanford University Press.
Coulter, Harris L.
    1973   *The Divided Legacy*. Washington, D.C.: Wehawken.
Daniels, A. K.
    1967   "The Low-Caste Stranger in Social Research." Pp. 267-96 in G. Sjoberg, ed., *Ethics, Politics and Social Research*. Cambridge, Mass.: Schenkman.
    1969   "The Captive Professional: Bureaucratic Limitations in the Practice of Military Psychiatry." *Journal of Health and Social Behavior* 10: 255-65.

Daniels, Shari
    1981a   "Legislation: Pro's and Con's." *National Midwives Association Newsletter* 4 (1) 7-9.
    1981b   "Editorial: Home Birth on Trial." *National Midwives Association Newsletter* 4 (1): 11.
Danziger, S. K.
    1978   *The Medical Context of Childbearing: A Study of Social Control in Doctor-Patient Interactions.* Unpublished Ph.D. dissertation, Boston University.
Davis, Fred
    1959   "The Cabdriver and His Fare: Facets of a Fleeting Relationship." *American Journal of Sociology* 65: 158-65.
    1961   "Comment on 'Initial Interaction of Newcomers to Alcoholics Anonymous'." *Social Problems* 8 (4): 364-65.
Davis-Floyd, R. E.
    1992   *Birth as an American Rite of Passage.* Berkeley: University of California Press.
DCA (California Department of Consumer Affairs)
    n.d.   *AB 1896—Fact Sheet.* Sacramento, Calif.: DCA.
    1977   *AB 1896—Background Information Paper.* Sacramento, Calif.: DCA.
    1979   *California Health Personnel Licensure Policy: New Approaches to Primary Health Care Practitioners.* Sacramento, Calif.: DCA.
DeClercq, Eugene
    1992   "The Transformation of American Midwifery: 1975-1988." *American Journal of Public Health* 82 (5): 680-84.
    1994   "The Trials of Hanna Porn: The Campaign to Abolish Midwifery in Massachusetts." *American Journal of Public Health* 84 (6): 1022-28.
DeLee, Joseph
    1920   "The Prophylactic Forceps Operation." *American Journal of Gynecology* 1: 34-44.
Department of Health (U.K.)
    1993   *Changing Childbirth* (Parts I and II). London: HSMO Publications.

Derbyshire, R. C.
1969   *Medical License and Discipline in the United States.* Baltimore: The Johns Hopkins University Press.

Deutscher, Irwin
1973   *What We Say/What We Do.* Glenview, Ill.: Scott, Foresman.

Devitt, Neal
1977   "The Transition from Home to Hospital Birth in the United States, 1930-1960." *Birth and the Family Journal* 4: 47-58.
1979a   "How Doctors Conspire to Eliminate the Midwife Even though the Scientific Data Support Midwifery." Pp. 345-70 in D. Stewart and L. Stewart, eds., *Compulsory Hospitalization: Freedom of Choice in Childbirth?* Marble Hill, Mo.: NAPSAC.
1979b   "The Statistical Case for the Elimination of the Midwife: Fact versus Prejudice, 1890-1935 (Part 1)." *Women and Health* 4 (1): 81-96.
1979c   "The Statistical Case for the Elimination of the Midwife: Fact versus Prejudice, 1890-1935 (Part 2)." *Women and Health* 4 (2): 169-86.

DeVries, Raymond G.
1979a   "Responding to Consumer Demand: A Study of Alternative Birth Centers." *Hospital Progress* 60 (10): 48-51, 68.
1979b   "The Development and Future of the Hospital-Based Alternative Birth Center." *Journal of Nurse-Midwifery* 24 (6): 37-38.
1980   "The Alternative Birth Center: Option or Cooptation?" *Women and Health* 5 (3): 47-60.
1981   "Birth and Death: Social Construction at the Poles of Existence." *Social Forces* 59: 1074-93.
1982   "Midwifery and the Problem of Licensure." Pp. 77-120 in J. Roth, ed., *Research in the Sociology of Health Care,* vol. 2: *The Changing Structure of Health Care Occupations.* Greenwich, Conn.: JAI Press.
1983   "Image and Reality: An Evaluation of Hospital Alternative Birth Centers." *Journal of Nurse-Midwifery* 28 (3): 3-10.
1984   "'Humanizing' Childbirth: The Discovery and Implementation of Bonding Theory." *International Journal of Health Services* 14 (1): 89-104.

1986   "The Contest for Control: Regulating New and Expanding Health Occupations." *American Journal of Public Health* 76 (9): 1147-51.

1996   "The Social and Cultural Context of Dutch Maternity Care: Lessons for Health Reform." *Journal of Perinatal Education,* forthcoming.

DeVries, Raymond G., and R. Barroso

1996   "Midwives among the Machines: Recreating Midwifery in the Late 20th Century." In H. Marland and A. Rafferty, eds., *Midwives, Society and Childbirth: Debates and Controversies, 1850-1995.* London: Routledge.

DHEW (Department of Health, Education, and Welfare)

1971   *Report of Licensure and Related Health Personnel Credentialing.* Publication No. (HSM) 72-11.

Divoky, Diane

1981   "Resistance: Midwives Move into Physician Territory." *The Sacramento Bee* April 29: A3.

Donegan, Jane

1978   *Women and Men Midwives: Medicine, Morality and Misogyny in Early America.* Westport, Conn.: Greenwood Press.

Donnison, Jean

1977   *Midwives and Medical Men.* London: Heinemann.

Douglas, J.

1976   *Investigative Social Research.* Beverly Hills, Calif.: Sage.

Dror, Yehezkel

1959   "Law and Social Change." *Tulane Law Review* 33: 749-801.

Durand, A. M.

1992   "The Safety of Home Birth: The Farm Study." *American Journal of Public Health* 82 (3): 450-53.

Ehrenreich, Barbara, and D. English

1973   *Witches, Midwives and Nurses: A History of Women Healers.* Oyster Bay, N.Y.: Glass Mountain Pamphlets.

Ehrlich, Eugen

1936   *Fundamental Principles of the Sociology of Law.* Cambridge, Mass.: Harvard University Press.

Ehrlich, Karen
1976   "The Santa Cruz Birth Center Today." *Birth and the Family Journal* 3: 119-26.
1981   "Editorial Response." *CAM Newsletter* July 21: 2-4.
Ellis, Shawn, Ellen Minkiff, and Patricia Weir
1980   *A Descriptive Study of Home Birth Attendants in San Diego County.* M.A. thesis, San Diego State University.
El Paso Times
1971   "Doctor Warns against Review of State Board." *El Paso Times* September 23.
Emmons, A., and J. Huntington
1911   "A Review of the Midwife Situation." *Boston Medical and Surgical Journal* 164: 251-62.
Engel, Gloria V.
1969   "The Effect of Bureaucracy on the Professional Autonomy of the Physician." *Journal of Health and Social Behavior* 10: 30-41.
Epstein, Janet, and Marion McCartney
1975   "A Home Birth Service That Works." *Birth and the Family Journal* 2: 71-75.
Erikson, Kai
1967   "A Comment on Disguised Observation in Sociology." *Social Problems* 14 (4): 366-73.
Evan, William
1962   "Law as an Instrument of Social Change." *Estudies de Sociologica* 2: 167-76.
Evenson, Debra
1982   "Midwives: Survival of An Ancient Profession." *Women's Rights Law Reporter* 7 (4): 313-30.
Ferguson, James H.
1950   "Mississippi Midwives." *Journal of the History of Medicine and Allied Sciences* 5 (1): 85-95.
Forbes, Thomas
1966   *The Midwife and the Witch.* New Haven: Yale University Press.
Forgotson, Edward, and John L. Cook
1967   "Innovation and Experiments in Uses of Health Manpower—

The Effect of Licensure Laws." *Law and Contemporary Problems* 32: 731-50.

Forgotson, E., C. Bradley, and M. Ballanger
1970   "Health Services for the Poor—The Manpower Problem: Innovations and the Law." *Wisconsin Law Review* 1970: 756-89.

Forman, Alice M.
1973   "Legislation and the Practice of Nurse-Midwifery in the United States: Patterns, Guidelines and Issues." Pp. 192-99 in A. Forman, S. Fischman, and L. Woodville, eds., *New Horizons in Midwifery*. Baltimore: Waverly Press.

Forman, Alice M., and E. M. Cooper
1976   "Legislation and Nurse-Midwifery Practice in the USA." *Journal of Nurse-Midwifery* 21 (2): 1-53.

Fox, Renee C.
1977   "The Medicalization and Demedicalization of American Society." Pp. 9-22 in J. H. Knowles, ed., *Doing Better and Feeling Worse*. New York: W. W. Norton and Company.

Freidson, Eliot
1970a   *Professional Dominance*. New York: Atherton.
1970b   *Profession of Medicine*. New York: Harper and Row.

Friedman, L. M.
1965   "Freedom of Contract and Occupational Licensing, 1890-1910: A Legal and Social Study." *California Law Review* 53: 487-534.

Friedman, Milton
1962   *Capitalism and Freedom*. Chicago: University of Chicago Press.

Gaskin, Ina May
1978   *Spiritual Midwifery*. Summertown, Tenn.: The Book Publishing Company.

Giacoia, George
1991   "Lay Midwives in Oklahoma." *Journal of the Oklahoma State Medical Association* 84 (4): 160-62.

Gibbs, Jack
1968   "Crime, Punishment and Deterrence." *Southwestern Social Science Quarterly* 48: 515-30.

Gill, D. G., and G. W. Horobin
1972   "Doctors, Patients and the State: Relationships and Decision-Making." *Sociological Review* 20: 505-20.
Glaser, B., and A. Strauss
1967   *The Discovery of Grounded Theory.* Chicago: Aldine.
Goer, Henci
1995   *Obstetric Myths versus Research Realities.* Westport, Conn.: Bergin and Garvey.
Goldthorpe, W. O., and J. Richman
1974   "Reorganization of the Maternity Services—A Comment on Domiciliary Confinement in View of the Experience of the Hospital Strike, 1973." *Midwife and Health Visitor* 10: 265-70.
Goode, W. J.
1960   "Encroachment, Charlatanism, and the Emerging Profession: Psychology, Sociology and Medicine." *American Sociological Review* 25: 902-14.
Goss, Mary E. W.
1963   "Patterns of Bureaucracy among Hospital Staff Physicians." Pp. 170-94 in E. Freidson, ed., *The Hospital in Modern Society.* New York: Free Press.
Gregory, Samuel
1974   *Man-Midwifery Exposed and Corrected* (1848) in C. Rosenberg and C. Smith-Rosenberg, eds., *The Male Midwife and the Female Doctor.* New York: Arno Press.
Gyarmati, Gabriel
1975   "The Doctrine of the Professions: Basis of a Power Structure." *International Social Science Journal* 27: 645-57.
Hafner-Eaton, C., and L. K. Pearce
1994   "Birth Choices, the Law and Medicine: Balancing Individual Freedoms and Protection of the Public's Health." *Journal of Health Politics, Policy and Law* 19 (4): 813-35.
Haire, Doris
1972   *The Cultural Warping of Childbirth.* Seattle: International Childbirth Education Association.
1981   "Improving the Outcomes of Pregnancy through Increased Utilization of Midwives." *Journal of Nurse-Midwifery* 26 (1): 5-8.

Hall, Jerome
1952   *Theft, Law and Society.* Indianapolis: Bobbs-Merrill.
Handler, Joel
1978   *Social Movements and the Legal System.* New York: Academic Press.
Hanson, Bill
1980   "An Ethnography of Power Relations: Consumers and Providers on a Health Systems Council." Pp. 137-78 in J. Roth, ed., *Research in the Sociology of Health Care,* vol. 1. Greenwich, Conn.: JAI Press.
Hart, Nicky
1977   "Parenthood and Patienthood: A Dialectical Autobiography." Pp. 98-114 in A. David and G. Horobin, eds., *Medical Encounters: The Experience of Illness and Treatment.* New York: St. Martin's Press.
Hazell, Lester
1974   *Birth Goes Home.* Seattle: Catalyst Publishing Company.
1976   *Commonsense Childbirth.* New York: Berkley Publishing.
Health Resources Administration
1977   *State Regulation of Health Manpower.* Washington, D.C.: Public Health Service.
Heaton, C. E.
1935   *Modern Motherhood.* New York: Farrar and Rinehart, Inc.
Heinz, John P., and E. Laumann
1982   *Chicago Lawyers: The Social Structure of the Bar.* New York: Russell Sage Foundation and Chicago: The American Bar Foundation.
Hendrix, Kathleen
1980   "Madera Midwife Faces Murder Charge." *Los Angeles Times* April 7: Part V, pp. 1, 7-9.
Her-Self
1976   "Santa Cruz Center Victory." *Her-Self* 5 (July): 4.
Hersey, Thomas
1974   *The Midwife's Practical Directory.* New York: Arno Press.
(1836)

Hinds, M., G. Bergeisen, and D. Allen
    1985   "Neonatal Outcome in Planned vs. Unplanned Out-of-Hospital
            Births in Kentucky." *JAMA* 253: 1578-82.
Hingstman, Lammert
    1994   "Primary Care Obstetrics and Perinatal Health in the Nether-
            lands." *Journal of Nurse-Midwifery* 39 (6): 379-86.
Hitchcock, James
    1967   "A Sixteenth Century Midwife's License." *Bulletin of the His-
            tory of Medicine* 41: 75-76.
Hodgson, Ellen L.
    1977   "Restrictions on Unorthodox Health Treatment in California:
            A Legal and Economic Analysis." *UCLA Law Review* 24:
            647-96.
Holmes, Linda
    n.d.   "Alabama Midwife Paper." Unpublished. Newark: University of
            Medicine and Dentistry of New Jersey.
Holmes, O. W.
    1897   "The Path of Law." *Harvard Law Review* 10: 457-78.
Holt, M.
    1969   "Mothers Don't Make Better Midwives." *Nursing Mirror*
            June 13: 24.
HOME (Home Oriented Maternity Experience)
    1976   *State Regulation of Lay and Nurse Midwives.* Washington,
            D.C.: Women's Rights Project of the Center for Law and Social
            Policy.
Horwitz, Eve
    1979   "Of Love and Laetrile: Medical Decision-Making and a Child's
            Best Interests." *American Journal of Law and Medicine* 5:
            271-94.
Hosford, E.
    1976   "The Home Birth Movement." *Journal of Nurse-Midwifery* 21:
            27-30.
Howard, J., F. Davis, C. Pope, and S. Ruzek
    1977   "Humanizing Health Care: The Implications of Technology."
            Medical Care 15: 11-26.

Hunter, Mark
1980   "Mothers and Outlaws." *New West* 5 (25): 61-77.
Hurst, J. W.
1950   *The Growth of American Law.* Boston: Little Brown and Company.
Hurst, John
1978   "Charges in Midwife Case Dismissed." *Los Angeles Times* October 21: Part II, p. 1.
Hyman, H., and P. Sheatsley
1964   "Attitudes toward Desegregation." *Scientific American* 211 (July): 16-23.
Illich, I.
1976   *The Medical Nemesis.* New York: Pantheon.
Iowa Law Review
1972   "Regulation of Health Personnel in Iowa—A Distortion of Public Interest." *Iowa Law Review* 57: 1104-62.
Jacobson, Paul
1956   "Hospital Care and the Vanishing Midwife." *The Milbank Memorial Fund Quarterly* 34: 253-61.
Jewson, Norman
1976   "The Disappearance of the Sick Man from Medical Cosmology, 1770-1870." *Sociology* 10 (2): 225-44.
Johnson, Amos N.
1968   "Comments." Pp. 94-95 in *Report of Macy Conference: The Midwife in the United States.* New York: Josiah Macy, Jr. Foundation.
Jordan, Brigitte
1978   *Birth in Four Cultures.* St. Albans, Vt.: Eden Press.
Josiah Macy, Jr. Foundation
1968   *The Midwife in the United States.* New York: Josiah Macy, Jr. Foundation.
Journal of Nurse-Midwifery
1975   "Joint Statement on Maternity Care." *Journal of Nurse-Midwifery* 20 (Fall): 15.
Kantorowicz, H.
1958   *The Definition of Law.* New York: Cambridge University Press.

Kaplin, William A.
1976   "Professional Power and Judicial Review: The Health Profes-
        sions." *George Washington Law Review* 44: 708-24.
Karlin, Rick
1994   "Midwives Stunned by Law." *Albany Times Union* Janu-
        ary 25: C1.
Katz, Barbara
1980   "Childbirth and the Law." *Colorado Medicine* 77 (2): 64-68.
Keplinger, John
1977   "$40 Million Spent to Influence State Government." Report.
        Sacramento, Calif.: Fair Political Practices Commission Au-
        gust 17.
King, Laura
1981   "Midwives' Uneasy Truce in Jeopardy." *Contra Costa Times*
        July 10: 4A.
King, Peter, and Richard Saltus
1978   "Midwife Faces Murder Charge in Home-birth Tragedy." *San
        Francisco Sunday Examiner and Chronicle* June 9: 4.
Klaus, Marshall, and J. Kennell
1976   *Maternal-Infant Bonding.* St. Louis: Mosby.
1981   *Parent-Infant Bonding.* St. Louis: Mosby.
Knoll, E.
1967   "Ten Years of Deliberate Speed." In H. Gold and F. Scarpetti,
        eds., *Combatting Social Problems.* New York: Holt Rinehart
        and Winston.
Knox, Richard A.
1984   "Midwife's RN License Suspended." *Boston Globe* January 29:
        21, 25.
Kobrin, Frances E.
1966   "The American Midwife Controversy: A Crisis of Professional-
        ization." *Bulletin of the History of Medicine* 40: 350-63.
Korte, Diana
1995   "Midwives on Trial." *Mothering* 76 (Fall): 52-63.
Kovit, L.
1972   "Labor Is Hard Work: Notes on the Social Organization of
        Childbirth." *Sociological Symposium* 8: 11-21.

Krause, Elliot
1977   *Power and Illness: The Political Sociology of Health and Medical Care*. New York: Elsevier.
Krisman, Michael
n.d.   Personal communication regarding California Assembly Bill, 1896.
Lang, Raven
1972   *Birth Book*. Palo Alto, Calif.: Genesis Press.
Larkin, G. V.
1978   "Medical Dominance and Control: Radiographers in the Division of Labour." *Sociological Review* 26: 843–58.
1981   "Professional Autonomy and the Opthalmic Optician." *Sociology of Health and Illness* 3: 15–30.
1983   *Occupational Monopoly and Modern Medicine*. London: Tavistock.
Larson, M. S.
1977   *The Rise of Professionalism*. Berkeley: University of California Press.
Lasch, C.
1978   *The Culture of Narcissism*. New York: Norton.
Laurillard-Lampe, Paula
1981   "Giving Birth in Holland in a Time of Changes." *Association of Radical Midwives Newsletter* 9 (February): 10–12.
Lee, F. E., and J. Glasser
1974   "Role of Lay Midwifery in Maternity Care in a Large Metropolitan Area." *Public Health Reports* 89: 537–44.
Lerner, Max
1943   *The Mind and Faith of Justice Holmes*. New York: Random House.
Linck, Kathy
1973   "Legalizing a Woman's Right to Choose." P. 26 in *Proceedings of the First International Childbirth Conference*. Stamford, Conn.
Litoff, Judy B.
1978   *American Midwives—1860 to the Present*. Westport, Conn.: Greenwood Press.

1980   Personal correspondence to author. July 16.
1986   *The American Midwife Debate.* Westport, Conn.: Greenwood Press.
Lofland, J.
1961   "Reply to Davis' Comment on 'Initial Interaction.'" *Social Problems* 8 (4): 365-67.
1971   *Analyzing Social Settings.* Englewood Cliffs, N.J.: Prentice-Hall.
Longbrake, Martha, and William Longbrake
1976   "Control Is the Key." Pp. 154-60 in D. Stewart and L. Stewart, eds., *Safe Alternatives in Childbirth.* Chapel Hill, N.C.: NAPSAC.
Lyon, Pamela
1979   "Truan Presses Investigation of Pregnant Woman's Death." *Corpus Christi Caller* March 17: 14.
McCallum, W.
1979   "The El Paso Maternity Center." *Birth and the Family Journal* 6: 259-66.
McCleery, Robert S., *et al.*
1971   *One Life—One Physician: An Inquiry into the Medical Profession's Performance in Self-Regulation.* Washington, D.C.: Public Affairs Press.
McKinley, John B.
1973   "On the Professional Regulation of Change." Pp. 61-84 in P. Halmos, ed., *Professionalization and Social Change.* The Sociological Review Monograph, No. 20.
McQuarrie, H. G.
1980   "Home Delivery Controversy" (editorial). *JAMA* 243: 1747-48.
MAACC (Maine Access to Alternatives in Childbirth Care)
1980   *MAACC Newsletter: A Survey of Current Midwifery Legislation Activity in the U.S.* No. 12. Dixmont, Me.: MAACC.
MAC (Midwifery Advisory Council)
n.d.   *The Midwifery Advisory Council.* Sacramento, Calif.: DCA.
Macintyre, Sally
1977   "The Management of Childbirth: A Review of Sociological Research Issues." *Social Science and Medicine* 11: 477-84.

MANA (Midwives' Alliance of North America)
n.d.   *The North American Registry of Midwives*. Newton, Kans.: MANA.

Marieskind, H.
1979   *An Evaluation of Caesarean Section in the United States*. Washington, D.C.: Department of Health, Education and Welfare.

Markle, G., and J. Peterson, eds.
1980   *Politics, Science and Cancer: The Laetrile Phenomenon*. Boulder, Col.: Westview Press.

Marsico, Teresa
1995   "All the News That's Fit to Print: The ACNM Sets the Record Straight." *Journal of Nurse-Midwifery* 40 (3): 253-55.

Martin, Emily
1987   *The Woman in the Body: A Cultural Analysis of Reproduction*. Boston: Beacon Press.

Massell, Gregory
1968   "Law as an Instrument of Change in a Traditional Milieu: The Case of Soviet Central Asia." *Law and Society Review* 2: 179-211.

Mathews, J. J., and K. Zadak
1991   "The Alternative Birth Movement in the United States: History and Current Status." *Women and Health* 17 (1): 39-56.

MCAP (Midwifery Communication and Accountability Project)
n.d.   "Midwifery: The Heart of Maternity Care Reform." Newton Highlands, Mass.: MCAP.

Mehl, L.
1976   "Statistical Outcomes of Homebirths in the United States: Current Status." Pp. 545-52 in D. Stewart and L. Stewart, eds., *Safe Alternatives in Childbirth*. Chapel Hill, N.C.: NAPSAC.

Mehl, L., L. A. Leavitt, G. H. Peterson, and D. C. Creevy
1976   "Home Birth versus Hospital Birth: Comparisons of Outcomes of Matched Populations." Paper presented at the meetings of the American Public Health Association, Miami.

Mehl, L., G. H. Peterson, M. Whitt, and W. Hawes
1977   "Outcomes of Elective Home Births: A Series of 1,146 Cases." *The Journal of Reproductive Medicine* 19: 281-90.

Mehl Madrona, M., and L. Mehl Madrona
1993   "The Future of Midwifery in the United States." *NAPSAC News*
        18 (3-4): 1-32.
Mendelsohn, R.
1979   *Confessions of a Medical Heretic.* New York: Contemporary
        Books.
Merton, Robert
1957   "The Role-set." *British Journal of Sociology* 8: 106-20.
Mertz, Thya
1977   "A Working Lay Midwife Home Birth Center, Madison, Wiscon-
        sin." Pp. 545-52 in D. Stewart and L. Stewart, eds., *21st Cen-
        tury Obstetrics Now!* Chapel Hill, N.C.: NAPSAC.
Milinaire, C.
1974   *Birth.* New York: Harmony Books.
Millman, Marcia
1977   *The Unkindest Cut.* New York: William Morrow and Company.
Mills, Nancy
1977   "A Midwife's Story." Pp. 47-52 in C. Ward and F. Ward, *The
        Home Birth Book.* Garden City, N.Y.: Doubleday.
Mitford, Jessica
1992   *The American Way of Birth.* New York: Penguin.
Mongeau, B., H. L. Smith, and A. C. Maney
1961   "The Granny Midwife: Changing Roles and Functions of
        a Folk Practitioner." *American Journal of Sociology* 66:
        497-505.
Montgomery, M. R.
1982   "Making Medicine News." *Boston Globe Magazine* March 28:
        12-13, 16, 20, 23, 27, 30.
Moorhead, Jean
1978   Speech delivered at Alternatives in Childbirth Conference, Na-
        tividad Hospital, Salinas, Calif., February 24.
Mothering
1979   "Legalities." *Mothering* 10 (Winter): 71-72.
Myers, Harold B.
1970   "The Medical-Industrial Complex." *Fortune* 81 (January):
        90-91ff.

Myers, S. J., and J. Myers-Ciecko
    1989   "Professional Midwifery." *American Journal of Public Health*
            79 (4): 520.
Myers, S. J., P. St. Clair, S. Gloyd, P. Salzberg, and J. Myers-Ciecko
    1990   "Unlicensed Midwifery Practice in Washington State." *American Journal of Public Health* 80 (6): 726-28.
Nader, L., and D. Serber
    1976   "Law and the Distribution of Power." Pp. 273-91 in L. Coser
            and O. Larsen, eds., *The Uses of Controversy in Sociology.*
            New York: Free Press.
NAPSAC (National Association of Parents and Professionals for Safe Alternatives in Childbirth)
    1980a   "Midwife Charged with First Degree Murder in Stillbirth." *NAPSAC News* 5 (Spring): 11, 23.
    1980b   "Midwife Exonerated of Murder Charge." *NAPSAC News* 5
            (Winter): 1-2.
    1981a   "The Conspiracy of Doctors Against Doctors." *NAPSAC News* 6
            (Spring): 1-9.
    1981b   "Midwife Brought to Court a 3rd Time for Same Incident."
            NAPSAC News 6 (Summer): 12.
Nash, A., and J. Nash
    1979   "Conflicting Interpretations of Childbirth: The Medical and
            Natural Perspectives." *Urban Life* 7: 493-511.
National Center for Health Statistics
    1969   *State Licensing of Health Occupations.* Washington, D.C.
    1979   *Health Resources Statistics, 1976-77.* Hyattsville, Md.
    1981   *Vital Statistics of the United States, 1977: Vol. 1 — Natality.*
            Hyattsville, Md.
    1983   *Monthly Vital Statistics Report* 32 (December 29): 9, supplement. Hyattsville, Md.
    1994   "Advance Report of Final Natality Statistics, 1992." *Monthly
            Vital Statistics Report* 43 (October 25): 5, supplement. Hyattsville, Md.
National Commission on Nurse-Midwifery Education
    1993   *Education of Nurse Midwives: A Strategy for Achieving Affordable, High-Quality Maternity Care.* Washington, D.C.: ACNM.

Newman, Eric
    1976   "Family Law—Constitutional Right of Privacy: The Father in the Delivery Room." *North Carolina Law Review* 54: 1297-1307.
Niemiec, Dennis
    1994   "Baby's Death Sparks Battle." *Detroit Free Press* October 3: 1A.
Oakley, Ann
    1976   "Wise Woman and Medicine Man: Changes in the Management of Childbirth." Pp. 17-58 in J. Mitchell and A. Oakley, eds., *The Rights and Wrongs of Women.* Harmondsworth, Eng.: Penguin Books.
    1977   "Cross-cultural Practices." Pp. 18-33 in T. Chard and M. Richards, eds., *Benefits and Hazards of the New Obstetrics.* Philadelphia: J. B. Lippincott.
    1979   "A Case of Maternity: Paradigms of Women as Maternity Cases." *Signs: A Journal of Women in Culture and Society* 4: 607-31.
    1980   *Women Confined: Towards a Sociology of Childbirth.* New York: Schocken Books.
Odessa (Texas) *American*
    1979   "Bill Calls for Midwife Training, Regulation." *Odessa American* April 5.
Office of Technology Assessment
    1978   *Assessing the Efficacy and Safety of Medical Technologies.* Washington, D.C.: Office of Technology Assessment.
Ortman-Glick, Stephanie
    1978   "A Look at Lay-Midwifery in Austin, Texas." *Journal of Nurse-Midwifery* 22 (4): 39-45.
Ostling, R. N.
    1984   "Matters of Faith and Death." *Time* 123 (April 16): 42.
Parker, Jennifer
    1994   "Ethnic Differences in Midwife-Attended US Births." *American Journal of Public Health* 84 (7): 1139-41.
Pearse, Warren H.
    1979   "Home Birth." *Journal of the American Medical Association* 241 (March 8): 1039-41.

1980   "Burden of Proof." *Montgomery County* (Texas) *Courier* August 10: 16.

1987   "Parturition: Places and Priorities." *American Journal of Public Health* 77 (8): 923-24.

Pel, M., and M. H. B. Heres
1995   *OBINT: A Study of Obstetric Intervention.* The Hague: CIP-Koninklijke Bibliotheek.

Peterson, Fred W.
1947   *Desert Pioneer Doctor and Experiences in Obstetrics.* Calexico, Calif.: Calexico Chronicle.

Peterson, Karen
1983   "Technology as the Last Resort in Home Birth: The Work of Lay Midwives." *Social Problems* 30 (3): 272-83.

Petit, Charles
1978   "Growing Dispute on Midwifery." *San Francisco Chronicle* July 19: 2.

Petrelli, Richard L.
1971   "The Regulation of French Midwifery during the Ancient Regime." *Journal of the History of Medicine* 26: 276-92.

Philpott, Loralee
1979   *A Descriptive Study of Birth Practices and Midwifery in the Lower Rio Grande Valley of Texas.* Ph.D. dissertation. University of Texas, Houston.

Pickens, Ace
1979   "Medicine and the Law: Attorney General's Opinions—Advanced Nurse Practitioners and Midwives." *Texas Medicine* 75 (April): 25-26.

Pott-Buter, H. A.
1993   *Facts and Fairy Tales about Female Labor, Family and Fertility.* Amsterdam: Amsterdam University Press.

Pound, Roscoe
1923   *Interpretations of Legal History.* New York: Macmillan Company.

Practicing Midwife
1981   "Regional Reports." *Practicing Midwife.* Summertown, Tenn.: 1 (12): 12.

Public Affairs Research Group
    n.d.   *Public Regulation of Health Care Occupations in California.*
             Sacramento, Calif.: Public Affairs Research Group.
Raboy, Barbara
    1980   Letter to the California Department of Consumer Affairs. May 8.
Ramsey, Matthew
    1977   "Medical Power and Popular Medicine: Illegal Healers in Nine-
             teenth-Century France." Pp. 183–210 in P. Branca, ed., *The
             Medicine Show.* New York: Science History Publication.
Record, Jane C., and Harold R. Cohen
    1972   "The Introduction of Midwifery in a Prepaid Group Practice."
             American Journal of Public Health 62: 354–60.
Record, Jane C., and M. R. Greenlick
    1976   "New Health Professionals and the Physician Role: An Hypoth-
             esis from the Kaiser Experience." *Journal of Nurse-Midwifery*
             21: 7–12.
Relman, Arnold S.
    1980   "The New Medical-Industrial Complex." *The New England
             Journal of Medicine* 303 (17): 953–70.
Rich, Adrienne
    1976   *Of Woman Born.* New York: W. W. Norton and Company.
Roback, Gene, L. Randolph, and B. Seidman
    1993   *Physician Characteristics and Distribution in the U.S., 1993
             Edition.* Chicago: American Medical Society.
Roberts, R. S.
    1962   "The Personnel of Medicine in Tudor and Stuart Times." *Med-
             ical History* 6: 363–64.
Roemer, Ruth
    1973   "Legal Systems Regulating Health Personnel: A Comparative
             Analysis." Pp. 233–273 in J. B. McKinley, ed., *Politics and Law
             in Health Care Policy.* New York: Prodist.
    1980   "Regulation of Health Personnel." Pp. 97–128 in R. Roemer
             and G. McKray, eds., *Legal Aspects of Health Policy.* Westport,
             Conn.: Greenwood Press.
Rooks, J. P., and K. C. Carr
    1995   "Criteria for Accreditation of Direct-Entry Midwifery Educa-
             tion." *Journal of Nurse-Midwifery* 40 (3): 297–303.

Rooks, J., S. Fischman, E. Kaplan, P. Leseynski, G. Morgan, and J. Witek
1978   *Nurse-Midwifery in the United States, 1976-1977.* Washington, D.C.: American College of Nurse-Midwives.

Rooks, J. P., N. Weatherby, E. Ernst, S. Stapelton, D. Rosen, and A. Rosenfeld
1989   "Outcomes of Care in Birth Centers: The National Birth Center Study." *New England Journal of Medicine* 321 (26): 1804-11.

Rosenberg, C., and C. Smith-Rosenberg, eds.
1974   *The Male Midwife and the Female Doctor.* New York: Arno Press.

Rosenberger, Lani
1983   "Peer Review?" *CAM Newsletter* September-October: 1.

Rosengren, W. R., and S. DeVault
1963   "The Sociology of Time and Space in an Obstetric Hospital." Pp. 266-92 in E. Freidson, ed., *The Hospital in Modern Society.* New York: Free Press.

Rosenthal, D. E.
1974   *Lawyer and Client: Who's in Charge?* New York: Russell Sage Foundation.

Roth, Julius A.
n.d.   "Comment on AB 1896." Unpublished report.
1962   "Comments on Secret Observation." *Social Problems* 9 (3): 283-84.
1963   *Timetables.* Indianapolis: Bobbs-Merrill.
1972   "The Necessity and Control of Hospitalization." *Social Science and Medicine* 6: 425-46.
1977   *Health Purifiers and Their Enemies.* New York: Prodist.

Rothman, Barbara Katz
1977   "The Social Construction of Birth." *Journal of Nurse-Midwifery* 22: 9-13.
1982   *In Labor: Women and Power in the Birthplace.* New York: W. W. Norton.
1983   "Midwives in Transition: The Structure of a Clinical Revolution." *Social Problems* 30 (3): 262-71.

Roush, Robert E.
1979   "The Development of Midwifery—Male and Female, Yesterday and Today." *Journal of Nurse-Midwifery* 24 (3): 27-37.

Roy, Donald F.
1959   "'Banana Time': Job Satisfaction and Informal Interaction." *Human Organization* 18: 158-68.
Rubin, Daniel
1976   *California State Policy for Home Birth, Nurse Midwives, and Lay Midwives.* M.A. thesis, University of California, Berkeley.
Rueschemeyer, Dietrich
1964   "Doctors and Lawyers: A Comment on the Theory of the Professions." *Canadian Review of Sociology and Anthropology* 1: 17.
Runnerstrom, Lillian
1968   "Midwifery and the Nursing Profession." Pp. 89-93 in *A Report of a Macy Conference: The Midwife in the United States.* New York: Josiah Macy, Jr. Foundation.
Russell, Keith
1987   "Midwives: A Review of *Regulating Birth: Midwives, Medicine and the Law." JAMA* 257 (2): 252-53.
Ruzek, Sheryl B.
1978   *The Women's Health Movement: Feminist Alternatives to Medical Control.* New York: Praeger Publishers.
Rybczynski, Witold
1986   *Home: A Short History of an Idea.* New York: Penguin.
Sacramento Bee
1980   "Editorial." *Sacramento Bee* July 8.
1981a   "Murder Charge against Midwife Refiled in Death of Newborn Boy." *Sacramento Bee* April 8: B14.
1981b   "Court Victory for Midwife." *Sacramento Bee* May 2: B8.
Sakala, Carol
1993   "Midwifery Care and Out-of-Hospital Birth Settings: How Do They Reduce Unnecessary Cesarean Section Births?" *Social Science and Medicine* 37 (10): 1233-50.
Sallomi, Pacia, A. Pallow, and P. O'Mara McMahon
1981   *Midwifery and the Law.* Albuquerque, N.M.: Mothering Publications.
San Antonio Light
1979   "Midwife Charged in Baby's Death." *San Antonio Light* February 25: 1.

San Francisco Chronicle
   1978a   "Midwife Cleared in Murder Case." *San Francisco Chronicle*
           October 21: 1, 14.
   1978b   "A Midwifery Crisis Case." *San Francisco Chronicle* Octo-
           ber 29: *This World Magazine.*
   1981   "30 Days in Jail for Midwife—Illegal Practice." *San Francisco
           Chronicle* May 24: 23.
Schama, Simon
   1988   *The Embarrassment of Riches.* Berkeley: University of Califor-
           nia Press.
Schatzman, L., and A. Strauss
   1973   *Field Research: Strategies for Natural Sociology.* Englewood
           Cliffs, N.J.: Prentice-Hall.
Schrag, Peter
   1978   "Midwifery: A Misdemeanor Called Murder." *The Sacramento
           Bee* July 16: F1.
Schramm, W. F., D. Barnes, and J. Bakewell
   1987   "Neonatal Mortality in Missouri Home Births, 1978–84." *Amer-
           ican Journal of Public Health* 77 (8): 930–35.
Schwartz, Richard D., and James C. Miller
   1964   "Legal Evolution and Societal Complexity." *American Journal
           of Sociology* 70: 159–69.
Scott, William C.
   1980   "Lay Midwives: Some Solutions to a Serious Problem." *Contem-
           porary OB/Gyn* 16 (3): 37–53.
Scully, Diana
   1980   *Men Who Control Women's Health.* Boston: Houghton Mifflin.
Serber, David
   1975   "Reforming Regulation: The Social Organization of Insurance
           Regulation." *Insurgent Sociologist* 5: 83–105.
Shaw, Nancy
   1974   *Forced Labor: Maternity Care in the United States.* New York:
           Pergamon.
Shorter, Edward
   1982   *A History of Women's Bodies.* New York: Basic Books.

Shyrock, Richard H.
    1967   *Medical Licensing in America, 1650-1965.* Baltimore: The
            Johns Hopkins University Press.
Sigerist, Henry
    1935   "The History of Medical Licensure." *Journal of the American
            Medical Association* 104 (March 30): 1056-60.
Skolnick, Jerome, and J. Dombrink
    1978   "The Legalization of Deviance." *Criminology* 16: 193-208.
Solares, Allan
    n.d.(a)   "A Birthing Renaissance." Unpublished manuscript.
    n.d.(b)   "The Struggle for Dominance: Orthodox vs. Unorthodox Medi-
               cine." Unpublished manuscript.
    1983   "Balancing the Goals of Consumer Protection, Self-Determina-
            tion and Competition in Health Occupational Regulation." M.A.
            thesis, University of California, Berkeley.
Sousa, Marion
    1976   *Childbirth at Home.* Englewood Cliffs, N.J.: Prentice-Hall.
Speert, Harold
    1968   "Midwifery in Retrospect." Pp. 163-77 in *Report of a Macy
            Conference: The Midwife in the United States.* New York:
            Josiah Macy, Jr. Foundation.
Springer, Eric
    1973   "Law and Medicine: Reflections on a Metaphysical Misalliance."
            Pp. 201-31 in J. McKinlay, ed., *Politics and Law in Health
            Care Policy.* New York: Prodist.
Stanwick, W.
    1977   Letter to Representative Chris Miller. March 29.
Starr, Paul
    1982   *The Social Transformation of American Medicine.* New York:
            Basic Books.
Stern, Susan
    1978   "Doctors vs. Midwives: The Crackdown on Home Birth." *In-
            quiry* 2 (December 25): 17-20.
Stevens, Rosemary
    1971   *American Medicine and the Public Interest.* New Haven: Yale
            University Press.

Stewart, David
    1981   "An Editorial Commentary on the New Law." *NAPSAC News* 6
            (2): 21.
Stewart, David, and Lee Stewart, eds.
    1976   *Safe Alternatives in Childbirth.* Chapel Hill, N.C.: NAPSAC.
    1977   *21st Century Obstetrics Now!* vols. 1-2. Chapel Hill, N.C.:
            NAPSAC.
Stone, Deborah
    1980   *The Limits of Professional Power.* Chicago: University of
            Chicago Press.
Streck, D. W.
    n.d.   *"Midwifery in Texas: An Overview."* Unpublished paper,
            Division of Maternal and Child Health, Texas Department of
            Health, Austin.
Sullivan, Deborah A., and Ruth Beeman
    1983   "Four Years' Experience with Home Birth by Licensed Mid-
            wives in Arizona." *American Journal of Public Health* 73 (6):
            641-45.
Sullivan, D., and R. Weitz
    1988   *Labor Pains: Modern Midwives and Home Birth.* New Haven,
            Conn.: Yale University Press.
Sumner, W. G.
    1960   *Folkways.* New York: New American Library.
    (1906)
Tew, M.
    1990   *A Safer Birth: A Critical History of Maternity Care.* New York:
            Routledge.
Texas Department of Health
    n.d.   "Legal Status of the Practice of Midwifery in Texas." Inter-office
            memo, Texas Department of Health, Austin.
    1976   *Vernon's Annotated Revised Civil Statutes of the State of
            Texas,* vol. 12C, Art. 4465-4477, Health-Public, St. Paul, Minn.:
            West Pub. Co.
Thomas, Jen
    1978   Personal communication to author.
    1979   "Extracts from a Review of the Fifth International Congress of

Psychosomatic Obstetrics and Gynecology." *Association of Radical Midwives Newsletter* 4: 14-15.

Tittle, Charles
1969   "Crime Rates and Legal Sanction." *Social Problems* 16: 409-22.

Tjaden, Patricia
1987   "Midwifery in Colorado: A Case Study in the Politics of Professionalization." *Qualitative Sociology* 10 (1): 29-45.

van Arkel, W. G., A. J. Ament, and N. Bell
1980   "The Politics of Home Delivery in the Netherlands." *Birth and the Family Journal* 7 (2): 101-12.

van Daalen, R.
1988   "De groei van ziekenhuisbevalling: Nederland en het buitenland" (The growth of hospital birth in the Netherlands and elsewhere). *Amsterdams Sociologisch Tijdschrijft* 15 (3): 414-45.
1993   "Family Change and Continuity in the Netherlands: Birth and Childbed in Text and Art." Pp. 77-94 in E. Abraham, ed., *Successful Home Birth and Midwifery: The Dutch Model.* Westport, Conn.: Bergin and Garvey.

Ventre, Fran
1976   "The Making of a Legalized Lay Midwife." *Birth and the Family Journal* 3: 109-15.

Wagner, Marsden
1995   "Don't Blame Midwives in Maternity Care Crisis." *The New York Times* March 13: A18.

Walker, Jean
1972   "The Changing Role of the Midwife." *International Journal of Nursing Studies* 9: 85-94.

Ward, Fred, and Charlotte Ward
1977   *The Home Birth Book.* Garden City, N.Y.: Doubleday.

Ward, Lester
1906   *Applied Sociology.* Boston: Ginn.

Wardwell, Walter
1972   "Limited, Marginal and Quasi-Practitioners." Pp. 250-72 in H. Freeman, S. Levine, and L. Reeder, eds., *Handbook of Medical Sociology.* Englewood Cliffs, N.J.: Prentice-Hall.

Warpinski, D. H., and C. J. Adams
1979   "Characteristics of Applicants to Nurse-Midwifery Educational Programs." *Journal of Nurse-Midwifery* 24 (4): 5-9.
Watson, J.
1979   "Attending Doctors, Lay Midwife Agree: Woman's Death 'Totally Preventable.'" *El Paso Times* July 19.
Weber, Max
1954   *Max Weber on Law in Economy and Society.* Max Rheinstein, ed. Cambridge, Mass.: Harvard University Press.
Wertz, Richard W., and D. C. Wertz
1977   *Lying-In: A History of Childbirth in America.* New York: Free Press.
White, William D.
1979   *Public Health and Private Gain.* Chicago: Maaroufa Press.
WICP (Women's Institute for Childbearing Policy)
1994   *Childbearing Policy within a National Health Program: An Evolving Consensus for New Directions.* Boston: WICP.
Wigginton, Eliot
1973   *Foxfire 2.* Garden City, N.Y.: Doubleday.
Wilcox, Donald P. "Rocky"
1981   "Medicine and the Law: Midwives in Texas." *Texas Medicine* 77 (February): 80-81.
Wile, Ira S.
1912   "Immigration and the Midwife Problem." *Boston Medical and Surgical Journal* 167 (4): 113-15.
Williston, C. Lincoln
1980   Letter to director of the Laredo-Webb County Health Department. January 30.
Wilson, Adrian
1995   *The Making of Man-Midwifery.* Cambridge, Mass.: Harvard University Press.
Wolfson, C.
1986   "Midwives and Home Birth: Social, Medical, and Legal Perspectives." *Hastings Law Journal* 37: 909-67.
Woodland Daily Democrat
1980   "Birth Attendant Cited." *Woodland* (California) *Daily Democrat* February 22: 2.

Woodward, B., and Scott Armstrong
  1979   *The Brethren.* New York: Simon and Schuster.
Woodward, C. V.
  1966   *The Strange Career of Jim Crow.* New York: Oxford University
          Press.
Yankauer, Alfred
  1983   "The Valley of the Shadow of Birth." *American Journal of Pub-
          lic Health* 73 (6): 635–38.
Yankelovich, Daniel
  1981   *New Rules: Searching for Self-Fulfillment in a World Turned
          Upside Down.* New York: Random House.
Yedida, M.
  1980   "The Lay-Professional Division of Knowledge in Health Care
          Delivery." Pp. 355–66 in J. Roth, ed., *Research in the Sociol-
          ogy of Health Care,* vol. 1. Greenwich, Conn.: JAI Press.
Zola, Irving K.
  1972   "Medicine as an Institution of Social Control." *Sociological Re-
          view* 20: 487–504.
  1975   "In the Name of Health and Illness: On Some Socio-political
          Consequences of Medical Influence." *Social Science and Medi-
          cine* 9: 83–87.

Index

A

"Abnormalization" of birth, xvi,
40-42, 143-44; and medicalization, 40
Acquired model of support for
medical licensure, 141
Akers, Ronald, 8
Allopathy, 11-12; cultural faith in,
47, 80, 85, 140, 143; defined,
184 n. 4; and political organization of practitioner associations,
80
Alternative birth centers (ABCs),
54; breathing techniques in,
112; certified nurse-midwives in,
90-92; compared to home and
hospital births, 186-87 n. 1; as
enclave, 114; limits on behavior
in, 114-15; and protocols and
rates of transfer, 111; as
response to home births, 54;
and territory issue, 114
Alternative birth movements, xi
Alternatives to licensure: "Health
Responsibility System," 152;
peer review, 152-53; self-
regulation, 152-53
American College of Nurse-Mid-

wives, 18, 39, 166, 174; and
midwife regulation, 18, 39
American College of Obstetricians
and Gynecologists (ACOG): and
alternative birth centers, 53-54;
and certified nurse-midwives,
39; and lay midwife licensure in
California, 76; study of home
birth by, 134-35
American Medical Association
(AMA): and alternative birth centers, 53-54; and Sheppard-
Towner Act, 30
Annas, George, 49, 53, 184 n. 5,
187 n. 1
Arizona: hospital and nonhospital
births in, 61; lack of lay midwife
training programs in, 58; lay
midwife license revocation hearings in, 130-31, 168 n. 1; lay
midwife licensure in, 18, 48,
55-61; provisional licenses for
lay midwives in, 59-60
Arizona Department of Health Services, and lay midwife licensure,
56-61
Arizona Medical Association, and
lay midwife licensure, 59-60

Women and Health Series
Rima D. Apple and Janet Golden, Editors

The series examines the social and cultural construction of health practices and policies, focusing on women as subjects and objects of medical theory, health services, and policy formulation.

The Selling of Contraception
The Dalkon Shield Case, Sexuality, and Women's Autonomy
Nicole J. Grant

And Sin No More
Social Policy and Unwed Mothers in Cleveland, 1855 - 1990
Marian J. Morton

Women and Prenatal Testing
Facing the Challenges of Genetic Technology
Edited by Karen H. Rothenberg and Elizabeth J. Thomson

www.ingramcontent.com/pod-product-compliance
Lightning Source LLC
Chambersburg PA
CBHW021554210326
41599CB00010B/432